SEAPOWER IN THE
POST-MODERN WORLD

Seapower in the Post-Modern World

BASIL GERMOND

McGill-Queen's University Press
Montreal & Kingston · London · Chicago

ISBN 978-0-2280-2087-5 (cloth)
ISBN 978-0-2280-2088-2 (paper)
ISBN 978-0-2280-2089-9 (ePDF)
ISBN 978-0-2280-2090-5 (ePUB)

Legal deposit first quarter 2024
Bibliothèque nationale du Québec

Printed in Canada on acid-free paper that is 100% ancient forest free
(100% post-consumer recycled), processed chlorine free

Financé par le   Funded by the   Canada   Conseil des arts   Canada Council
gouvernement   Government   du Canada   for the Arts
du Canada   of Canada

We acknowledge the support of the Canada Council for the Arts.

Nous remercions le Conseil des arts du Canada de son soutien.

McGill-Queen's University Press in Montreal is on land which long served as a site of
meeting and exchange amongst Indigenous Peoples, including the Haudenosaunee and
Anishinabeg nations. In Kingston it is situated on the territory of the Haudenosaunee
and Anishinaabek. We acknowledge and thank the diverse Indigenous Peoples whose
footsteps have marked these territories on which peoples of the world now gather.

Library and Archives Canada Cataloguing in Publication

Title: Seapower in the post-modern world / Basil Germond.

Names: Germond, Basil, author.

Description: Includes bibliographical references and index.

Identifiers: Canadiana (print) 2023056173X | Canadiana (ebook) 20230561780 |
 ISBN 9780228020875 (cloth) | ISBN 9780228020882 (paper) | ISBN 9780228020899
 (ePDF) | ISBN 9780228020905 (ePUB)

Subjects: LCSH: Sea-power. | LCSH: International relations.

Classification: LCC V27.G47 2024 | DDC 359/.03—dc23

This book was typeset by Marquis Interscript in 10.5/13 Sabon.

To Bryony and Heather

Contents

Tables and Figures

Preface

As this book goes to press, the Russian invasion of Ukraine is well into its second year. This sinister war of aggression, the first of this scale on the European continent since 1945, is a historical turning point. I wonder how twenty-second-century historians will reflect on this war. Will the consensus be that the twenty-first century started in 2022 like the twentieth century started in 1914 with World War I and the nineteenth century in 1815 with the Congress of Vienna? Or will the period from 1989 to 2022 be remembered as a mere bracket in the history of the (Cold) War between the West and Russia (and China) that started in 1947?

These questions are deeply connected to a book devoted to seapower. Indeed, if 2022 confirms the start of a new phase in the global rivalry between Russia, China, and the West, will it also cement the over-arching confrontation between the continental Eurasian Heartland and the maritime nations of the crescent (Mackinder 1904; Spykman 1944) anticipated by classical geopolitics scholars? And if this happens, will China's increasing seapower be instrumental in initiating a change in global leadership? Ukraine's military successes against Russia – David against Goliath – cannot be dissociated from Kyiv's adoption of a Western-informed agile, strategic thinking that has, so far, proven effective against the continental mindset of Russian military planners. Although the naval dimension of the war remains minimal, seapower (in its broadened interpretation) is playing a role. Whereas commenta-tors focus solely on the Ukrainian successes against Russian naval forces (which indeed are remarkable, such as the sinking of the cruiser *Moskva*, flagship of the Black Sea Fleet), Western control of the global supply chain is playing a more discreet role, one that will be crucial in the longer term by undermining Putin's Russia's ability to attack its neighbours via the profound and enduring effects this control exerts on Russia's economy, finance, and industrial-military base. This strategic effect of seapower does not result from any encounter between the North Atlantic Treaty Organization (NATO) and Russia but from Western command of the global maritime order, including an organic relationship with civilian maritime stakeholders.

Seapower has been the object of many studies since its popularisation by Captain Alfred Thayer Mahan in the late nineteenth century. However, most of these studies have either sparingly discussed or circumvented or even plainly avoided the question of defining seapower as a concept. Seapower is often conflated with maritime strategy or command of the sea; it has acquired an almost mythical status, and thus it is, for many authors, beyond the need for any conceptual definition. However strange it may sound, seapower has still not been comprehensively defined in the academic literature. After all, in the words of Paul Kennedy who was referring to Mahan: 'if generalizations about the nature of sea power are risky, then, it would be a bold author who would claim to have detected certain "immutable" laws concerning naval affairs and navies that were applicable to all ages' (2022, 98). Far from being 'bold', I endeavour with this book to contribute to defining the concept of seapower. I also discuss the continuity and changes in the practice of seapower throughout history, and as such, the text contributes to existing debates about the role of seapower in explaining what Modelski and Thompson (1988) call hegemonic cycles.

Such a scholarly endeavour is based on my engagement with a wide variety of authors, from Greek philosophers to twentieth-century strategists and historians. I owe them all a debt of thanks. And in the famous words of Isaac Newton: 'if I have seen further, it is by standing on the shoulders of giants'. Among those giants are two academics who played an important role at the beginning of my intellectual journey on the seven seas in the 1990s and early 2000s: Eric Grove and Geoffrey Till. Eric has now left our shores, but I fondly remember time spent with him, eating oysters and drinking champagne on the Blackpool Promenade while revisiting British naval history in passionate discussions. Both scholars have inspired a then young student of naval power, who has since grown into a confident scholar of seapower. I hope to follow in their footsteps with my humble contribution to this fascinating field of study. I also warmly thank the three anonymous reviewers whose exceptional scholarship and sharp suggestions have ever improved this book.

Writing a book is a long commitment, and many people deserve my cheers: Lancaster University has supported me and even promoted me to chair in international security. My wife, parents, and beloved daughters who have always been there for me. My thanks to the editors of the *Australian Naval Review* in which a previous iteration of chapter 6's section on "the solidaristic society of maritime nations" was published. This book has also benefited from an interdisciplinary approach that would not have been possible without intellectual engagement with scholars in various disciplines, from security studies to critical political geography, and from history to marine biology. I cannot list them all here, but I would like to express my special thanks to Christian Bueger, Timothy Edmunds, Kimberley Peters, and Philip Steinberg. Finally, my thanks to my commissioning editor at McGill-Queen's University Press, Richard Baggaley, whose proactivity and support have been instrumental in my delivery of this book.

Writing a book remains a solitary endeavour though, and at the end of a long process, it is important to self-reflect on the intellectual journey and the subject matter of the book itself. Early naval historians, among them Mahan, Colomb, and Corbett, have focused their attention on naval power in the context of imperialism without questioning the practice itself. Indeed, 'in their day it was empire which made nations great, and navies which made empires' (Rodger [1997] 2004, xxii). There are three steps toward decolonising seapower studies: first, recognising the contribution of seapower to imperialism, colonisation, and their wrongdoings. This effort is well on track with studies having reflected on seapower's contribution to colonial empires (e.g., Münckler 2007) as well as exploitative capitalism (Campling and Colás 2021). It is nevertheless crucial to continually reflect on the past and on the way it has been studied when engaging with a book that is as much about the past as it is about the present. Second, accounting for the existence of non-European, non-Western naval thought that has run parallel with the traditional European thought. The scope of this book only permits a superficial engagement with such sources of seapower thought, which will be the subject of a next book. Finally, seapower via maritime endeavours is also about accepting differences and fostering them in the spirit of what former First Sea Lord, Admiral Sir George Zambellas, called the 'brotherhood of the sea'.

Abbreviations

C4ISTAR system	Command, control, communications, computers, intelligence, surveillance, target acquisition, and reconnaissance
EEZS	Exclusive economic zones
GDP	Gross domestic product
IMO	International Maritime Organization
IR	international relations
IISS	International Institute for Strategic Studies
MDA	Maritime Domain Awareness
MPAS	marine protected areas
NATO	North Atlantic Treaty Organization
SLOCS	sea lanes of communication
UNCLOS	United Nations Convention on the Law of the Sea
VPDS	vessel protection detachments

SEAPOWER IN THE
POST-MODERN WORLD

Introduction

The subject matter of this book is seapower (also written as sea power, in this case usually as a synonym for naval power). The concept of seapower is delineated in chapter 1, but it is important to make the distinction between naval power and seapower clear from the beginning. Naval power refers to what navies – or, more broadly, forces operating at, under, or above the sea – can do at or from the sea that contributes to states' defence and security and serves states' broader interests. Seapower refers to the maritime milieu that is the sea and infers a positive link between the sea and states' power, which transcends naval power to include economic, civilian, and ideational forms of power, whose impacts are not limited to short-term and/or military considerations. The concept of seapower accounts for the mutually beneficial relationship between seafaring culture, naval power, economic growth, and global dominance.

Since the classical writings of Captain Alfred Thayer Mahan (1890), Vice-Admiral Philip Colomb (1891), Sir Julian Corbett (1911), and other pioneers in the field of naval history and maritime strategy, seapower has been discussed sparingly in the academic literature regardless of disciplines, especially during the Cold War era, when scholars' attention was focused on nuclear power, the defence of the European continent, and guerrilla-type proxy wars. French strategist Hervé Coutau-Bégarie, the last and seemingly only contemporary French naval strategist, explains that when he started to study maritime affairs in the 1980s, he was essentially the only scholar in the French academic community to be interested in naval strategy; almost everything had to be written. Actually, 'we could write anything on the topic', he remarks (quoted in and translated from Kouar 2010, 17).

The end of the Cold War did nothing to increase scholars' attention toward naval affairs. It is fair to say that 'sea blindness', a lack of awareness of the sea and a lack of consideration for the role it has played (and still plays) for security and prosperity, has particularly affected continental scholars.

This gap in the literature on seapower is less pronounced in the English-speaking world, whose seafaring traditions and maritime outlook have contributed to produce more naval scholars. Even so, seapower is certainly a forgotten topic in international relations (IR) and political science. Naval historians have been more prolific, including such recent examples as Eric Grove (1990), John B. Hattendorf (2000a; 2011), Paul Kennedy ([1976] 2017; 2022), Andrew Lambert (2000; 2018), N.A.M. Rodger ([1997] 2004; 2004), and Ian Speller (2014). Strategists have mainly focused on navies, naval warfare, and maritime strategy, including Bernard Brodie (1943), Norman Friedman (2001), Colin S. Gray (1992; 1994), and Geoffrey Till (1987, 1994, 2004, 2022), while nevertheless discussing the concept of seapower (see especially Till 2004, 2018). Political scientists have rather sparingly studied seapower. Some have focused on naval diplomacy, for example Hedley Bull (1976b), Ken Booth (1979, 1985), and Christian Le Mière (2014), others on global leadership and cycles of dominance such as Modelski and Thompson (1988). Some critical geographers have also discussed the ideational dimension of seapower and deconstructed the traditional representation of the ocean as a void, such as Steinberg (2001).

In the twentieth century, several naval practitioners have made important contributions to seapower studies, notably French admiral Raoul Castex (1931–39), British admiral Herbert Richmond (1934, 1946), British captain Stephen Roskill (1962), British admiral Peter Gretton (1965), US admiral Stansfield Turner (1974), Soviet admiral Sergey Gorshkov ([1976] 1979), US rear admiral Henry Eccles (1979), British rear admiral J. Richard Hill (1986), and US admiral James Stavridis (2017), to name but the most prolific thinkers. The shrinking number of substantial academic contributions by naval practitioners since the end of the Cold War demonstrates the lack of academic interest in the maritime domain, which further underscores that contemporary naval practitioners have not been encouraged (even for career purposes) to engage with the topic of seapower outside their professional environment, contrary to their predecessors.

The above (non-exhaustive) enumeration of authors may give the erroneous impression that seapower has not been neglected in the academic literature. However, the meaning, attributes, scope, and effects of seapower have not been much discussed since most of these naval scholars and practitioners have focused on navies, naval missions, and naval operations as well as naval strategy and not on seapower itself. Even Modelski and Thompson (1988), whose book makes an important contribution to the field by demonstrating that seapower is instrumental in explaining hegemonic cycles, mainly use quantitative indicators based on *naval* strength. In addition, due to the fragmentation of the debate spanning various disciplines, we have not witnessed the development of any particular 'seapower school of thought'. There is a 'command/control of the sea school of thought', which finds its origins in Mahan's work and was then further developed by various scholars and practitioners, as well as a so-called British School (Till 2006) interested in the *exercise* of the command of the sea, inspired by the works of Corbett (1911). But their work mainly relates to maritime or even naval strategy, not seapower, despite regular use of the term in their book titles.

Furthermore, in the twenty-first century, except for Till's seminal work *Seapower: A Guide for the 21st Century* (2004), which was re-edited in 2009, 2013, and 2018, as well as Andrew Lambert's *Seapower States* (2018), seapower is mostly studied from a regional and naval perspective, such as China and India (see for example various academic pieces by Toshi Yoshihara and James Holmes). I contributed to this trend with my 2015 book *The Maritime Dimension of European Security*, although I framed my analysis within a broader discussion of seapower in the twenty-first century. Finally, an important contribution to knowledge in the field is the literature on seafaring and the importance of the sea in economic, political, or cultural terms. However, these anthologies spanning historical eras, such as Abulafia (2020), Paine (2013), and de Souza (2001), do not focus on seapower itself.

Thus, the general aim of this book is to fill the existing gap in the literature by comprehensively discussing the concept and practice of seapower and strictly focusing on seapower rather than seafaring or naval/maritime strategy. The objective is to explain how, despite its evolving characteristics, seapower still shapes world politics in the twenty-first century and demonstrate why it deserves further attention from academics and practitioners alike. Understanding the tenets, advantages, and limitations of seapower is crucial in the context of the new Cold War taking shape between the West and Russia (and

China). In other words, in a period of impending global leadership challenges, seapower is likely to play a significant role and thus warrants due attention.

The title of this book is a nod to Admiral Sir Herbert Richmond's *Sea Power in the Modern World* (1934). Richmond claimed that many changes occurred between the periods Mahan studied – roughly from the seventeenth century to the Napoleonic Wars – and the early twentieth century. Richmond thus wanted to address the resulting gap in our understanding of seapower by accounting for the new economic, technological, political, and military realities of his time. Similarly, my book situates our understanding of the concept and practice of seapower within a technological, societal, and political context that differs from those both Mahan and Richmond studied.

The last couple of decades of the twentieth century and the early decades of the twenty-first century have witnessed a rising interest in post-modern approaches and the concept of post-modernity in the field of IR. First, at the epistemological, ontological, and methodological levels, post-structuralist and deconstructive approaches have emerged within the discipline of IR, notably since the 1980s. Influenced by the continental philosophical movement associated with philosophers such as Michel Foucault and Jacques Derrida, post-structuralist approaches to IR claim that the main determinant of IR is not the material distribution of power among states or non-state actors but rather knowledge, how it is produced, constructed, reproduced, and perceived and how such constructions contribute to normalising policies and practices. This constitutes a major advancement in the discipline, which has induced the ongoing so-called fourth debate in IR between the proponents of such post-positivist approaches and the positivist/rationalist scholars opposing them. Consequently, in academics' imaginaries, the concept of post-modernity has been linked to this major epistemological, ontological, and methodological opposition between scholars in IR and beyond.

However, beyond IR theorists, many scholars interested in world politics and security, notably historians, have taken post-modernity into account in their analyses without themselves adhering to the post-modern academic agenda. In fact, a post-modern label has been attached to many actors and processes to acknowledge that their characteristics, objectives, means, or strategies are not aligned with modern (materialist) principles. As such post-modernity is a concept employed to account for the changing reality and the evolution of the subject matter of world politics. For example, Anderson (1996) talks about 'post-modern territorialities' to refer to the geo-politico-legal reality emerging from the European Union integration process and the resulting 'unbundling of territoriality'. In another example, post-modern diplomacy refers to public diplomacy, whose main goal is to interfere with foreign public opinion's perception as well as to account for the growing role played by non-state actors in diplomacy for the past decades (e.g., Melissen 1999). In the very field of maritime studies, Till (2007) stresses the existence of 'post-modern navies' (along with modern ones), which have 'different assumptions, sets of missions and acquisition programs' (569) and 'have an internationalist, collaborative and almost collective world outlook. They see their role as defending the system, directly at sea and indirectly from the sea' (571).

In sum, the modernity/post-modernity debate has informed scholars across disciplines and far beyond the positivist/post-positivist epistemological/methodological debate. The realisation that the practice of IR bears post-modern characteristics is the starting point of this book. However, Russia's territorial war in Ukraine demonstrates that modern or neo-modern practices coexist with the post-modern features of the current world order. And as for seapower, post-modern elements go alongside neo/modern ones.

Classical seapower scholars have mainly based their arguments on evidence from the modern era, starting with the Age of Discovery, such as Mahan ([1890] 2007), Colomb (1899), and Corbett (1911). Later authors focus on the more recent modern period since the second industrial revolution, such as Richmond (1934) and Brodie (1943), and beyond, for instance Gretton (1965), Roskill (1962), and Grove (1990). This book discusses seapower through the prism of pre-modernity/modernity/post-modernity/neo-modernity. By doing so, it is possible to highlight not only the changes but also the permanencies associated with seapower that transcend historical eras far beyond a classical Mahanian analysis of the advantage of maritime over land power. What are the constant features of seapower? And which ones are subject to change depending on the period under scrutiny? Post-modern elements of seapower may well have already been present during the modern era, such as the principles of freedom of the seas. Similarly, current post-modern dimensions of seapower such as good governance at sea and cooperative maritime security initiatives tend to lead to neo-modern forms of practice at sea, such as an increasing territorialisation of the maritime domain.

In sum, this book seeks to contribute answers to the following questions: to what extent are seapower's characteristics timeless? To what extent have the socio-economic-cultural characteristics associated with the pre-modern, modern, and post-modern eras influenced seapower? For instance, the values associated with modernity, such as liberal values, must be differentiated from those associated with seapower, such as seafaring and trade values, since the latter seem to transcend historical periods (Till 2004, 22). This book critically assesses the extent to which the permanencies associated with the concept of seapower transcend these historical periods. The aim is to enhance our understanding of seapower as a concept and a practice, while reflecting at the theoretical level on the enduring relevance of the framing of IR within pre-modernity, modernity, and post-modernity. Whereas the discourse on seapower has certainly varied depending on places and time, this book shows that seapower as a concept indeed bears some timeless characteristics, although the concept, narrative, and practice are mutually constitutive. Seapower in the twenty-first century combines traditional modern elements, such as naval power, with post-modern elements, such as collective and civilian seapower, and neo-modern elements, such as the process of territorialisation of the sea and new naval arms races.

This book also contributes to the broader discussion about the 'destiny' of seapower. Indeed, current debates mostly focus on the future of seapower by examining changes in its constitutive elements and effects. The broader question is the extent to which seapower will remain the dominant feature of IR, defence, and security. Paul Kennedy is sceptical of the timelessness of seapower in light of 'immense technological, political and demographical changes' (2017, 6). He suggests that if dominant naval forces are prevented from freely operating close to the shore due to land-based anti-access/access-denial weapons systems, then 'seapower's capacity to affect land outcomes may have been short-lived' (P. Kennedy 2017, xl). Modelski and Thompson argue that although seapower has been the 'higher-order power medium' since the modern era (1988, 13), it might eventually be replaced by outer space power. Interestingly, these two interpretations of seapower's fate account for the dominant role it has played in global politics since at least the Age of Discovery but consider its future as contingent on technological changes. The modernity/post-modernity framework of this book accounts for technological but also ideational factors in assessing the future of seapower.

Beyond its main contribution to seapower scholarship, this book aims to add to the literature on the oceans' role in IR. Naval and geopolitical considerations are indeed just one aspect of the broader 'turn to the ocean' that is taking place both in academic and practical terms with the gradual move away from 'sea blindness' (Bueger 2022; Peters et al. 2022). In particular, the systemic challenges posed by climate change and ocean sustainability, and the ways climate and the oceans interact (the ocean-climate nexus), cannot be dissociated from their security dimension, from climate change-induced increase in illegal fishing practices and fisheries conflicts to the geopolitical tensions arising from the melting polar ice cap. This book situates military, security but also governance and sustainability challenges at sea, within the evolving context of modernity/post-modernity/neo-modernity and, as such, offers a framework for the analysis of the centrality of the oceans in international politics that can be employed beyond the field of seapower.

The first three chapters construct a framework for analysis. Chapter 1 offers a preliminary definition of seapower based on the historiography of the concept and debates regarding the preponderance of seapower, the relationship between naval power and seapower, as well as the connection between seapower and maritime strategy. Chapter 2 introduces the central concepts of power in IR and situates the concept of seapower within the discipline of IR and international security studies. Since power (and seapower) can be measured and interpreted in many ways, chapter 2 offers a conceptual clarification.

Then, chapter 3 reveals how seapower can be analysed through the prism of the modernity/post-modernity debate. Modernity and post-modernity are also debated concepts, whose scope spans disciplines. By bringing together the two concepts of seapower and modernity/post-modernity, chapter 3 proposes an original framework for analysis that accounts for both changes and permanencies. The framework endorses a comprehensive approach to seapower that accounts for its naval, economic, civilian, and ideational dimensions at three different levels: the elements, the enactment, and the consequences/outcomes of seapower. It shows that the ideational factors are central to understanding the evolution of seapower, but states and human agency still constitute important determinants since seapower is ultimately about operating at, via, and from the sea as well as controlling human activities at sea.

The next two chapters apply the framework for analysis to the evolution of seapower from ancient times to the contemporary era to grasp the extent to which, and how, the evolution from pre-modernity to modernity and from modernity to post-/neo-modernity has impacted both the concept and practice of seapower. Chapter 4 starts with a review of the characteristics of pre-modern seapower. The purpose is to discuss the extent to which the so-called pre-modern political, social, and cultural features have influenced the practice of seapower in the pre-modern era. Seapower as a concept and a practice – and to some extent even a narrative – emerged during the pre-modern era. Technological and material factors more than ideational ones explain the limitations of seapower during this era. Then, the chapter discusses the extent to which modern features such as the belief in technology, the compression of time-space, and the development of nation-states have impacted on the nature, narrative, and practice of seapower since the Age of Discovery. The chapter concludes on the mutually reinforcing link between (nation) state building, empire building, and seapower but cautions against associating the development of seapower too closely with modern characteristics, since the main characteristics of seapower could already be found in the pre-modern era.

After debating the extent to which we currently live in a post-modern world, chapter 5 questions the impacts of post-modern features such as a further compression of time-space, an over-reliance on technology and communication, the re-emergence of non-state actors, and the rising power of supranational institutions that influence the practice of seapower. The practices of maritime security and ocean governance are deconstructed to illustrate the consequences of the dominant narrative that justifies practices of control beyond one's territorial waters. Indeed, the ongoing dynamics of the deterritorialisation of security are completed by a territorialisation of the sea that has initiated a movement towards a neo-modern form of seapower, which demonstrates the existence of enduring permanencies such as the control of human activities and flows at sea. Additionally, neo-navalism in Asia and the use of 'grey zone' tactics at sea contribute to the centrality of seapower in the context of an impending global leadership challenge.

Chapter 6 introduces two new concepts. First, the notion that collective seapower accounts for the increasingly integrated and cooperative dimension of naval operations, maritime security, and global governance of the oceans. The chapter discusses how maritime nations, led by the West but forming a distinct category of like-minded seafaring partners, have formed a 'solidaristic society of maritime nations' (Germond 2022c). Second, the chapter discusses the civilian dimension of seapower, that is to say the economic use of the sea and the role played by non-state actors, such as merchant marines, shipping companies, port authorities, which exercise forms of seapower in their own interests and in conjunction with states and sub-state actors. The chapter concludes that the preponderance of the West as a collective of maritime nations that structurally dominates the global order is intimately linked to civilian assets and interests. Control of the global supply chain and global reach capabilities are central to global leadership. As such, seapower is likely to play a crucial role in the forthcoming global leadership challenge.

The book concludes with the fact that permanence more than change characterises the evolution of seapower as a concept and a practice. It is thus necessary to go beyond the debate on modernity/post-modernity to grasp the nature of seapower as well as its relevance for states, international organisations, and non-state actors. In the context of a rising strategic competition akin to an impending global leadership challenge, and in light of outer space's increasing role, the balance between permanencies and changes is likely to characterise the future of seapower as much as the future of the world order.

The conclusion proposes some next steps in seapower studies. In particular, an important question is the extent to which the timelessness of seapower is also universal in that it applies to non-Western actors, past and present. Although this question is discussed in this book, which highlights the universality of seapower both as a concept and a practice, the European/Western lens needs to be deconstructed. Further research is needed to grasp the similarities between Western and non-Western experience of seapower from an ideational perspective. By demonstrating the timelessness of seapower in the Western world, the central role of ideational factors, and the implications in terms of framing studies within the modernity/post-modernity debate, this book paves the way for future comparative studies between regions or at a sub-level. The book also opens the door for further efforts to decolonise seapower studies by recognising and integrating the contributions of non-European, non-Western thinkers, texts, and practices. Scholars interested in seapower, or more generally in the maritime dimension of world politics, are encouraged to consider the sea beyond a placeless void to account for individuals', economic agents', and political actors' timeless efforts to operate, trade, travel, connect, and fight at sea as well as to control and regulate human activities and flows at or from the sea.

A Historiography of the
Concept of Seapower

Seapower is a form of power based on a variety of determinants, which proceeds from maritime or maritime-related assets, such as commercial shipping, navies, maritime culture, and geographical realities, and is enacted at or from the sea. Its effects and consequences are felt at sea and on land, although the effects on the latter realm are ultimately more significant. Since one of this book's objectives is to develop an under-standing of seapower by studying it through the prism of modernity/ post-modernity, a preliminary definition of seapower at this stage will allow for development of the analytical framework and serve as a conceptual basis for the rest of the book. This definition will then evolve throughout the analysis. To begin, the historiography of seapower offers insight, for it shows the extent to which the concept has been closely associated with modernity since its inception.

The concept of seapower, or sea power – cf. below for a discussion of the distinction between the two expressions – has been popularised by the writings of US Navy captain Alfred Thayer Mahan at the end of the nineteenth century.[1] Mahan is commonly considered the 'father' of seapower theory. He certainly popularised the concept with his series of books published since the 1890s, and as Francis Sempa shows, he elaborated a proper 'philosophy of sea power' (2002, 105). Indeed Mahan's extensive corpus of scholarly works tends towards justifying if not advocating seapower as a way to (positively) 'exercise effects … upon the welfare of the people' (Mahan [1890] 2007, 89). His main argument was, however, more pragmatic, that is, the importance of obtaining command of the sea, usually following a 'decisive' naval bat-tle. Mahan has thus been associated with the proponents of navalism (or naval militarism) not unlike the 'Fleet Professors' in Germany, among them geographer Friedrich Ratzel (1911).

Although several of Mahan's books, including the seminal *Influence of Sea Power* series, have 'sea power' in the title, he did not focus his attention on the definition of the concept itself but rather proposed a historical demonstration of its characteristics and relevance. His *Influence of Sea Power upon History* starts with a chapter discussing the 'elements of sea power' though. But as Jon Sumida reveals, this was a last-minute addition suggested by his publisher so as to make the book 'more palatable to general readers' (Sumida 1999, 46). Consequently, the attention of many readers and commentators has focused on geopolitical rather than operational considerations, such as the importance of the decisive battle or the concentration of forces, which were the real focus of Mahan's work (Sumida 1997, 25).

Apart from defining some 'elements' of seapower, that is, the factors that determine countries' likeliness to develop seapower (cf. chapter 2), Mahan only partially defined the concept, making it clear that seapower rests on 'the connection between a flourishing maritime trade that generates the nation's wealth and a powerful navy to protect it' (Germond 2015, 5). This lack of a full definition clearly indicates that Mahan considered the concept to be beyond question, even obvious. He nevertheless argued that seapower goes beyond naval power since it rests on the economic use of the sea at least as much as on the military use of it, and seapower is relevant in peace as well as in war (Mahan [1890] 2007, under introduction and chapter 1). Admiral Cyprian Bridge was one of the first to acknowledge the ambiguity of the term, recognising that it was often used as a synonym for 'naval power' rather than to express mastery of the seas (1910, 2). This point is crucial. As Hew Strachan points out, naval battles have been more the exception than the rule; today, as in the nineteenth century, 'sea power [serves] national policy, more than it [serves] strategy' (Strachan 2007, 30). In other words, the military dimension of seapower is often overemphasised, a fact which is reinforced by terminological confusion (see below).

Despite Mahan's enduring popularity, it must be noted that he was not the first advocate of seapower, and certainly not the first scholar or practitioner to acknowledge the existence of a reciprocal link between economic and naval power. Contemporaries such as Admiral Philip H. Colomb in Britain and Admiral Richild Grivel in France also proposed comparable ideas. Colomb's *Naval Warfare* focuses on the importance of obtaining and exercising command of the sea, but he nevertheless makes it clear in his introductory chapter that 'true naval warfare' has developed when commerce has truly become the source of 'a large proportion [of] the riches of a country' (Colomb 1899, 1). Naval power can only be sustained if the economy is flourishing, and for the economy to flourish naval power is required. Such a notion illustrates how seapower scholars of the nineteenth century closely connected seapower with (economic) modernity.

Modernity also emerges from Colomb's argument that 'the sea is regarded more and more as a territory necessary to be held by the nation' (9). Colomb's influence on Corbett and thus on the development of a so-called British School (Till 2006) cannot be denied. However, his influence on British naval thinking has not been fairly acknowledged to the extent that, in 1962, Roskill wrote that Mahan's works had limited impact in Britain (1962, 95), which practically ignores the influence Colomb had on Corbett as well as the fact that Colomb's book *Naval Warfare* proposes principles and ideas that are rather close to those of his US colleague, if more focused on what to do once command is secured, in particular mounting 'attacks on territory from the sea' (Colomb 1891, 227–430).

In France, Grivel also emphasised the importance of maritime commerce and stressed that naval preponderance originates in peoples' mores and vocation (Grivel 1869, 278); however, contrary to Mahan, he stressed that naval battles, even decisive ones, cannot generate immediate peace settlement (254). In addition to the contextual balance of power that naturally pushed France towards favouring *guerre de course* over the concentration of forces, Grivel was influenced by the modern liberal thought of the nineteenth century: 'in this century of free trade, neighbouring nations have become too interdependent for the misfortune and the ruin of some not to fatally make the misery and suffering of others' (7–8). Thus, his writings appear less 'warmongering' than those of contemporaries, and he stressed the importance of 'brother nations' at sea (7). Interestingly, it is debatable whether Mahan was a proponent of developing a navy and a merchant fleet in order to dominate the world, since he was well aware of the transnational nature of seapower and the need to cooperate (e.g., Sumida 1999, 52–4).

Although George Grote is credited with the first occurrence of the expression 'sea-power' in his comprehensive *History of Greece* ([1849] 1857), earlier European authors outside the cast of naval practitioners had discussed the correlation between maritime commerce and naval power well before Mahan's time. For instance, in 1754 – that is

130 years before Mahan's writings and well before the inception of the 'Second' British Empire – the Marquis D'Angeul noted in reference to Great Britain that 'the most maritime Power was naturally the properest to become the most commercial one, whilst her commerce, and marine, ought naturally to procure reciprocally one another's augmentation' (D'Angeul 1754, 53).[2] Similarly, twelve years before, Spanish high-level civil servant Don Gerónymo de Uztáriz stressed that a commercial fleet is a necessary condition for a powerful navy since it generates the necessary operating funds and acts as a cradle for navigation skills ([1742] 1752, 275) and, in turn, a navy contributes to active commerce (545). Geoffrey Till recently brought to light the often-forgotten work of Henry Maydman titled *Naval Speculations and Maritime Politicks* (1691), in which the Royal Navy's warrant officer stresses that 'the very Welfare of the Politick Body of this nation [England] does hang upon' building maritime power (quoted in Till 2022, 1). The following 1688 quote, of a similar tenor, is attributed to George Savile, Lord Halifax: 'the first Article of an Englishman's political creed must be, that he believeth in the Sea' (quoted in Foxcroft 1896, 723).

In the same vein, during the reign of Queen Elizabeth I – the very beginning of Britain's maritime success story – this limpid quote was attributed to Sir Walter Raleigh: 'for whosoever commands the sea commands the trade; whosoever commands the trade of the world commands the riches of the world, and consequently the world itself' (Raleigh [c. 1600] 1829, 325). And to control trade one has to control sea lanes of communication (SLOCS). Similarly, Andrew Lambert reminds us in a quote from Mahan himself who acknowledged that Francis Bacon proposed a definition of seapower in 1597, based on Thucydides's account of Pericles's funeral oration: 'he that commands the sea is at great liberty, and may take as much and as little of the war as he will; whereas those that be strongest by land are many times nevertheless in great straits' (Lambert 2010, 81). Chapter 2 explores the importance of Ancient Greece's naval thought in understanding the concept of seapower.

It is noteworthy that even in 'continental' France, an understanding of the preponderance of seapower (or at least naval power) existed at the time of Renaissance. For example, in 1515, the Bishop of Marseille, Claude de Seyssel, an ardent defender of an absolute monarchy, argued that 'polities that have historically been powerful at sea have done bigger things and more swiftly than those who only had a terrestrial army [for example] the Romans did not achieve substantial conquests before they became powerful at sea' (de Seyssel [1515] 1558, 65, translation from old French mine). Tommaso Campanella, an Italian utopian philosopher, made a similar point when he wrote in 1601 that 'the lord of the sea has always been the lord of the land' ([1601] 1997, 228). However, this must not be understood as a simple tribute to the power resulting from the mastery of the sea. Rather, it was about Campanella's recognition that the unbound sea was a unifying factor that transcends time and space as well as artificial boundaries, in other words, an additional argument in favour of the universal credential of the catholic (Spanish) monarchy (Fournel 2006, 441).

The limited account of references to seapower ideas in the Middle Ages contrasts with the proliferation of references since the Renaissance. Whereas this discrepancy in part results from the 'local' (as opposed to 'global') nature of politics during this era (cf. chapter 4), the roles played by naval battles and maritime commerce both in medieval Mediterranean and Asia shall not be neglected. The absence of elaborated reflections on the importance of seapower is also explained by the constraints of the pre-printing era. Thus, it is not surprising to witness an increase of references to seapower in the century following the invention of the modern printing press since this simply follows the increase of printed materials still available to consult today. This shall not, however, instil the idea that seapower as a concept had been relegated to brackets between Ancient Greece and the Renaissance. A short and often neglected contribution comes from the Arab historian and thinker Ibn Khaldun, who, in his work *Muqaddimah* (1377), demonstrates an understanding of the push-and-pull factors in regard to seafaring and naval power, in particular cultural conventions versus geopolitical rationales, as well as trade versus conquest motives for seafaring.

There is no denying that Mahan's impact on naval thought and scholarship has been immense and continues to be so. Admiral Sir Herbert Richmond's introduction to his book *Sea Power in the Modern World* (1934) is titled "Mahan and Sea Power", which not only acknowledges the origin of the term but also contributes to presenting Mahan as the father of seapower studies. This is interesting when one knows that Richmond rather followed a Corbettian view in that he wanted 'the Royal Navy to move on from its obsession with battle, to concentrate on securing its sea lines of communication, to prepare for expeditions' (Till 2004, 55). Admiral Raoul Castex sparingly refers to Mahan in his *Strategic Theories*, but nevertheless introduces him as 'America's most influential naval writer' ([1931–39] 1994, 7), and 'disparage[s] Corbett's challenges to Mahan as serving only as a check on and reaffirmation of Mahan's principles' (Kiesling 1994, xxxvi). Today, Mahan constitutes an undeniable reference point. For instance, twenty-first-century scholars interested in Chinese expanding naval power refer to China's seapower as taking a Mahanian turn (see notably Holmes and Yoshihara 2008).

It must be noted that some important naval scholars have rather downplayed Mahan's importance or even questioned the relevance of some of his arguments. Mahan's conception of seapower has been influenced by, or at least is linked to, his emphasis on decisive naval battles and the need to gain command of the sea. His general argument is that command of the sea will lead to victory in war and wealth in peace. Other contemporaneous and later authors have adopted contrasting views, while still stressing the importance of seapower and naval forces. Grivel (1869), for example, acknowledges that a dominant sea Power can proceed with attacks on land, expeditions, and blockades but stressed that if confronted with a superior navy, one has to opt for a *guerre de course* (sea denial) strategy, which is not only more likely to succeed in disrupting the enemy's commerce but also is less likely to result in a severe loss.

In other words, Grivel was not in favour of gaining command of the sea at all costs, he was wary of force concentration, and he acknowledged that strategies should be adapted to opponents. For instance, France, allied with the dominant (British) sea Power at the end of the nineteenth century, could envisage taking part in expeditionary warfare thanks to the preponderance of the Royal Navy, which implied that no other contender would obtain command of the sea. So, in Grivel's view, alliances are very important at sea as well as on land, since (outside the dominant sea Power) the balance of naval power determines the strategy to adopt. Grivel's moderate approach could well have applied to the US at the end of the nineteenth century, illustrating his differentiation with Mahan's navalist arguments, which better aligned with contemporary US decision makers' own perception, most notably Theodore Roosevelt. Indeed, in a period of growing tensions 'the international scene was favourable for just such a book as his' (P. Kennedy 2022, 100).

In Britain, Colomb rather diverged from Mahan: he emphasised exerting command by launching attacks onto the land. In other words, command is important, but not in itself; what really matters is what states make of their command of the sea and how this can influence the situation ashore. Similarly, Sir Julian Corbett's criticisms of Mahan were rather focused on sea mastery versus exercising command of the sea, less so on the notion of seapower. Corbett only mentions Mahan three times in his book *Some Principles of Maritime Strategy* (1911), which rather challenges Mahan's claim about mastering the sea, notably the importance of concentration and the decisive naval battle that Corbett downplays in favour of protecting ships along slocs. In other words, for Corbett, seapower is 'about getting merchant ships safely to port' (P. Kennedy 2022, 102), which reflects an emphasis on the centrality of seafaring, commerce, and supply (i.e., broader strategic considerations), rather than naval strategic principles (see also Eccles 1979).

Corbett also emphasises the interdependence between the sea and the land much more than Mahan does, and as such stresses that 'it is almost impossible that a war can be decided by naval action alone' ([1911] 1988, 15), hence the importance of coining maritime strategy as a component of general strategy rather than something superior to it in a deterministic form. Rear Admiral Wylie re-emphasises the point when he stresses that maritime strategy is eventually about exploiting one's command of the sea to produce effects onto the land (1989, 34). Captain Hughes Jr similarly reminds us that 'the navy [is] a means towards the end of controlling an enemy on the ground', and 'sea power's greatest payoff comes from the highly efficient movement of "goods" and services' (2000, 9–10). This echoes German naval thinker Wolfgang Wegener's argument that seapower primarily rests on exercising control of slocs ([1929] 1989).

For Corbett, national strategy must integrate all elements of state power from naval assets to maritime trade and from law of the sea to maritime culture. For him, the 'British way of waging war' is about making the most of what maritime power can offer, including in a limited or asymmetrical way, such as economic sanctions and long-term strategic effects that 'exert pressure on the citizens and their collective life' (Lambert 2017; 2021, 5). Similarly, Callwell argues that 'the stronger navy is to a certain extent tied to the land' ([1905] 1996, 164), since it depends on depots, shipyards, and so forth. He also qualifies the relevance of 'command of the sea' as an expression having 'limited signification' and prefers to employ 'maritime preponderance' to account for the fact that command is rarely total, global, or sustained (1–2).

Admiral Richmond's contribution to seapower studies has surprisingly been overlooked, notably his works *Sea Power in the Modern World* (1934) and *Statesmen and Sea Power* (1946). Nevertheless, he is one of the few twentieth-century authors who further discusses the concept of seapower rather than focusing on maritime strategy. Interestingly, he differentiates the 'causes' of seapower from the 'elements' of seapower. Whereas the latter refers to material constituents, the former accounts for the factors explaining states' acquisition of seapower, either as a result of economic and social realities (such as a predominantly trade economy) or as a result of politicians' decisions to acquire seapower to benefit from 'the added wealth and strength and influence which it would confer' (Richmond 1934, 17). This distinction is interesting since he argues that maritime culture and maritime socio-economic bases were not necessary conditions for the development of seapower as long as this absence was offset by political and Grand Strategy incentives: 'the Roman people were not maritime; they were under no pressing economic need to seek their fortunes at sea. That which brought Roman sea power in existence was the political question of who should rule in Sicily' (25).

This is not dissimilar to Lambert's argument that rulers of sea states need to nurture seafaring identity and maritime culture, which are not intrinsically natural attributes of human beings, if they want to develop (or maintain) seapower (Lambert 2018). Indeed, Richmond (1934) also highlights how predominantly land Powers (e.g., the US) can decide to develop seapower. His understanding of the elements of seapower is more restricted than Mahan's, since geographical factors and people's character have more to do with what he calls the causes of seapower. Richmond's elements of seapower consist in three material constituents, namely merchant shipping, overseas possessions, and naval power. Shipping is a condition for trade, which is a condition for wealth (39); seafaring also contributes to providing 'a reserve of seafaring officers and men' (41). This latter point shows that maritime culture and nautical experience were still conceived as mutually beneficial in the 1930s, despite the existence of institutionalised navies, which were maintained in peacetime. However, Richmond considered cultural preferences, an 'outlook' to the sea, as causes of seapower rather than elements of it.

In his *Strategic Theories*, Admiral Castex agrees with Mahan's argument about the importance of seapower in history but further emphasises that navies are also useful for states unable to pursue a

Mahanian seapower strategy (Kiesling 1994, xxxi), such as France. Seapower is not conceived as a means to an end of reaching hegemony but as a tool at states' disposal, parallel with other non-maritime tools. This conception fits with a continental outlook that is also found in Soviet admiral Gorshkov's writings. As such, Castex was not keen to separate maritime strategy from general strategy. Castex was, however, interested in strategy in general and naval strategy in particular, though less so in further discussing seapower as a concept.

Scholars' interpretations of Mahan's work strongly depend on whether they think his arguments were context-dependent or rather timeless. British political scientist Ken Booth went as far as saying that 'much of what Mahan wrote became obsolete rather quickly [and that] Mahan was, however, an effective publicist for a great and coming navy' (1979, 76), basically reducing Mahan to a successful proponent of navalism in the US at the end of the nineteenth century. This perspective contrasts with Colin S. Gray's argument about Mahan's "timeless words" regarding the sea as the safest and cheapest highway: 'a general economic truth whose validity has been eroded only at the margin in the twentieth century' (1992, 4–5).

Technological developments may well influence the principles of maritime strategy; they do not render obsolete the importance of seapower understood as more than naval (military) power. Booth's scholarly visibility in the naval field mainly came from his work on the evolution of naval missions. He devised a so-called trinity of naval missions, which was then endorsed by Eric Grove (1990) and even the British Maritime Doctrine in a slightly modified version (MoD 2011): military missions (mainly wartime missions such as securing command of the sea, naval expeditions, amphibious operations, etc.), diplomatic missions (such as naval presence, coercion, deterrence, etc.), and constabulary missions (such as fisheries protection, counter-narcotics, etc.) (Booth 1979, 15–25; cf. figure 2).

This model is very useful since it allows taking the geopolitical and strategic context into account. Indeed, depending on time and places, the emphasis was put on one or another category of missions. At the end of nineteenth century, Mahan's emphasis was on military missions (and especially obtaining command of the sea via the concentration of forces and decisive naval battle); diplomatic missions were acknowledged, and police missions overlooked. In the 1970s and 1980s, Booth's emphasis was on diplomatic missions, which, in a Cold War context, constituted navies' most important contribution to the peacetime security and deterrence effort. In the twenty-first century, the importance of police missions has increased due to the emphasis put on maritime security and ocean governance following the proliferation of non-state actors at sea and the expansion of the security agenda (cf. chapter 5).

In sum, various authors have either celebrated Mahan's 'wisdom' or criticised his propositions, depending on their own ideas and aims when writing. The extended nature of Mahan's work facilitates selective bias with scholars facing an extended choice of quotes from Mahan with at least one that can confirm their own thesis. Mahan's own style, which includes long historical case studies and few analytical summaries, opens the door to many interpretations, which has led to the frequent misuse of quotes, as well as dubious appropriations of the concept of seapower. Since Mahan's writings, the concept of seapower has indeed been employed indiscriminately by scholars, commentators, and practitioners, most of them more interested in drawing lessons from the past to understand current maritime affairs and to justify naval programmes, naval strategies, and maritime policies.

A noteworthy exception is the work of George Modelski and William R. Thompson, two American political scientists who agreed with Mahan's historical analysis of the advantage resulting from the mastery of the seas. However, they conducted a systematic quantitative study that corroborated the correlation between seapower and global leadership. In their *Seapower in Global Politics* (1988), they demonstrate that seapower as a resource and a function has been instrumental (i.e., a necessary but not sufficient condition) for winning global wars, thus gaining hegemonic status and then maintaining this dominance over long periods of time thanks to the control of the global ocean. As such, they validate Mahan's claim that the advantage of seapower is timeless.

Another issue is that many scholars in the twentieth and twenty-first centuries have continued to use the terms 'naval power', 'maritime power', and 'seapower' interchangeably and actually discuss naval power while referring to seapower. For example, Luttwak's *Political Uses of Sea Power* actually tackles 'the political impacts of naval deployments' (1974, 2). Similarly, Bernard Brodie's *Sea Power in the Machine Age* is 'a story of the industrial revolution in the implements of sea warfare' ([1943] 1969, 13) that focuses on the tactical and strategic impacts of technological inventions on naval warfare and their eventual implications in terms of power balance in the world. Friedman's

Seapower and Space (2000) details the impacts of space-based weapons and systems (missiles, satellites, etc.) on the evolution of *naval warfare* but does not even mention the term 'seapower' beyond the book's title. Paul Kennedy ([1976] 2017) tries to avoid the conceptual trap by focusing on what he calls 'naval mastery' instead of 'sea power' that he considers unfit for quantification; however, since he delves into the broader economic, financial, and organisational components of seapower, this contributes to the existing lexical confusion.

As a matter of semantic clarification, note that naval power is limited to the power enacted by navies while maritime (or sea) power refers to something broader: the connection between a thriving maritime culture, a prosperous maritime economy, and a powerful navy. As discussed in chapter 3, seapower has ideational elements that are not necessary to develop naval power that mainly rests on technology and finance. Seapower refers to the power emanating from the sea, or rather from what the sea makes it possible to achieve (mainly on land). Whereas pioneers in the field of maritime strategy, such as Mahan and Corbett 'focused largely on the role of navies in wartime ... today, there is a much larger theoretical understanding ... Maritime strategy is the direction of all aspects of national power that relate to a nation's interests at sea' (Hattendorf 2000, 235).

Confusion as to the naval focus of maritime strategy has also added to semantical ambiguity when it comes to the definition of seapower itself. Richmond makes a clear distinction between 'a navy and sea power. A navy is a constituent ... in sea power. But a state which possesses a navy will not necessarily possess sea power' (1934, 29–30). In other words, the navy as one constituent element of seapower is a necessary condition but certainly not a sufficient one. Lambert goes a step further when he explains that the Mahanian conception of 'sea power' [in two words] (which encompasses more than naval power) refers to a 'strategic tool' at states' disposal and misses the 'soul of seapower' (2018, 2), or in other words the cultural reality of being a seapower state' (2018, 2, 14). An example often discussed in the literature is the Soviet Union, which managed under the leadership of Admiral Gorshkov to develop a powerful oceanic navy but failed in its attempt to convert this into proper seapower, since the Soviet Union's economy and culture did not become more maritime as a result of the development of Soviet naval power. The gains were limited to naval diplomacy in a Cold War context and potential strategic, operational, and tactical advantages in case of a general war with the West.

However, the Soviet navy continued to be considered an extension of the army, perhaps not subordinate to it but whose purpose was not higher than enacting naval power, something which still characterises the Russian Navy in the twenty-first century.

Lambert's definition of a 'seapower state', or a state that overcomes its weaknesses (especially in comparison to large continental Powers) by harnessing maritime power to deliver strategic effects, highlights that seapower, for some scholars 'maritime power' (e.g., Eccles 1979), is much more than naval power and encompasses commercial, legal, and cultural elements. Such a distinction and the emphasis on agile, limited (maritime) power able to deliver strategic effects in a way that serves maritime states was initially advocated by Corbett whose contribution to the conceptualisation of a 'British Way of War' can still be felt today (Lambert 2021; also see chapter 6). This is particularly salient in regard to the UK's response to Russia's war of aggression in Ukraine and to the global leadership challenge posed by the Chinese Communist Party that focuses on the long-term stability and security of the global supply chain (Germond 2023).

A common misunderstanding, certainly since discussions about seapower have been dominated by strategists and strongly influenced by Mahan's own vision, is that whoever wants to pursue seapower politics has to aim at commanding the sea. Further, authors have thus considered sea control as the main function of seapower. For example, Roskill says that 'the function of maritime power is to win and keep control of the seas for one's own use, and to deny such control to one's adversaries' (1962, 15). Rosinski also stresses that seapower rests on the command of the sea above all, be it command of the open ocean or command of the 'narrow seas' (1977, 121–39). In reality, whereas seapower indeed rests on the command of the relevant SLOCs, seapower and command of the sea refer to two distinct processes. Command of the sea, or control – the latter acknowledging the spatially and temporally restricted extent to which any navy, even the US Navy today, can control the sea (S. Turner 1974) – refers to one's ability to dominate portions of the sea or, as Corbett (1911, 320) puts it, 'the necessary lines of communication'. Once obtained or secured, command can then be 'exercised' or 'exerted', for example by projecting power and forces abroad onto the land or pressuring the enemy's economy in a Corbettian way (i.e., with sanctions whose efficiency depends on one's control of SLOCs/global supply chain). Similarly, Rear Admiral Wylie (1989) made it clear that the preponderance of seapower results from one's ability to produce effects onto the land and thereby increase one's political, economic, and psychological control of the enemy in the long term.

Command of the sea is thus a strategic objective and, until recently, has mainly referred to wartime situations, although it becomes more frequent to acknowledge the importance of sea control in peacetime for a variety of security purposes, such as policing the seas against transnational criminal actors, naval diplomacy, freedom of navigation operations, and so forth. Seapower, since it has both civilian and military components and rests on both material and ideational grounds, transcends the notions of peacetime and wartime. As Castex reminds us, Mahan 'introduced a "peacetime strategy", composed of all measures serving to augment naval forces' (Castex [1937] 1994, 15) and the maritime power of a nation. Furthermore, in practice, seapower does not exclusively depend on naval means or on one's ability to exercise the monopoly on the legitimate use of violence at sea. After all, it is not exclusively a form of ostentatious power, and Mahan's writings stress that seapower 'acts indirectly, often silently' (Friedman 2001, 6).

The main British naval thinkers of the Cold War period, notably Captain Roskill and Admiral Gretton, held the objective to discuss maritime (and especially) naval strategy, which means their works do not tackle seapower as such and tend to conflate the term 'seapower' with 'maritime strategy', focusing on attacking the enemy's trade, protecting one's commerce, and exercising command by attacking the enemy's land – always bringing the discussion back to sea control, notably control of the SLOCs. Gretton went as far as using Richmond's definition of 'seapower' (Richmond 1946, ix) to describe 'maritime strategy' (Gretton 1965, 21). Such lexical and conceptual misinterpretation coming from someone as cultivated and experienced as Gretton illustrates the extent to which seapower remains an ill-defined and misunderstood concept. Rear Admiral Eccles explains that 'maritime strategy is a national strategy based on the full use of maritime power'. However, he considers 'seapower' a component of 'maritime power' related to 'naval strategy' (1979, 205). This enduring confusion and elusiveness in the literature has not served the concept of seapower, which has often been either wrongly interpreted as a synonym for maritime strategy or simply ignored by practitioners and scholars interested in naval warfare or, more broadly, maritime affairs.

Beyond the scholarly debates about the relevance of Mahan's theses and the interpretations of his works and those attempts of later authors to understand the concept of seapower, the very relevance of seapower or of the sea (and naval forces) as an enabler of states' power has also been criticised by various scholars. Despite recognising that England's acquisition of Malta bestowed crucial geostrategic advantage to control, along with Gibraltar, the Western Mediterranean, Eyre E. Crowe argues that 'an island power is a sea power; and the fate of empires – begging pardon of English prejudice – was never decided on sea' (1853, 18). Ahead of Corbett's own interpretation, Crowe's point is that seapower was useful only in regard to what it eventually achieved on land.

Paul Kennedy, in his *Rise and Fall of British Naval Mastery* ([1976] 2017), argues that already in the nineteenth century the leverage of seapower was diminishing in comparison with other forms of power. For example, the development of railway networks throughout Europe was supposed to allow continental Powers to concentrate forces in the right place at the right time, including to repel a naval expedition. The development of airpower engendered a debate about the obsolescence of surface ships rather than of seapower itself. Indeed, the question was whether command of the sea could be secured and disputed by aircrafts alone (e.g., Brodie 1943), not whether airpower could entirely replace seapower. In other words, could airplanes become the main instruments of seapower? This debate shows the extent to which seapower is linked to technological developments and thus to the debate about modernity (industrial revolution) and postmodernity (information revolution).

In 1906, Fred T. Jane, the founding editor of *Jane's Fighting Ships*, published a controversial book titled *Heresies of Sea Power*, which argues that seapower may not have played such an important role in history and the 'winning nation rather happened to make use of the sea in winning' (1). Instead Jane, otherwise passionate about ships, proposes a controversial theory emphasising the 'fitness to win' of the victor, whose neo-Darwinian nature has since been criticised (Zellen 2012, 27). Jane also argues that naval officers were not good historians and the proponent of seapower may well 'select his instances by a process of eliminating any facts that go to contradict his pet theories' (1906, 14). Jane's book is not the only instance of social Darwinism in this era's seapower literature. For example, in his history of British seapower (with a preface by Admiral Sir Beatty), Colonel William

Table 1.1
Contributors to seapower scholarship (twentieth to twenty-first centuries)

Author	Main contribution(s)	Main background
C.E. Callwell	*Military Operation and Maritime Preponderance* (1905)	Practitioner
J. Corbett	*Some Principles of Maritime Strategy* (1911)	Academic
W. Wegener	*The Naval Strategy of the World War* (1929)	Practitioner
R. Castex	*Strategic Theories* (1931–39)	Practitioner
H. Richmond	*Seapower in the Modern World* (1934); *Statesmen and Seapower* (1946)	Practitioner
B. Brodie	*Sea Power in the Machine Age* (1943)	Academic
S. Roskill	*The Strategy of Sea Power* (1962)	Practitioner
P. Gretton	*Maritime Strategy* (1965)	Practitioner
S. Turner	"Missions of the U.S. Navy" (1974)	Practitioner
E.N. Luttwak	*The Political Uses of Sea Power* (1974)	Academic
S.G. Gorshkov	*The Sea Power of the State* (1976)	Practitioner
H. Rosinski	*The Development of Naval Though* (1977)	Academic
H. Eccles	*Military Power in a Free Society* (1979)	Practitioner
K. Booth	*Navies and Foreign Policy* (1979); *Law, Force and Diplomacy at Sea* (1985)	Practitioner
H. Moineville	*Naval Warfare Today and Tomorrow* (1983)	Practitioner
J. Cable	*Diplomacy at Sea* (1985); *Gunboat Diplomacy 1919–1991* (1994)	Practitioner
J.R. Hill	*Maritime Strategy for Medium Powers* (1986)	Practitioner
J.C. Wylie	*Military Strategy: A General Theory of Power Control* (1989)	Practitioner
E. Grove	*The Future of Sea Power* (1990)	Academic
C.S. Gray	*The Leverage of Sea Power: The Strategic Advantage of Navies in War* (1992); *The Navy in the Post-Cold War World: The Uses and Value of Strategic Sea Power* (1994)	Academic
N.A.M. Rodger	*The Safeguard of the Sea: A Naval History of Britain, vol. 1, 660–1649* (1997); *The Command of the Ocean: A Naval History of Britain, vol. 2, 1649–1815* (2004)	Academic
N. Friedman	*Seapower and Space* (2000); *Seapower as Strategy* (2001)	Academic and practitioner
J.B. Hattendorf	*Naval History and Maritime Strategy: Collected Essays* (2000); *Talking about Naval History* (2011)	Academic (with naval background)
H. Coutau-Bégarie	*Traité de stratégie* (2002)	Academic (with naval credentials)
G. Till	*Seapower: A Guide for the 21st Century* (2004); *How to Grow a Navy* (2022)	Academic
A. Lambert	*Seapower States* (2018)	Academic

Wood states that Britain's successful seapower is an outcome of having 'bred the greatest race of seamen [themselves] mostly bred from those hardy Norsemen' (1919, 24).

Three nineteenth-century pioneering seapower scholars – Grivel, Mahan, and Colomb – were naval officers, but in the twentieth century most of the 'big names' in the field are found in the academic sector with Corbett, Brodie, Rosinski, Booth, Grove, Gray, Till, and Lambert, among others (see table 1.1). Whether practitioners-turned-academics, policy advisers, or pure academics, naval scholars have discussed the extent to which 'those who control the sea control the world', or the preponderance of sea over land Powers, and the debate on the advantage and disadvantage of seapower versus land power. Most of the classical authors have focused their answers on wartime considerations. The advocates of seapower over land power have thus emphasised the fact that command of the sea allows not only for protecting commerce and carrying out projection operations but also preventing the enemy from using the sea and disrupting commerce. Most importantly, maritime preponderance first enables securing control of the sea (rarely total, more likely regional, local, and/or temporary) and then exercising pressures on the land, whether via forces projection or economic suffocation that has long-term effects on one's ability to control the enemy (Eccles 1979, 203–5; Wylie 1989).

Authors have thus discussed the relevance of the preponderance of seapower over land power across the centuries and sorted out factors that explain why seapower cannot be considered a panacea. Richmond (1934, 71) recognises that seapower is limited in war by the need to ally with land (Great) Powers (such as Britain and France during the World War I): 'single-handed sea power can do little against any Great Power'. Rosinski notices the brevity of conflicts since the nineteenth century that could prevent seapower from having time to exert influence on others' economy and railways across the continent that helped quicken responses to any landing (1977, 126). Roskill stresses that 'although many wars have been decided mainly by sea power, rarely, if ever, have they been decided by sea power alone', hence contention between advocates of seapower to weaken the enemy's economy and those of land battles to defeat the enemy (1962, 20) given that 'war operations ... belong essentially to the land' (Moineville 1983, 13). Lambert (2018) argues that the ability to exercise seapower in the long term rests on rulers' sustained advocacy of a maritime culture, which is never a given.

Whereas seapower may not be sufficient to win wars, there has been a consensus (based on historical and quantitative facts) that seapower bears advantages in war as in peace. The preponderance of seapower is based on the following assumptions, beautifully exposed by C.S. Gray: 'command of the sea tends to yield a more absolute and extensive superiority at sea than command on land does on land [and] command at sea yields possibilities for influence on land superior to the influence at sea that can flow from command on land' (1994, 14). Similarly, Admiral Stavridis explains that continental Powers which have neglected the sea will eventually be contained by sea Powers (2017, 314). Seapower grants agility and the ability to seize opportunities and 'deliberately chang[e] the character or the scene of the war' (Wylie 1989, 158).

Modelski and Thompson's systematic quantitative analysis of the crucial contribution of seapower to cycles of global dominance demonstrates in a falsifiable way (and thus with high academic validity) that seapower is instrumental both in winning global wars and in cementing hegemonic status. One of their central arguments is that global power depends on global reach and that this is contingent to mastering the seas. Thus, seapower 'represents a higher-order medium of interaction in world politics' (1988, 13). If we follow this argument, seapower is indeed going to have 'a sound and secure future' (Grove 1990, 241) as a 'great enabler' (Gray 1994, 13) in war as in peace. That said, Till makes it clear that dividing nations between 'maritime' and 'continental' is of limited analytical relevance, since this binary categorisation is no more than an ideal-type model, countries must rather be classified along a maritime-continental spectrum, and their position is open to variations over time due to political decisions and/or geopolitical changes (2022, 10–11).

This mirrors Spykman's argument that 'there has never really been a simple land power-sea power opposition' (1944, 43) in that the determining factor was which 'rimland' or 'crescent' Powers would ally with the dominant sea Power or the dominant land Power. Modelski and Thompson also note that naval victories pave the way for winning long wars and denying continental Powers the opportunity to change the system, but they need to be supplemented by sustained land warfare (1988, 22). That said, sea Powers tend to win decisive naval battles more often than land Powers, which grant them with long-term strategic advantage, since 'those defeated in the naval contest could not expect to win at the global level even if they did score regional and/or continental victories' (12).

In peacetime, seapower bears different advantages beyond strategic considerations. For example, James Kraska notes the mutually reinforcing and beneficial relationship between being the main sea Power and shaping the international order at sea (2009, 117). In other words, seapower allows influencing the system at sea and the norms applied at sea, including defining naval war laws (such as the 1856 Paris Declaration, the 1907 Hague Convention, and the United Nations Convention on the Law of the Seas [UNCLOS]). This illustrates the ideational dimension of seapower in the form of soft power. As Friedman notices, seapower, especially in the post–Cold War era, 'can exert its influence without resorting to force' (2001, 227). This is the case with naval diplomacy (e.g., prepositioning of forces) or as mentioned above as a form of 'power to define' or normative power (e.g., maritime law).

In another example, naval forces can control activities by third parties, including non-state actors, at sea in one's territorial waters, exclusive economic zones (EEZs), or even on the high seas, that is to say beyond one's jurisdictional waters (Moineville 1983, 17). Controlling the movement of goods and people at sea in peacetime is crucial, and the ability to do it is a form of seapower, albeit more assimilated to the Weberian notion of the monopoly on the legitimate use of violence (Germond 2015, 75). Thus, seapower is not only about operating at, through, or from the sea but also about controlling human activities at sea. Whereas traditional studies have emphasised the control of SLOCs (purview of naval scholars) or maritime spaces (purview of critical geographers), it is worth reiterating that ultimately the control is exercised over other actors, which eventually are individuals (although operating within private or public structures).

This historiographical discussion of seapower illustrates that the concept, used indiscriminately, is open to various interpretations and subject to many misinterpretations. Whereas most authors agree that seapower is a form of power enacted at or from the sea, they disagree about what constitutes seapower (i.e., the elements or determinants of seapower) and the outcomes of seapower (i.e., what is possible to achieve when exerting seapower). In a bid to further explore the nature of seapower, the discussion in chapter 2 turns to IR theories to discover how competing theoretical approaches tackle the concept of seapower.

2

Seapower in
International Relations

Maritime and naval studies scholars such as Hill (1986, 14), Till (2004, 2), and Speller (2014, 5) are right when they say the concept of 'power' has been widely discussed and remains a contested one. However, in the field of naval and maritime studies, scholars have rather avoided the debate about the meaning of power and have tended to implicitly adopt a decidedly very materialist conception of power, which reflects in the limited number of attempts to link seapower to cultural elements. This shortcoming needs to be addressed in order to clarify the meaning and scope of this central concept for seapower studies.

The concept of power, central to the study of international relations (IR), has often been presented as one of the most important concepts in the discipline, although it remains 'one of the most troublesome in the field of international relations' (Gilpin 1981, 13). As discussed, there is indeed no consensus about the concept's definition, and it has been employed indiscriminately to refer to state and (progressively) non-state actors' capabilities (means to an end), achievements, and goals, as well as to the relationship and balance between actors on the world stage. With a capital *P* the term is even used to refer to powerful states, (e.g., 'Great Powers', *les Grandes Puissance* in French). Naval scholars have tended to avoid the debate about the meaning or nature of power for the very reason that the concept is controversial. Mahan himself never defined the concept of power, even loosely. This is definitely a shortcoming of the maritime/naval studies literature, since studying seapower without previously defining the concept of power seems somewhat flawed. Whereas IR theories have dominated the debate about power in international relations, other approaches shed light on the complex nature of the concept.

INTERNATIONAL RELATIONS THEORIES,
POWER, AND THE SEA

Beyond the definition of the elements of power (and how to quantify them), the debate about power in IR has been dominated by discussions related to the dichotomy and links between the various material and ideational forms of power. This stems from the evolution of the discipline of IR, which has resulted in a number of dominant debates between contending approaches: first between the realist, liberalist, and eventually Marxist schools of thought (contending assumptions about the subject matter), and then between the advocates of positivism or rationalism and post-positivism (epistemological and methodological debates). Contending approaches towards the concept of power usefully stress the multifaceted nature of the concept, even if they may not all be commensurable (Germond 2015).

Scholars from the realist tradition tend to define power from a state-centric and materialist perspective. States possess quantifiable leverages, such as financial, economic, human, and military resources. From a realist perspective, power can be reduced to a sum of material capabilities originating in the possession or the existence of certain material elements or assets (such as natural resources endowment, demography, and geographical realities). If military power is usually considered as the main form of power by the realists, socio-economic elements that contribute to the development and sustainability of military power are also generally taken into account as prerequisites, for example political systems' stability or national demographic trends. Indicators of material forms of power allow comparison between states, resulting in quantitative statistical comparisons, such as the famous *Military Balance* published annually by the International Institute for Strategic Studies (IISS) since 1961. Power is considered in relative terms by many (structural) realist scholars: for example, in a world with only two states, state A can have only as much power as state B does not have. In other words, power is distributed within a zero-sum game. Power is considered a finite resource. If one state has 'lots' of power, the other states have only the remaining share of power left. The distribution of (material) power between states, which is rarely equal, constitutes an important determinant of world politics from the realist perspective, notably for Kenneth Waltz's structural realist school of thought (Waltz 1979).

Scholars have extensively discussed the naval elements of seapower from a quantitative perspective, resulting in the elaboration of naval hierarchies based on the order of battle and reach of navies (e.g., Morris 1987; Grove 1990). Although qualitative criteria have also been increasingly employed to classify navies, such as sailors' morale or the type of missions assigned by the political elites, the very act of hierarchising navies contributes to the binary narrative surrounding them; ranking navies is a process of 'othering' (Germond 2014). At the top of the scale there are the so-called *blue water* navies that have the capabilities to operate far from home on a sustainable basis (and to perform any type of tasks assigned to them), and at the bottom of the scale are those that cannot, of which the less enviable are the so-called *token* navies.

The ranking of navies goes beyond classification according to their capabilities in absolute terms; 'what is ... important is the position of each navy relative to the others' (Jackson 2010, 12). Till stresses that navies have traditionally been an indicator of states' power and have thus contributed to their prestige (Till 2004, 116). Thus, ranking navies contributes to the construction of states' international reputation, since 'there is a general correlation between ranking of a nation's navy and a nation's status in the international system' (Hickey 2006, 46). Scholars influenced by the realist school of thought do not only focus on naval capabilities and the balance between navies; they also take economic (maritime) power into account (e.g., Hill 1986; Grove 1990) but principally as a form of quantifiable power.

Liberal theorists emphasise the primacy of trade and thus cooperation between individuals, groups of individuals, and eventually states. Power is understood as the capacity to create and sustain well-being and the necessary conditions for wealth (including military capabilities since stability and security are prerequisites for economic growth). But power is not relative. Absolute gains are what matters when states cooperate. The world is not seen as a zero-sum game, and thus interdependence and cooperation can lead to the absolute increase of states' wealth and individuals' well-being. From that perspective, British and then US seapower have been seen as guarantors of the stability of the international liberal order, which relies on the freedom of the seas for trade. In fact liberal democracies' policies and strategies are inextricably linked to seapower (Grygiel 2012, 33; Strachan 2005, 39). For example, the so-called *Pax Britannica* in the nineteenth century did not prevent wars and conflicts between European Great Powers, but the Royal Navy was in a position to secure freedom of the seas, contributing to Britain's wealth in particular and to the stability of the capitalist imperial world order in general. The same can be said of the so-called *Pax Americana* since the end of World War II, which (regardless of the fact that 'half of the world' was not allied to the US) is characterised by the US hegemony on the seas that has contributed to both the prosperity of the US and the stability of the liberal world order.

Captain Henry Hendrix employs the term '*Pax Oceania*' to account for the fact that *Pax Americana* has first and foremost been characterised by a stable maritime order that enables prosperity, whereas the land is still subject to war and conflict (2020, 5). In other words, from a liberal perspective, seapower is instrumental in creating the necessary conditions for trade and prosperity by guaranteeing freedom of the seas. In this sense, Till's argument that seapower is 'relative', given that 'some countries have more [seapower] than others' (2004, 5), can be challenged from a liberal perspective, because within the liberal international order if one's seapower increases, it does not mean that others' seapower decreases, since wealth is understood not in relative but in absolute terms (Germond 2019). Thus, in theory, seapower can be shared between like-minded states engaged in cooperation, all the more since seapower contributes to spreading liberal values (Germond 2022c). Dominant sea Powers have encouraged democracy and democratisation in a bid to limit the risk of war between states sharing an interest in peace and trade (cf. chapter 4), which in turn incentivised the development of a solidaristic society of maritime nations (cf. chapter 6).

Soft power is also a form of power that liberal scholars emphasise. Indeed, liberal states are supposed to conform to liberal principles. Thus, legitimacy – central to the liberal project – is considered a form of ideational power. Promoting democracy by initiating wars with non-democratic states complies with a liberal approach to IR only as long as the intervention is presented as legitimate (here, meaning in accordance with liberal norms and values), which can derive from prior human rights violations taking place in the target country (e.g., responsibility to protect). Maintaining the freedom of the seas and securing the 'global commons' are presented as legitimate activities, and fit with the liberal principles and ideals, even if they imply the use of force. Whether they rest on some states' capacity to exercise hegemony on the high seas is another question, which has been discussed by critical scholars.

Critical IR scholars have devoted their attention to power inequalities within societies and at the international level. Marxist-informed theorists tend to focus on economic inequalities, which, according to them, are the main source of power inequalities and the main determinant of IR. Capitalist elites own wealth and directly or indirectly control states, which in turn act in favour of capitalist interests when interacting with other states. Power is thus seen as a form of control: control over the means of production, control over states' structures, and eventually control over the destiny of the world. Other critical scholars, such as feminists or green theorists focus their attention on gender or environmental inequalities and the resulting power inequalities. Critical approaches to seapower tend to highlight the contribution seapower makes to the dominance of the capitalist world order and the resulting global system of exploitation. In the mid-nineteenth century, British seapower was instrumental in securing not only Britain's hegemony but also free trade over protectionism (Cox 1980, 378–9).

The hegemonic nature of seapower is also illustrated by the link between the command of the global commons and the current US hegemony as discussed by Barry Posen (2003). From that perspective, the very link between wealth and seapower contributes to demonstrating that seapower is instrumental in perpetuating the global system of dominance. This is not incompatible with Till's own observation that 'for better or worse, the Europeans created new empires and changed the world. And they did it by sea' (2004, 16). The sea has been recognised by critical IR scholars and critical political economists as a vector and facilitator of exploitative capitalism (e.g., Campling and Colás 2021; Steinberg 2001). Marxist-informed scholars believe in the primacy of the 'economic' over the 'political' and thus consider that naval bureaucracies, warship industries, naval strategy, and the normative/legal structures (such as the principle of the free sea or UNCLOS) have been subordinated to underlying capitalist interests. In other words, they do not neglect the role that seapower plays in sustaining global hegemony, but they tend to downplay states' agency in this process.

Proponents of systemic theories who do not focus on 'world-economy' but rather on 'global political systems' have emphasised the centrality of seapower in explaining hegemonic cycles (Boswell and Sweat 1991, 129–2). Within the systemic but not necessarily critical tradition,

Modelski and Thompson are the only scholars to have proposed a systematic quantitative analysis of the correlation between seapower and cycles of global dominance. However, as political scientists, their study has been neglected by traditional scholars of seapower in the fields of naval history and maritime strategy. According to Modelski and Thompson, seapower 'or more generally the development of capabilities for global reach constitutes one of four necessary conditions for leadership' (1996, 52), along with the existence of a global political system, the growth of the system's lead economy, and its capacity to respond to global problems in a perceived legitimate way. Seapower is crucial for winning wars but also 'in enforcing the new, postwar order; in policing sea lanes; and in deterring potential attacks on the world power and its allies and clients' (52). In other words, seapower is not just about winning global wars, it is also key to stabilising the post-war order and making it beneficial to the hegemonic Power of the time.

The flourishing of critical IR theories especially since the 1970s and 1980s has also fuelled the debate between positivist and post-positivist scholars. Positivist scholars, whether from the realist, liberal, or even Marxist traditions tend to focus on the material aspects of power: power as a sum of financial, economic, and military assets (and the capacity to assure one's security); power as wealth (and the capacity to create it); power as a form of control (re-enforcing inequalities, maintaining hegemony). Post-positivists tend to focus on the ideational elements of power. Norms, beliefs, and identities shape the definition of interests and the implementation of policies. Thus, there is a direct relationship between knowledge – more precisely the capacity to create knowledge (to construct 'truths') – and power. Power is understood as the power to define such things as norms, what is 'good' or 'bad', what is 'right' or 'wrong', how to characterise world politics in a particular way, which varies depending on time and place. The power to define helps normalising practices and thus contributes to perpetuating certain structures and belief systems, which will in turn contribute to legitimising certain practices.

Following this approach, seapower can be understood as an ideational power, that is, the capacity to set up agendas. Seapower has been idealised in the collective imaginaries, as the source of wealth, the method by which to acquire wealth, and the normal state of affairs in the maritime domain, which tends to stabilise and legitimise the liberal world order. Critical scholars thus denounce this construction and the resulting practice discussed above: 'water is capital's element. The bourgeois idealization of sea power and ocean borne commerce has been central to the mythology of capital' (Connery 1995, 40). Naval hierarchies contribute to representing the international order as also highly hierarchical. As discussed by Kearsley, ranking navies combines the desire 'by both authors and practitioners of naval power alike to compare and contrast navies on a global scale with the desire of obtaining a linear list that reflects an international maritime pecking order' (1992, 32). Critical geographers, led by Philip Steinberg (2001), denounce the representation of the sea as an empty space devoid of any social relationships, given that this contributes to the projection of both material and normative power, including modern and liberal values.

Table 2.1 shows that regardless of IR traditions, seapower can be analysed as a capacity and a consequence/outcome (a subject discussed by Till in 2004, see below). However, depending on the approach adopted, more emphasis is put on ideational factors, and the consequential power relationship is either presented as a fact (realism), beneficial to everybody (liberalism), or beneficial to the hegemonic Power(s) (critical and systemic approaches). Ongoing debates over the concept of power within the field of IR theories have been highly informative and have contributed to the academic scholarship. However, they have directed the discussions towards epistemological and methodological questions rather than the very meaning and scope of power, especially since the 1980s and the emergence of constructivist and post-structuralist approaches in IR. Beyond the field of IR, other definitions of the concept centre on the very nature of power in IR.

INTRINSIC AND EXTRINSIC SEAPOWER

A relevant alternative conception of power distinguishes intrinsic from extrinsic power. Intrinsic (i.e., inner) power accounts for actors' inherent capabilities, often quantified in absolute terms. In other words, intrinsic power is not dependent on other agents' perception and behaviour. Measure of states' intrinsic power can consist of their order of battle and gross domestic product, or GDP (numerical measures). However, political factors that sustain military and economic capabilities, such as internal stability, also constitute forms of intrinsic power, albeit more difficult to quantify. Intrinsic power still depends on other actors' potential vulnerabilities, or at least on other actors' propensity to be influenced by its elements. For example, nuclear weapons and

Table 2.1
A summary of IR theories' take on seapower

IR approaches	Approach to seapower	Nature of seapower
Realist tradition	Sea (naval) power as a tool at states' disposal; balance of naval assets; naval ranking	• Sum of assets/quantifiable capabilities • Consequential relationship (hierarchy, balance of power)
Liberal tradition	Seapower as the capacity to create wealth and stabilise the liberal world order	• Capabilities (soft and hard) • Consequential relationship (stability, wealth)
Critical traditions	Seapower as a tool at states' disposal (and an instrument of capitalism) to maintain their control over the system	• Material and/or ideational capabilities • Consequential relationship (control, hegemony)
Systemic approaches	Seapower as instrumental in explaining global cycles of dominance (via global reach and control of global supply chains)	• Material and institutional capabilities • Consequential relationship (dominance)

the means to deliver them, such as ballistic missiles, constitute elements of intrinsic power for those who possess them, but this is the case only if, and since, other actors are vulnerable to nuclear strikes, in terms of individuals' and states' survival. Thus a state which possesses millions of water squirt pistols has no more intrinsic power than a state which does not possess any (except if water pistols constitute an indicator of economic wealth ...). In practice, this criterion of vulnerability is complex since it may be difficult to sort out which assets or resources must be taken into account when quantifying actors' intrinsic power. Additionally, intrinsic power can be constrained by the context, including structural forces (e.g., the distribution of intrinsic power between various actors) and geographical realities (e.g., a landlocked country's maritime power, for example via a thriving commercial high sea fleet, will at best remain limited).

Intrinsic elements of seapower include the naval order of battle, sailors' training, commanders' experience, the strength of the domestic naval industry, the strength of the domestic commercial shipping sector, countries' underlying economic performances, demography, as well as various ideational elements, such as sailors' morale, the existence of a maritime strategic culture, and good governance. Geographical elements may also be taken into account to measure intrinsic seapower, such as the presence of a long coastline and states' positioning on the global grid. Interestingly, intrinsic forms of seapower transcend the traditional boundaries between material and ideational elements. In other words, intrinsic seapower depends on both material and ideational factors (cf. chapter 3).

For its part, extrinsic (i.e., outward) power is a form of power that comes from one's ideational relationship with other agents within the system. It refers to one's influence and one's position as perceived by other actors. It is not a capacity that needs to be material but one that is attributed to an actor. It is thus dependent on social relations (Crespi 1988, 8) and on the meaning associated with attributes. For example, when French general Pierre Gallois emphasised the 'equalizing power' of the atomic bomb, he did not only refer to the ability to deter much more powerful states (such as the Soviet Union) because of the devastating effects of a handful of nuclear bombs but also to the fact that once a country had acquired nuclear capabilities, it is de facto considered a 'Great Power' and is thus respected as a member of this 'club' (see also Sagan 1997). Permanent membership of the UN Security Council or membership of the G-7 are other examples of extrinsic power. Although based on actual attributes, such as nuclear bombs and large industrial sector, extrinsic power generates behaviours by other actors that respond to the socially created meaning of these attributes.

The extrinsic power of navies depends on their possession of certain classes of ships that, based on the technical, tactical, and operational realities of the time, bear strong symbolic power: first-rate ships of the line in the age of sail, battleships until World War II, and aircraft carriers since then. In the twenty-first century, the very possession of an aircraft carrier symbolises the high status of a given navy; it demonstrates 'blue water' capabilities (intrinsic power) but also a state's intents in terms of power projection and as such is a form of extrinsic power, since power and forces projection represent the ultimate form of military power in the collective imaginaries. China's first aircraft carrier (the Type 001 *Liaoning* launched in 2012 and based on the Soviet-era Kuznetsov class) is a case in point. At the time it had been constructed it represented a symbol of China's move towards being a proper contender to the US hegemony, although in practice it did not modify the naval balance of power in the Pacific. Another example is Thailand's light aircraft carrier, the HTMS *Chakri Naruebet*, which rarely leaves her base and is mainly used for transportation and humanitarian purposes; its function is thus mainly symbolic in the form of extrinsic power projected into Southeast Asia; Thailand being the only Association of Southeast Asian Nations country whose navy operates a carrier. Russia's current inability to operate an aircraft carrier is highly detrimental to its perceived/assigned status as a Great Power and Putin's regime's claim of global power.

Naval ranking is a common practice in the academic literature (Morris 1987; Grove 1990; Lindberg 1998; Coutau-Bégarie 2002; Barber and Sipos 2004; Haydon 2007; Germond 2014). The resulting hierarchies are also popular among naval practitioners, certainly due to the human nature's inclination to rank, categorise, and benchmark everything (Surminski and Williamson 2014). The outcome of these hierarchies is that navies reaching the 'upper' categories, even by the most limited margin, increase their extrinsic power, which can virtually happen 'in a snap' following the release of a new ranking, even though it does not really fit with the material/operational realities. In this sense we can wonder about the extent to which Grove's *Future of Sea Power*, which placed the Soviet navy one category above the French and the British ones (1990, 237–8) would have resulted in an increase of the extrinsic power of the Soviet navy should the USSR not have imploded one year after the book was published.

Extrinsic power can be distributed or delegated to actors by the authority holding the (perceived) legitimacy to do this. For example, states hold intrinsic power but can delegate extrinsic power to multilateral bodies such as NATO (Falcon y Tella 2004, 353). The link to constructivist ideas is clear; international institutions exist by the will of states (and individuals within the states); their power is thus only extrinsic since states' will/agreement can stop or change at any time, and their power depends on their legitimacy to 'hold' power (i.e., the social construction of international organisations). At sea, such a form of extrinsic power can be found in the way NATO standards and operating procedures are employed by the great majority of navies, even those considered traditional NATO competitors. As an alliance of the most powerful naval actors, NATO combines collective intrinsic and extrinsic power.

POTENTIAL AND KINETIC SEAPOWER

Another relevant distinction is between so-called potential and kinetic power, a classification borrowed from the terminology of Newtonian physics, which differentiates potential from kinetic energy. Potential power is the power, intrinsic and/or extrinsic, associated with an actor, even if it is not put to use. It can be quantified but remains potential as long as it is not delivered, or enacted. Kinetic power refers to the power actually delivered, which impacts on other actors, or in other words the 'enactment of power' (Coleman, Deutsch, and Marcus, 2014, 140). It is about physically, or kinetically, producing effects on or influencing other actors' behaviour or the system itself. For example, state A's order of battle and G D P are indicators of its potential power. If state A actually uses its military capabilities and financial resources to attack state B, this converts part of its potential power into kinetic power. Cyber-attacks are not physical and thus are often referred to as non-kinetic. Launching a cyber-attack is nonetheless a form of 'kinetic' power as opposed to potential power, that is, an enactment of power with 'concrete' consequences/effects.

Prepositioned naval forces and supply ships are a form of potential power, that is, a Damocles sword placed above the head of other states. On the other hand, prepositioned forces exert power by deterrence, which is a form of enacted power that is accounted for by the concept of ideational kinetic power. Indeed, kinetic power can be the result of a material enactment of potential power (for instance a military campaign) or of an ideational enactment of power (for instance state A threatening to use nuclear weapons against state B resulting in state B renouncing to attack states A and C). In another example, state A's possession of an aircraft carrier can constrain state B's decisions via its symbolic power. Ideational kinetic power can be linked to Joseph Nye's notion of soft power, that is, 'the ability to shape the preferences of others' (2004, 5). Actors can exercise normative power (i.e., defining the acceptable norms or normal behaviour) or normalising, or transformative, power (i.e., the power to make other actors change their behaviour to align to the norm). Again, naval diplomacy is a case in point. Naval presence can certainly coerce other states. More subtly, naval confidence-building measures and maritime capacity building can help propagate certain norms via the adoption of certain standards and common procedures, which consist in the first step towards the development of security communities. Indeed, the naval signals, procedures, and tactics of the US and NATO have become global (Tangredi 2002, 27), which facilitates interoperability, but also reinforces Western leadership over maritime affairs. In sum, the enactment of seapower is as important as its elements.

As mentioned, when discussing critical I R approaches and seapower, from a Foucauldian perspective power is not an essence; rather, it is

Table 2.2
Typology of power and the nature of seapower

Types of power	Related elements/attributes of seapower (examples)	Nature of seapower
Intrinsic power (material)	Naval order of battle, naval bases, naval industry, shipping industry	Sum of (material) assets
Intrinsic power (ideational)	Maritime culture, seafaring culture, trade value	Sum of (ideational) assets
Extrinsic power	Possession of certain ships, naval ranking, NATO standards	Sum of assets and (perceived) capabilities
Potential power	Fleet-in-being, forward presence, order of battle	Sum of assets
Kinetic power (material)	Anti-ship missile strikes, land-attacked cruise missile strikes, amphibious operations, policing the seas, etc.	Enactment
Kinetic power (ideational)	Naval diplomacy, deterrence at sea, ocean governance norms and regulations	Enactment
Power as a consequential relationship	Command of the sea, stability of the liberal world order, law of the seas regime	Power as a consequential relationship

a relationship of domination, which is subject to change (Foucault 1982, 788–9). Power can be understood as a context-influenced consequence, a state of affairs (i.e., a snapshot of the power relation at a given time, and perhaps also in a given place), which reflects a given world order. The enactment of material and ideational kinetic power results in a certain power relation, usually at the advantage of the most powerful actor or the one that has succeeded in applying its potential power to its relationship with other actors. This power relation normalises and consolidates a certain political order. For example, the domination of Western navies over the world's ocean since the end of the Cold War (and before the rise of any serious contender) has translated into a stable liberal world order dominated by trade relations. Table 2.2 summarises how alternative understandings of power can help us better grasp the meaning and scope of seapower beyond IR theories, and thus help complement the initial definition of seapower.

In sum, the definition of seapower needs to account for three layers of analysis: the elements, enactment, and outcomes of seapower. This framework for analysis is discussed in chapter 3.

3

Seapower and (Post)Modernity:
A New Framework for Analysis

Power (and seapower) can be measured and interpreted in many
different ways. Modernity and post-modernity are also controversial
concepts, whose scope spans disciplines. By bringing the two concepts
together this chapter proposes an original framework for analysis.
The chapter introduces the concept of modernity and the way
seapower can be analysed through the prism of the modernity/
post-modernity debate. The framework endorses a comprehensive
approach to seapower that accounts for its naval, economic, civilian,
and ideational dimensions at three different levels: the elements, the
enactment, and the consequences/outcomes of seapower. Whereas
the ideational factors are central when it comes to understanding the
evolution of seapower, states and human agency still constitute an
important determinant, since seapower is ultimately about operating
at, via, and from the sea as well as controlling human activities and
flows at sea.

REASSESSING THE NATURE OF SEAPOWER:
ELEMENTS, ENACTMENT, AND OUTCOMES

Chapter 1 offers a preliminary discussion of seapower from a historiographical perspective. Then, chapter 2 frames seapower within IR
approaches and alternative conceptions of the nature and features of
power. With that in mind, we can now further explore the characteristics of seapower. One of the greatest contemporary thinkers who
discussed the concept of seapower is Geoffrey Till. His main contribution to the debate is his valuable distinction between two complementary
understandings of seapower: (1) seapower as an input, that is, a variety

of quantitative assets broadly related to the ability of one state to operate at sea, and/or (2) seapower as an output (a consequence), that is,
'the capacity to influence the behaviour of other people or things by
what one does at or from the sea' (Till 2004, 4). This is closer to Herbert
Rosinski's understanding that seapower can 'shift freely between the
various contending naval powers' (1977, 124) and is thus the result of
a certain balance of naval power at a given time.

Although Till's focus is on maritime strategy, thinking in terms of
consequences of seapower also enables accounting for non-material
elements. In 2015, I proposed that seapower as a consequence shall
also be understood as a process or a relationship, that is, a relationship
of domination resulting from an efficient use of the sea (Germond
2015, 11). This accounts for the fact that those who master the sea
become sea Powers, but this status is not immutable; it remains subject
to change. And, as Lambert (2018) reminds us, maintaining a maritime
outlook is both crucial and arduous over long periods of time.
Accounting for the outcomes of seapower also shows that beyond its
close link to the liberal international order and to the stability of this
order, seapower can also be understood as a form of dominance, as
proposed by critical and systemic scholars. In the following section,
the nature of seapower is examined by focusing on three different
layers: the elements, the enactment, and the outcomes/consequences
of seapower.

The Elements of Seapower

The elements of seapower refer to the main determinants of seapower,
that is to say the factors that contribute to the development and success of seapower. Mahan famously identifies six conditions affecting
the seapower of nations, namely the geographical position, the physical conformation, the extent of territory, the size of population, the
character of people, and the character of the government ([1890]
2007, 25–89). Later authors and commentators have mainly discussed
Mahan's geographical and geopolitical elements, thus missing a crucial
point: 'Mahan's main concern in the *Influence of Sea Power* series was
the critical importance of decision making by statesmen and admirals,
not the power of geographical factors to determine the course of
history' (Sumida 1999, 57). This argument does not differ from
Richmond's main claim in *Statesmen and Sea Power* that seapower is
made of three main material elements (merchant shipping, overseas

possessions, and naval power), but the crucial role is played by statesmen who have the power to determine 'the policy of national defence
and the part which sea power plays in it; deciding the standard of
naval strength in relation to other Powers; providing and maintaining
the fighting instruments at the required strength and efficiency, the
bases necessary for their use, and the shipping and seamen which
transport the armies and the commerce' (1946, ix). The influence of
ideational elements on decisions related to maritime policies is crucial,
and the role of decision makers is further discussed in relation to the
enactment of seapower. In this sub-section, three main categories of
determinants are considered, which are not all fixed and immutable:
natural/geographical (immutable) factors, geopolitical and material
(context-dependent) factors, and ideational factors.

Natural factors refers to geographical 'permanencies', such as the
shape and length of coasts. Such elements were considered 'immutable'
on a human timescale (hundreds to thousands of years) and moving
only on a geological timescale (millions to billions of years). However,
the effects of climate change on sea level rise (with the planned
disappearance of entire islands in the medium term) mean that we
have to qualify the so-called immutability of some geological features,
including the shape of coasts. States or societies, such as landlocked
countries, without access to the sea will not *naturally* develop
seapower. This needs to be qualified, at least in theory. First, international law does not formally prevent landlocked countries from
operating naval forces; they only need to secure allies who will want to
harbour their warships. For example, in the late 1990s and early 2000s,
Belgium and Luxembourg launched a common acquisition programme
for a large amphibious ship that would be financed at 25 per cent by
Luxembourg and could accommodate Luxembourgian crew. The
project was eventually cancelled for financial reasons. It nevertheless
shows that a small landlocked country is not prevented from developing some form of naval power. And in 2010, Luxembourg participated
in the EU counter-piracy operation Atalanta at the Horn of Africa
with a patrol aircraft. This shows the importance of multilateral operations and the post-modern political environment, in this case the EU,
which allow a landlocked country to operate, almost 'naturally', within
a naval coalition.

Beyond the development of a navy or the participation in coalition
operations (which will at best remain anecdotal for a landlocked
country) seapower refers to seafaring and maritime commerce as well;

it is thus interesting to note that landlocked countries can also own and operate a merchant navy and then acquire some form of civilian seapower (cf. chapter 6). For example, as of 2021, eighteen ocean-going ships operated by four companies were flying the Swiss flag. During World War II, when the Swiss merchant marine was created, it had an important role in terms of critical supply and political neutrality, which illustrates the non-exclusively military dimension of seapower (Germond 2022b). In 2020, Switzerland was also firmly in the world's top twenty in terms of the number of ships owned by Swiss companies, with 416 ocean-going ships (Federal Department of Foreign Affairs 2021). In particular MSC, the largest container shipping company since 2022, has its headquarters in Switzerland. A 2018 study of 'leading maritime nations' (quoted in Abreu de Moura 2022, 61–2) that uses indicators such as fleet size management, fleet size by owner country, maritime finance (but also shipyards and ports) placed Switzerland in the top-tier group of maritime nations along with China, the US, Greece, Singapore, and others.

This shows how the globalisation of finance has rendered irrelevant the link between owning, or even operating, a merchant marine and the geographical position of the owner's, or operator's, country. At the cultural level, Switzerland does have a sailing nation tradition. In 2003, a Swiss team became the fifth nation to win the coveted America's Cup sailing competition, which is regarded as one of the most prestigious and difficult nautical competitions to win; the team's headquarter was situated on the shores of Lake Geneva. Interestingly, Royal Navy historian Captain Roskill emphasised the role of 'yachtsmen and amateur sailors' in addition to fishermen and sailors to provide the necessary base for maritime strength (Roskill 1962, 19). It is also telling that sailing as a sport (including competitions) grew in popularity in the mid-nineteenth century, which coincides with the vanishing role played by sailing ships both for trade and warfare (Lavery 2013, 366).

In sum, it is pointless to deny that landlocked countries are less likely to become sea Powers, but they can nevertheless acquire some elements of seapower, notably economic ones. Actually, as Till (2004, 5) points out, seapower is not restricted to 'a handful of largely Western countries' or large, powerful maritime states. In his discussion of maritime strategy for so-called medium Powers, admiral J. Richard Hill stresses that 'if power is the ability to influence events, all states with a seacoast have some maritime power' (1986, 30). Now if seapower is to be understood as more than national navies and encompass participation in multilateral naval operations and maritime economic power, then even landlocked countries can develop some form of limited, mainly civilian seapower.

The length of the coastline is also critical, since it impacts on other elements of seapower, such as the maritime culture and maritime economy. Indeed, we can infer a logical correlation between the length of a country's coastline and the importance of maritime commerce and culture. However, this also needs to be qualified since countries with rather short coastlines may well develop a disproportionate interest in maritime trade. For example, Venice in the ninth to twelfth centuries, and, the Netherlands, with a longer coastline, in the sixteenth and seventeenth centuries, translated into naval power as well. Island countries and those with long coastlines were traditionally thought to be in a better position to concentrate naval forces where and when needed. However, since the late nineteenth century, the densification of railway networks has impacted on the strategic advantage of seapower since it became possible to quickly concentrate power on land.

The further development of airpower also rendered the length of the coastline somewhat redundant as a factor accounting for the development of naval power. Economic liberalism and especially states' economic integration have also globalised the patterns of world trade; in peacetime, even landlocked countries' commerce is not much limited by the lack of direct access to a coastline. That said, from an identity perspective, the length of the coastline is associated with a maritime outlook, which is part of the important ideational elements of seapower.

Another 'natural' element is one country's location on the global grid and especially one's access to the main SLOCS. This is linked to the concept of insularity, a geographical position that commands access to many SLOCS and offers protection from invasion: 'Islands in the world ocean have had privileged access to global traffic routes and opportunities to develop trading fleets, fisheries, navies and explorations. For continental powers these could be seen as luxuries; for insular states these would be necessities and therefore the object of sustained interest and major investment' (Modelski 1987, 221). In his *Seapower States*, Lambert (2018) shows that a high dependence on seafaring and maritime trade has incentivised seapower upon which maritime states' survival was based, due to their relative weakness compared to continental Powers.

States with limited access to the high seas may well be limited in their development of seapower. But this point is linked to geopolitical considerations, thus context-dependent factors, since even if one's access to the sea is via a narrow strait, whether this strait is controlled by an ally or an enemy will eventually determine one's ability to develop seapower, not the fact that this strait actually exists. This is akin to what Wegener ([1929] 1989) calls 'strategic position'. Russia's limited access to the sea is, on the one hand, due to the climate in the Arctic and on the other hand to the enclosed geography of its Baltic Sea and Black Sea facades. However, the Turkish and Danish straits act as limits to Russia' seapower only if we consider the antagonistic nature of the relationships between Russia and NATO. In other words, and to paraphrase the well-known IR constructivist scholar Alexander Wendt (1992), one could say that geography is what states make of it: a strait will prevent state A's seapower to develop only as long as state B, which controls said strait, is antagonistic to state A. Decision makers' willingness to harness geographical constraints and develop seapower remains central, illustrating the role of agency along with that of geography. For Elizabethan England, 'the fact of geography had not changed, but England had learned to exploit them' (Rodger [1997] 2004, 430). In sum, the geographical position really matters only when linked to political considerations, which are context-dependent and thus not immutable. Figure 3.1 shows geographical elements of seapower do not influence seapower directly; geographical permanencies rather indirectly impact seapower via their influence on geopolitical, material, and ideational elements of seapower.

Context-dependent determinants can be broadly divided between geopolitical elements and purely material elements. Geopolitical elements of seapower refer to the political/military/security spatial environment of a given state and are thus susceptible to change over the course of history. The case of France, which had to deal with continental threats while England could concentrate on the sea, has been widely discussed. Despite its navy being second to none but the Royal Navy, Admiral Grivel made it clear that France is first and foremost a land Power. He stressed that 'all Frenchmen possess a more or less exact knowledge of military matters and art [but] an understanding of the naval art and the condition of maritime power is only rarely found in France' (Grivel 1869, 280). This shows that geopolitical elements of seapower can be mutually constitutive with ideational ones, such as maritime culture and identity (discussed below).

Another context-dependent geopolitical element of seapower is one's possession of overseas bases or one's ability to secure access to friendly harbours or coaling/fuelling stations, since this allows sustaining deployments overseas for longer periods of time and increases one's navy's reach, while contributing to developing/securing a network of s l o c s for maritime trade. This is, for example, what China is currently trying to achieve with its strategy of acquiring or getting access to naval facilities along the sea route from China to the Gulf – Spratly and Paracel Islands, Cambodia, Thailand, Myanmar, Bangladesh, Sri Lanka, Maldives, and Pakistan – a strategy that has been labelled as the 'string of pearl[s]' (Pant 2012, 365). Western commentators consider this a strategic move by Beijing although, in the Chinese Communist Party's narrative, it is presented as 'benevolent' within its Maritime Silk Road initiative. Thus, whether China's initiative represents a threat depends on the contextual strategic relationships between China and the West.

Material determinants of seapower include a variety of assets, such as the naval order of battle, a seafaring economy, a shipbuilding industry, a thriving fishing sector, and, upstream, a strong enough economy and a stable enough political system to allow seapower to flourish. In the twenty-first century the existence of a merchant navy is not a prerequisite for seapower, as long as one's economy is maritime-oriented, and one has enough leverage to guarantee its sustainable growth. The main sea Powers of the twenty-first century are no longer those with the largest merchant marine (flag states), the most striking example being the US, which is outside the world's top twenty merchant navy chart that is topped by Panama, Liberia, and the Marshall Islands (open registers). However, the US remains one of the main actors in terms of ownership of ships and is one of the major places of origin of, and destination for, the goods transported by sea. Material elements such as the naval order of battle also depend on material prerequisites, which are quantifiable and influence the ability to develop seapower, including demography, political stability, states' institutional structures, and so forth. The distribution of naval power within the international system (structure) is another context-dependent factor that realist authors have taken into account, since according to this approach one's naval power is limited by the amount of naval power other states have developed (zero-sum game). As discussed in chapter 2, this argument can be criticised since it implies an understanding of seapower in relative terms, and thus downplays the role of coalition and cooperative behaviours in explaining the success of the West in dominating the global maritime order.

Ideational factors are what Sørensen (2008) calls social programming that influences states' actions. As with the discussion of geography and geopolitics, ideational factors are mutually constitutive with the structural and material elements. Ideational elements of seapower include political will, norms, maritime culture, and collective imaginaries, as well as geo-representations. The role of decision makers is discussed in the next sub-section on the enactment of seapower, but it is worth mentioning here that their cognitive programming influences the development of seapower, as does the existence of a maritime culture (or lack thereof). Mahan himself assigned significant importance to his fifth and sixth elements of seapower: the national character and the character of government that impact 'upon the development of sea power' ([1890] 2007, 50, 58). This is not dissimilar to Wegener's ([1929] 1989) emphasis on the 'strategic will' of a nation as a crucial enabler of seapower. The idea is that the material elements of seapower rest on the existence of a maritime culture, which includes seafaring values and, generally, an attraction to the sea rather than a fear of it (notably for the fear that it can bring 'foreign', subversive values). Roskill stresses that 'the need for a maritime nation to foster the profession of the sea' is vital (1962, 18). Indeed, whereas governments can 'decree' the need to build warships, know-how and naval traditions result from a long-term practice, including by the civilian maritime sector.

The Soviet bid to develop a (balanced) oceanic navy since the late 1960s–70s and the failure to become ever close to the US Navy has often been linked in the academic literature to the lack of a proper maritime strategic culture in Russia (e.g., Brooks 1986). Even strategist C.S. Gray admits that in addition to a navy and a merchant marine, a sea Power needs 'an influential sea-oriented community for the advancement of maritime aspects' (1992, 7). This is a point made very clear in Lambert's *Seapower States* (2018): seapower is underpinned by a maritime identity that has to be nurtured, what Till calls 'sea-mindedness' (Till 2022, 6). The need for proactive rulers to advocate the importance of the sea for the nation had already been recognised in the nineteenth century by George Grote, who explained that Athens's conversion 'from a land-power into a sea-power' necessitated Themistocles, as the initiator of this policy change, to instil it 'in the mind of the people' ([1849] 1857, 51).

A maritime culture (or the absence thereof) is somewhat linked to the importance of trade values within one community, which, according to Till (2004, 22) have to be differentiated from Western values, since they can be found in non-Western cultures as well. Although seafaring and trade values can be found in any culture, maritime culture seems to be linked to the 'free spirit of humanity' (Dehio 1962, 272), for it encompasses a greater degree of openness and freedom that is less frequently encountered in totalitarian or even authoritarian states. Opposing democratic seafaring Athens with authoritarian land-oriented Sparta or opposing Enlightened Europe sailing the world's ocean with obscurantist Russia stuck on the land-mass has too many times resulted in caricatures rather than demonstrated anything concrete about the role of values and identity in seapower politics. Indeed, the relationship goes both ways: whereas progressive values have been instrumental in fostering maritime outlooks, a maritime identity has to be nurtured for economic, financial, and political elites to back investment in seapower. Only a few proper sea states (most notably England) have managed to do this for extended periods of time (Lambert 2018). In other words, agency and identity cannot be separated when reflecting on the development of seapower.

Beyond trade values, a maritime culture more generally depends on nations' level of integration between their economy and the sea. For example, the EU's maritime culture is intrinsically linked to economic considerations; something perfectly illustrated by the Blue Growth discourse within the Union. Indeed, the over-emphasis on maritime economy (trade, tourism, fisheries, etc.) explains the need for the EU to develop its own seapower to maintain security in the maritime domain: 'The Sea is a valuable source of growth and prosperity for the European Union and its citizens. The EU depends on open, protected and secure seas and oceans for economic development, free trade, transport, energy security, tourism and good status of the marine environment' (Council of the EU 2014, 2). As mentioned above, dominant sea Powers have the necessary material and ideational leverage to shape the international maritime order and its underlying institutions and norms. In turn, the maritime legal culture, norms, and regime play in favour of the dominant sea Powers: 'the expanded notion of sea power as against purely naval power is dependent upon the regimes created by progressive maritime law' (Kraska 2009, 121). The international law of the sea guarantees the freedom of the seas for commercial and military purposes, while increasingly allowing states to steward and police the ocean even beyond their territorial waters. Although small states might find it useful (e.g., UNCLOS extended jurisdictional rights over EEZs), this mainly serves dominant sea Powers' interests and increases their leverage (cf. chapter 5).

Ideational elements of seapower also include collective imaginaries, that is to say the way people within one community (e.g., a state) tend to construct something (such as the sea and seapower) through a series of representations. This is obviously linked to maritime culture since positive representations form the basis of maritime identity. For example, since the Elizabethan era, the sea and what it brings to England's power have constantly been romanticised and glorified in arts and discourses (e.g., Baker 2010), contributing to the myth of British seapower in the collective imaginaries. On the contrary, the sea and seafaring values have traditionally been represented sceptically by China's central government (especially since the decision to stop maritime exploration).This contributes to China's limited maritime outlook even today and the difficulty in moving beyond a continental outlook, despite the current development of naval power (e.g. aircraft carrier programme) and civilian endeavours such as the Belt and Road Initiative and its strong maritime dimension.

As figure 3.1 shows, ideational factors cannot be taken into account without linking them to geographical, geopolitical, and material factors. The relationship is twofold, that is, ideational factors via decision makers influence the development of material components of seapower, such as a navy, and the will to obtain overseas bases and maintain the ability to dominate the global supply chain, which in turn influences geopolitical elements of seapower. But geography and geopolitical realities also affect the development of a maritime culture over a long-term period, since proximity to the sea is perhaps the most important factor constraining the development of a maritime identity.

In sum, the four elements of seapower are interdependent but the geographical elements only affect other elements – not seapower directly – and thus constitute some sort of pre-elements due to their permanence on a human-time scale (barring the effects of climate change on marine geography). At first glance, geographical elements do not depend on other elements since geographical permanencies cannot be changed. However, this may be debatable, since the building of canals, such as Suez and Panama, has impacted on geographical

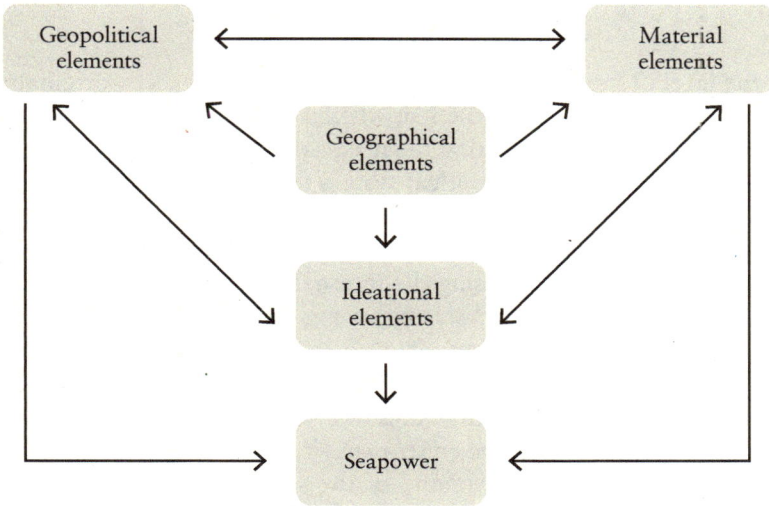

Figure 3.1 The elements of seapower

elements of seapower (notably some states' facilitated access to, and control of, global shipping lanes) by de facto modifying geographical features of the Earth. Similarly, China's building of artificial islands in the South China Sea for strategic, political, and legal reasons constitutes some sort of a modification of the natural geography, which definitely impacts on China's elements of seapower. Whether this modifies geographical permanencies or simply creates different geopolitical realities is open to debate.

Although geographical permanencies cannot easily be 'changed' (and only to some extent), as discussed above, states' agency has room for developing practices that overcome the 'negative' or limiting aspects of geography, since the conception of 'positive' or 'negative' geography often depends on the behaviour and perception of other states within the system. For their part, geopolitical, material, and ideational elements influence each other reciprocally. For example, the development of a blue water navy may well result from the need to acquire bases far away from home and/or from the growing maritime character of the people and government. Then, the very development of new ships capable of remaining at sea for longer periods of time can modify the maritime identity of a given country, with long-lasting effects on their seapower politics.

The Enactments of Seapower

At the level of its enactment, seapower is an act of power, originating in the sea and one's use of the sea, which consists in influencing other actors' behaviour and creating the necessary conditions for one's own economy to flourish and political system to stabilise and thrive. From a realist perspective, the enactment of seapower allows fulfilling one's national interests (notably security). From a liberal perspective it allows creating wealth and stabilising the international liberal order. From a critical perspective it allows strengthening the hegemony of dominant Powers via an efficient and cost-effective use of the 'great void' (Steinberg 2001) for power projection and the free flow of capital and ideas. From a systemic perspective it contributes to cycles of global dominance.

In purely naval terms, the enactment of seapower consists in securing (global or limited) command of the sea and exploiting/exerting command of the sea, which practically consists in protecting one's sovereignty and trade and/or projecting one's power beyond one's external boundary. In fact, seapower is largely enacted by navies, which are a crucial vector of seapower (Germond 2015, 33), but this enactment is not limited to the naval dimension. Enacting seapower is about using the sea to impact the situation on land: carrying out interventions, blockades, but also fostering trade and cooperation as well as governing the oceans and stabilising the world order. Ultimately, the enactment of seapower is also about controlling and managing the flow of goods and people at/from the sea: controlling the global supply chain and controlling the maritime space under one's sovereignty and beyond, securing the maritime domain, projecting norms and ocean governance.

The enactment of seapower at the naval level has been the object of study of maritime/naval strategy, that is, 'the principles which govern a war in which the sea is a substantial factor' (Corbett 1911, 15). Discussions have revolved around the maritime strategic principles, such as sea control, sea denial, projection, forward presence, fleet-in-being, force concentration, and decisive naval battle. The aim of this book is not to revisit maritime/naval strategy (for that see Germond 2015; Speller 2014, 2022; Till 2004). It is, however, interesting to briefly discuss the recent evolution of naval missions during war as well as in peacetime. Indeed, naval missions are the strategic or policy objectives or tasks assigned to the naval forces. They are also called naval functions by some authors (e.g., Booth 1979), to refer to the inherent role, or even nature, of naval force. There are peacetime and wartime naval missions as well as missions that are relevant in both contexts. Naval forces can perform widely varied missions due to their mobility, versatility, and freedom of action; all of these features are inherent to the milieu in which they operate, that is the sea (Germond 2015, 34–8).

Naval missions are a good indicator of how seapower is conceived by high-level political and military decision makers at a given time and in a given place. Indeed, statements of naval missions serve two aims: (1) to set up the boundaries of what the navy is supposed to contribute to in terms of military, strategic, security, and policy objectives; (2) to tell the public opinion, home and abroad, a story about one's navy's role, thus constructing the navy's image, which is a form of soft power. The triangle developed by Booth (1979, 15–25) and Grove (1990, 234) is still a relevant starting point (figure 3.2).

Whereas diplomatic and police (constabulary) missions have gained in importance since the end of the Cold War, within the military missions there has been a clear shift from sea control (in defence of commerce and in view of potential naval battles and force projection in case of war) to power and forces projection in a peacetime context, that is, in the framework of foreign interventions, where the intervening actors de facto possess sea control in the theatre of operation. Discussions about potential opposition between China and the US in the Pacific region have led to a new emphasis on area denial and anti-area denial (e.g., Tangredi 2013). Russia's annexation of Crimea in 2014 had led NATO to discuss the extent to which its main role shall be to prepare for the defence of the European continent (including its maritime approaches) rather than (or in addition to) foreign interventions. Russia's illegal invasion of Ukraine in 2022 has cemented this strategic reorientation: 'The Russian Federation is the most significant and direct threat to Allies' security and to peace and stability in the Euro-Atlantic area' (NATO 2022, para. 8). The Alliance's maritime strategy will eventually be revised accordingly.

In peacetime, seapower can still be enacted by navies in the case of 'benign' naval operations, meaning operations that do not involve the use of force (or a minimal use thereof), as well as contribute to naval diplomacy and exercise extrinsic power: naval presence, port visits, prepositioning of forces, intelligence gathering, deterrence, capacity building, peacekeeping, and, at the far end of the peacetime spectrum, limited combat operations during peace enforcement or counter-piracy operations. In addition to what the navy can do, peacetime seapower

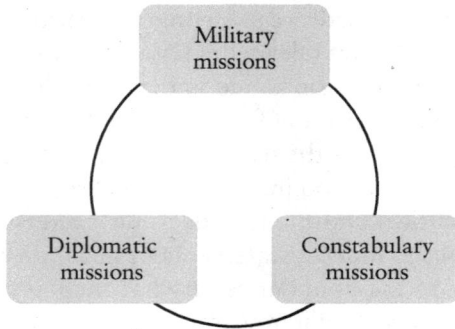

Figure 3.2 The trinity of naval missions
Source: Adapted from Booth (1979), Grove (1990), and Germond (2015).

can be enacted in two main specific ways. First, states monitor and control the seas under and beyond their jurisdiction. Surveying and policing the maritime domain 24/7 enables control of human activities at and from the sea. This form of seapower involves state actors, which still hold the monopoly on the legitimate use of violence, but also includes economic and civilian actors via self-imposition of standards and behaviours across sectors. For example, shipping companies are expected to assure the security of their systems and operations. Second, ideational seapower can be enacted in peacetime that is, setting up international norms and frameworks for governance of maritime spaces, essentially the rules of the game at sea. These two elements together contribute to a process of territorialisation of the sea akin to the situation on land (cf. chapter 5). Overall, dominant sea Powers aim at controlling the global supply chain in peacetime since this is how 'wealth accumulates' (Eccles 1979, 205), which necessitates the enactment of a combination of naval, police, and civilian power at, towards, and from the sea.

The role of decision makers is crucial when it comes to the enactment of seapower. The existence of a strong maritime culture among the ruling elites is instrumental in that it will contribute to constructing seapower (and its enactment) as something 'natural', a 'normal' tool at states' disposal to fulfil their national interest (cf. chapter 2). Chapter 4 shows that even rulers who had a negative opinion of the sea, seafaring, and maritime values have tended to be pragmatic towards seapower or, at least, towards naval procurement. Mahan notes that government influence upon seapower is felt in wartime via direct effects on combat readiness and sustainability of forces but also in peacetime: 'making or marring the sea power of the country' (Mahan [1890] 2007, 82). Seapower cannot be ordered at will; some material elements of seapower, such as the order of battle, have to be planned, developed, and maintained. As Richmond points out, 'it is the duty of the statesman to make provision for the fulfilment of all these needs' (1946, x). Given the resource-heavy nature of navies, those decisions cannot have immediate effects (Grove 1990, 321), and thus seapower politics must be based on long-term considerations and investments that vary depending on the existence of a maritime culture versus sea blindness. For example, the UK's enhanced naval power in the 2020s with two major aircraft carriers that are at the forefront of the post-Brexit 'Global Britain' strategy is the result of strategic and procurement decisions made at the turn of the millennium by the Blair cabinet.

It must also be noted that navies are usually heavy bureaucracies that have to operate within a competitive institutional framework. The competitive relationships between the naval establishment, other branches of the armed forces, and ministries can result in entrenched, bureaucratic politics, which have a direct impact on a state's ability or willingness to enact seapower. Whereas the intra-service competition between the navy and the air force in the US is well documented, such processes are as much if not more important in the case of smaller countries with fewer resources to devote to the armed forces in general.

The Outcomes/Consequences of Seapower

At the level of its outcomes or consequences, seapower creates a relationship of dominance or superiority (depending on the level of seapower enacted and the degree of success of such enactment) that concretises one actor's or one system's preponderance or hegemony. The consequences of seapower are linked to Aristotle's fourth cause, the final cause, in other words, the end towards which seapower tends that can be interpreted very differently, depending on one's positioning within the analytical framework/epistemological spectrum: security and power maximisation (realism), prosperity and stability of the system (liberalism), or hegemony and exploitation (critical approaches) (cf. figure 3.3). The difference between naval power and seapower is thus clear in the sense that naval power alone, as strong as it could be, cannot on its own create those conditions for success and engender these outcomes. The consequences of naval power include wining a battle or successfully conducting a military campaign in a foreign country. The consequences of seapower are deeper and felt in the longer term. They are found at the systemic and structural level with regard to the balance of power and control of the global supply chain and the maritime order, or hegemonic power of agents. Each of these outcomes tends to reinforce the others.

Understood as a consequential relationship, seapower is also context-dependent since the conditions for its enactment can change in the form of varying elements of seapower (geopolitical, material, and ideational factors). Till's virtuous maritime circle (2004, 20; 2022, 3), argues maritime trade engenders maritime resources, which allow developing naval power, which in turn contributes to maritime supremacy, helping to sustain maritime trade. To build on Till's circle, I propose that the elements and the enactment of seapower can mutually reinforce each other in a virtuous circle of seapower via the outcomes/consequences of seapower, which create or sustain these necessary conditions (see figure 3.4).

The elements of seapower are subject to change (and so are the capacity and willingness to enact seapower and the way it is enacted), but there is no inconsequential seapower. Seapower can be poorly enacted resulting in minimal or even negative outcomes, but if and when successfully enacted it will have consequences in terms of power relationships and global dominance. Changes and permanencies in terms of elements but also enactment and consequences are thus crucial to understand the evolution of seapower.

The next stage in building the analytical framework involves the application of concepts of modernity/post-modernity to discuss the three layers of seapower in the context of historical evolution, so as to identify and isolate the changes (e.g., technological advances) and the permanencies (in elements, enactment, and consequences) and analyse how they impact the concept and practice of seapower.

MODERNITY, POST-MODERNITY, AND SEAPOWER: A NEW FRAMEWORK FOR ANALYSIS

As with power, the concepts of modernity and post-modernity have been subject to various debates and interpretations. To begin, the difference between modernism/post-modernism and modernity/post-modernity has been the source of much confusion in the academic

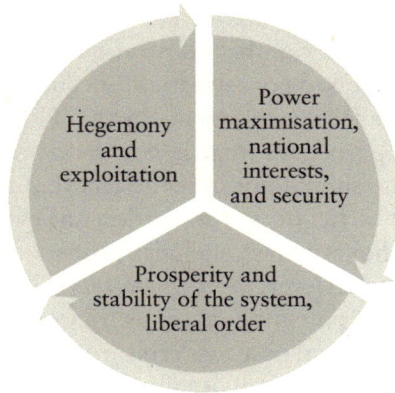

Figure 3.3 The consequences of seapower

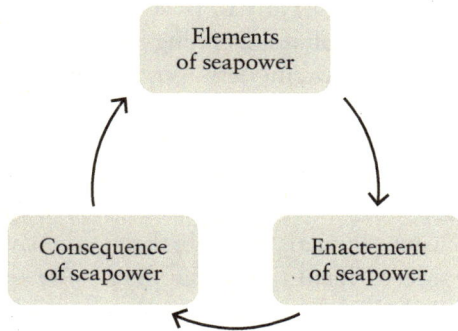

Figure 3.4 The three layers of seapower and the virtuous circle of seapower

literature. The first set of terms refers to artistic, philosophical, and eventually epistemological/methodological movements, while the second set refers either to a normative goal, that is, modernity as the normal endpoint of societies (e.g., Rostow's 1960 modernity thesis) or to historical periods, which are used by positivist and post-positivist scholars alike as research/analytical tools to facilitate the analysis of the evolution of states' and societies' characteristics across historical periods.

Since the birth of IR as an academic discipline in the 1920s and especially since the 1970s, academic debates in the field have been dominated by epistemological and methodological disagreements, which mainly centre around the opposition between rationalist theorists and those informed by normative and post-structuralist concepts and philosophies (leading to the so-called fourth debate in IR). However, the fact that post-structuralist approaches (that is *post-modernism*) are contested within the discipline should not hide the fact that the object of study (or subject matter) of IR, or world politics, has evolved in the recent past, and now, without contest, includes post-modern features at the structural and ideational levels (*post-modernity*). This is what Cahoone (1996) calls historical post-modernism as opposed to methodological post-modernism. Historical post-modernism acknowledges the fact that the social, political, and cultural organisation of the world has fundamentally changed (17). In this book, I employ the terms 'modernity' and 'post-modernity' to refer to the changing social, political, and cultural characteristics of the world order, and I reserve 'modernism' and 'post-modernism' for the epistemological and methodological debates within the discipline.

When this shift from modernity to post-modernity occurred is still highly debated across disciplines. Defining historical periods along the division between pre-modern, modern, post-modern, and neo-modern eras is academically hazardous, since there is no consensus on the definition of the time periods associated with the various states (if not 'stages') of modernity. As Zygmunt Bauman notices, the problem is that modern and post-modern practices currently coexist and thus such historical divisions (and all the more their successive development) can only be considered ideal types (Bauman 1987, 3). In addition, modernity is closely linked to modernisation and thus holds a prescriptive or normative meaning framed within binaries such as past/bad versus present/good, which contributes to constructing the reality as a linear evolution towards something 'better'. In the same vein, Peter Osborne rejects the idea that modernity could be a chronological category and stresses that it is actually a qualitative category:

Modernity, then, plays a peculiar dual role as a category of historical periodization: it designates the contemporaneity of an epoch to the time of its classification, but it registers this contemporaneity in terms of a qualitatively new, self-transcending temporality, which has the simultaneous effect of distancing the present from even that most recent past with which it is thus identified. (1992, 73)

It is then questionable whether post-modernity is just the beginning of what will then be considered modern in an endless process of cultural and societal redefinitions. According to Jean-Francois Lyotard, 'post-modernity consists in the rewriting of modernity and, particularly, of the grounding of its legitimacy on the emancipatory project through science and technology' (1988, 202–3). Gavin Hyman explains that 'postmodernism, then, "begins" with the modern and cannot be understood in isolation from it' (2001, 11). Thus, post-modernity finds its roots in modernity and eventually merges into what becomes modern (or contemporary). Modern and post-modern traits can thus become difficult to differentiate and isolate.

Also noteworthy is that scholars tend to refer to different historical periods depending on their discipline when they talk about modernity (and post-modernity). For example, in arts and humanities the evolution from one historical period to another is generally based on architectural and artistic productions (hence the importance placed on post-modernism as an artistic movement), while historians and political scientists refer to the evolution of world politics' structures, mechanisms, and determining factors, as well as to the ideational elements sustaining these evolutions. Whereas defining a clear distinction between what is (or was) modern and what is (or could be) post-modern can only be of limited relevance, it is crucial to discuss the qualitative factors that are considered to lead to modernity (i.e., a departure from pre-modernity) and post-modernity (i.e., a departure from modernity), and to then apply those criteria to seapower in the next chapters.

Whether in the arts, culture, philosophy or politics, the pre-modern order centres on traditions. Since the opposition between tradition and modernity results from the ideas of Enlightenment, tradition is sometimes simplistically associated with obscurantism (e.g., feudalism, superstitions) and inertia, for instance, if 'everything and everyone occupied a pre-ordained place in the grand scheme of things. Ranks, hierarchies and "the great chain of being" were all part of the divine order' (Howe 1994, 513). However, traditional or pre-modern societies are not static and are actually subject to changes (Germond-Duret 2016), and this is why modernity cannot be defined in opposition to tradition, since it actually originates in traditional societies and practices.

With the end of the Middle Ages and the beginning of the Renaissance, factors of modernity emerged. They can roughly be classified into two groups: the material and the ideational factors. Material factors include the (pre)industrial revolution (and especially the mechanisation of production), urbanisation, and the compression of time/space (due to progress in transportation and printing). Ideational factors include more progressive societies and the affirmation of civil rights; the breakthrough of rationalism, such as 'Man' becomes the centre of interest; Bauman's 'withdrawal of God' and 'triumphant entry of Man' (1992, xii); reflexivity that according to Giddens prevents traditions from functioning 'as normative structures contextualising all activities and experience' (quoted in Mellor 1993, 118); the rise of capitalism (first mercantile then commercial) and the belief in free market; the belief that machines and technology will generate wealth and better social conditions; the rise of nationalism not as much as an ideology but rather an ideational element shaping the structure of world politics (i.e., nation-states, the Westphalian system); and the inception of mass culture. Modernity can thus be associated with industrialisation and rationality, which are considered the drivers of either progress (liberal vision) or inequalities (Marxist vision), depending on one's perspective, during the so-called modern era.

Post-modernity constitutes both an evolutive form and a rejection of modernity. Material factors include the information revolution (further time/space compression: telegraph, telephone, television, then more recently electronic, computer, and cyber technologies, as well as automation and artificial intelligence); the growth of the third sector and a de-industrialisation process; further globalisation of the world economy and finance; and hyper-consumerism. Those material factors are somewhat more prominent in Western societies but in no way limited to them. Ideational factors include more cosmopolitanism (again at least within the Western world); a certain rejection of the belief in progress and transcendence and a rejection of rationalism (i.e., there is no 'one truth', truths are constructed and interpreted – an influence of continental philosophy); and a fragmentation of identity (even poly-identity).

So again, there is both a material component of modernity, that is, post-industrialisation and (hyper)globalisation, and an ideational one, that is, the rejection of the idea that the Enlightenment project is the way to emancipation and rejection of norms imposed as truth, such as one vision about world politics, what is 'right' or 'wrong'. In a post-modern world, state actors increasingly complement their material power, such as military capabilities, with ideational forms of power, such as symbolic, soft, normative, or transformative power.

Since the transition from modernity to post-modernity is not about to be completed anytime soon, the emergence of neo-modern

Elements

Seapower as a
sum of material
and ideational
assets

- Geography
- Naval order of battle
- Shipbuilding industry
- Seafaring economy
- Flourishing economy
- Stable political order
- Maritime identity and culture

Outcomes

*The cycle
of seapower*

Seapower as a
consequential
relationship

Domination or superiority
that translates into
flourishing economy
and stable political
system, or hegemony

Enactment

Seapower as
a capacity

Creating the necessary conditions
for one's own economy to flourish
and political system to stabilise
via the control of the maritime
flows and using the sea to create
effects onto the land

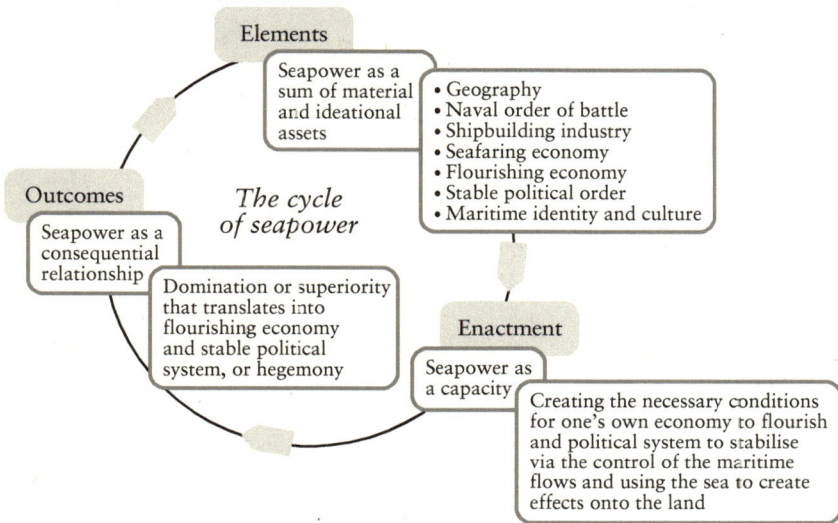

Figure 3.5 Three-layer analysis of seapower

characteristics only further complicates the picture. Neo-modernity finds solutions to problems linked to modernity but without rejecting the notion of progress: 'in some ways neo-modernity represents a continuation of the drive for progress, but like postmodernity it also represents a response or backlash to prior periods' (Knox-Hayes 2010, 954). In other words, neo-modernity finds solutions to problems originating in modernity but without rejecting the principal tenets of modernity, notably technology and rationality. Thus, neo-modernity can also be considered a form of revival of modernity in the post-modern era.

Although the transition from one era to the other is not straightforward, the material and ideational elements that characterise the evolution from the pre-modern era to the modern and then from the modern era to post-modern can be analysed in relation to seapower. The next chapters discuss how (if at all) the three layers of seapower presented above (i.e., the elements, the enactment, and the outcomes/consequences of seapower, cf. table 4.1 for a summary) have been affected by the material and ideational evolution from the pre-modern to the modern and from the modern to the post-modern (or even neo-modern) eras. This will enable concluding on the balance between permanencies and changes in seapower and the timelessness of the concept and practice thereof.

4

From Pre-modern to Modern Seapower

This chapter starts with an examination of the characteristics of pre-modern seapower. The aim is to discuss the extent to which the so-called pre-modern political, social, and cultural features have influenced the practice of seapower in the pre-modern era, or from Antiquity to the Middle Ages. Then, the chapter discusses the extent to which (and how) material and ideational modern features, such as a belief in technology, the compression of time-space, and the inception of nation-states, have impacted on the nature and practice of seapower since the so-called Age of Discovery (circa 1500). The reciprocal connection between seapower and modernity is highlighted by the discussion of the role seapower plays in modern state building. The chapter concludes on the limited relevance of associating too closely the development of seapower politics since the sixteenth century with modern characteristics, and instead shows that modernity was a catalyst for the development of seapower rather than a condition, and that in turn seapower was instrumental in providing the material, and to some extent cultural, bases for modernity to flourish.

PRE-MODERN SEAPOWER:
A STORY OF THE LAND AND THE SEA

Seapower as a scholarly concept is inherently linked to modernity, since the term was first used in the late nineteenth century at the height of the modern era, notably popularised by the seminal works of Captain Alfred Thayer Mahan, as discussed in chapter 1. As a practice, though, seapower can be traced as far back as history goes, albeit found at a different and much more limited scale than in later eras, for the sea was a dangerous place. Technological constraints and a burgeoning mastery of seafaring techniques did not prevent Bronze Age societies in Oceania, South America, Mesopotamia, India, and the Mediterranean from navigating very long distances, driven by curiosity, survival, or trade incentives (Paine 2013; de Souza 2001). However, military and commercial ships' operations were de facto limited by the technology available at that time.

Naval power, the military use of the sea, or the use of warships specifically designed for military purposes, dates back to at least the first millennium BCE, including in Ancient Greece, Persia, and Egypt, in this latter case perhaps as far back as circa 3500–3000 BCE according to various Egyptologists (Vinson 1994; A. Wood 2012). China also operated warships at least as far back as the fifth century BCE during the Chun Qiu period (Turnbull 2002, 4). Early naval thought was significant in Ancient Greece and Rome (Pagès 1991, 1992, 1993). Furthermore, there is evidence not only of tactical thinking (e.g., Egyptians' use of riverine ships to harass fluvial cities; and Romans' ship boarding techniques to make the most of their comparative advantage in hand-to-hand combat) but also of strategic thinking, including on the preponderance of maritime empires (Coutau-Bégarie 2002, 534) and the debated 'strategic advantages of sea-power over land-power in forming and holding an empire' (Momigliano 1944, 2). In other words, pre-modern scholars (such as Herodotus) and decision makers (such as Themistocles or Pericles) had already assimilated the importance of the link between the sea, maritime affairs, naval power, and (political) power.

That said, compared to land warfare, (big) naval battles although not rare (especially in the Ancient Greek world) were almost never decisive in the pre-modern era. History is made up of exceptions though. For example, the battles of Salamis and Plataea (480 and 479 BCE) marked the beginning of a new era in the Greek-Persian conflict, with the Greeks taking the upper hand; the battle of Actium (31 BCE) allowed Octavian to decisively defeat Anthony and Cleopatra. Admiral Colomb believes that those 'sea fights do not of themselves constitute naval warfare [and that] the ancient sea-fights were the result of military expeditions by sea and not of naval considerations' (Colomb 1899, 1), such as gaining command of the sea in order to secure one's commerce. This must be qualified since Greeks and Romans were well aware of the necessity to gain limited command to proceed with other military objectives, which is no less than exercising command. It may well be that Admiral Colomb started his book with such a statement to emphasise his main argument: 'proper' seapower could only develop when two conditions are fulfilled, that is, a striving maritime trade and a certain level of nautical and naval technological advances – two conditions that according to him were not present before the Elizabethan era. In fact, the limited impact of naval power during the galley era (which roughly coincides with the pre-modern era) can-not be separated from the technological limitations of that time. As Julian Corbett points out: 'Since men live upon the land and not upon the sea, great issues between nations at war have always been decided – except in the rarest cases – either by what your army can do against your enemy's territory and national life or else by the fear of what the fleet makes it possible for your army to do' (1911, 15).

In ancient times, navies were able to gain command of portions of the sea but had limited means in terms of *exercising* this command to produce strategic effects on land. Apart from moving and disembarking troops, navies' leverage and strategic contribution, such as enforcing blockades, was limited and the outcomes of wars were mainly decided on land and by land factors (and actors). For example, what was the point of a blockade when war supplies were mainly dependent on land transportation? In other words, more than in later eras, securing command of the sea was not at all a guarantee of victory and the advantage of naval power over land power was not considered obvious. Some Greek and Roman scholars and politicians (see Herodotus III.122; Thucydides I.143; Plutarch V.50) who were aware of the maritime origin and nature of the power of some 'thalasso-cracies', including Athens since the era of Pericles and until its fall during the Peloponnesian War, overtly praised seapower (understood as maritime commerce and naval strength), but most did not. For example, Plato's and Aristotle's disdain for maritime endeavours is well documented (Paine 2013, 105).

As a result of the limited impact of navies on the outcome of war (or at least the perception thereof), commanding the sea was not considered an enduring priority, even for dominant Powers, which tended to 'for-get' the sea when wars were won and over (see below). This vision varied from polities to polities and over time. For some, defending commerce at sea was not of uttermost importance given the limited proportion of riches that maritime trade represented for them. Others, such as Ancient Greek cities, had an interest in developing some form of naval power in peacetime to combat piracy and secure the SLOCS important for them and prevent pirates' raids (see Thucydides I.4–5). In another example, in the second century BCE, maritime trade played an important role for the Han dynasty in China, but the need to address piracy helps explain its naval turn (Abulafia 2020, 136). Successful maritime trading networks also depended on the ability of rulers (or merchants) to deter enemies or competitors. For example, both the Republic of Venice and the Kingdom of Aksum on the Red Sea could rely on substantial naval assets, whereas the Hanseatic League could rapidly assemble naval vessels in order to impose their commercial objectives (de Souza 2001). In other words, naval power politics was linked to peacetime for economic/commercial interests at least as much as wartime objectives. In peacetime, control of SLOCs (for trade and for supply of land forces) remained an important but costly task.

Fleets were expensive, not only to build but also to operate and maintain (which is still true in the twenty-first century). Given the limited impact of naval warfare, the expense often resulted in decisions not to maintain any 'fleet-in-being' during periods of peace. This mirrors contemporary sea blindness, when public opinion and decision makers demonstrate a lack of awareness of the sea's role in prosperity and security (Bueger and Edmunds 2017). For example, after its victory over the Athenians in the Peloponnesian War, Sparta maintained a fleet only for about two decades, and thus never truly replaced Athens as a sea Power. In other words, after securing hegemony in Greece, Sparta neglected the maritime component of its new empire, which shows the extent to which political elites overlooked one important component of their power base. Even the Roman Republic, after its final win over the other Mediterranean Powers (Carthage and then the Greek monarchies), did not, for a time, maintain the fleet in operational conditions and was content with its control of the land territories bordering the Mediterranean.

Then, once the need to possess a fleet resurfaced, only the civilian maritime sector could provide the necessary expertise: 'in the pre-modern times, the sources of naval expertise, and eventually of military shipping, lay with the merchant marine, and here it appears that the Romans and Latins were always weak' (Eckstein 2009, 65). Thus, Rome had to rely on non-Romans with a seafaring culture to man their ships. Rome's pragmatism trumped its sea blindness, but 'both in commerce and in the imperial fleets, then, the secret to Roman success lay not so much in maritime transformation of Roman culture but in the ability of the Romans to attach to themselves those polities and cultures that did have strong naval traditions' (Eckstein 2009, 65). The same was true of Sparta whose navy during the Peloponnesian War was principally manned by mercenaries and allies. Even Athens before the Peloponnesian War struggled to maintain the fleet due to financial constraints and relied on the tribute paid by members of the Delian League, including in ships (Starr 1978, 348). Interestingly, in the 1930s Admiral Richmond still noticed that 'no nations can maintain in peace the force which is needed in "great" war' (1934, 41), hence the crucial importance of the civilian seafaring sector to provide continuous manpower and knowledge of the sea. Maintaining a fleet required 'an enormous civic commitment' (Paine 2013, 95) that few rulers had at the time, not least because of the disregard for maritime activities that permeated most political elites.

This discussion shows that in the pre-modern era the cultural dimension of seapower was already important. Naval power could theoretically be 'ordered' at will since it was always possible to rely on the expertise of allies or mercenaries with a maritime tradition. However, neither Sparta nor the Roman Republic could be considered as true sea Powers, notably due to the lack of a proper maritime culture that translated into land-oriented policies and, to employ a twenty-first-century expression, some form of sea blindness. In other words, if the importance of the sea is only taken into consideration when the need to possess a fleet arises, then seapower is not likely to develop and consolidate. Then even those aware of the importance of the sea, such as Athens or Carthage whose power was dependent on the sea (if not on the control of it), were limited in their leverage for technological and financial limitations were at play. Consequently, even for ancient sea Powers such as Athens or Carthage, naval fights were rather a continuation of land battles and lacked a dynamic of their own, which led nineteenth- and twentieth-century scholars to downplay the role of seapower in the pre-modern era, not least since their studies' emphasis was on naval power rather than broader maritime power.

Whereas naval power was rarely decisive in war in the pre-modern era, the sea, as a means of transportation, has nevertheless been important in war as in peace in economic terms (trade) and cultural terms (cross-penetration between civilisations). For example, Pompey's campaign against the pirates in the Mediterranean was not motivated by defence concerns but by the need 'to allow trade to take place smoothly between east and west, north and south' (Münkler 2007, 60). Moreover, the Romans in the empire era referred to the Mediterranean

Sea as *Mare Nostrum* not only to denote the military and economic power 'gathered along the shores of the Mediterranean, [but also the] role of that sea as a medium for transportation and communication in the transmission of ideas, religion and culture' (Hattendorf 2000b: xxi). In fact, the Roman Empire enjoyed centuries of uncontested domination, hence the paucity of great naval battles, but naval power was nevertheless instrumental in stabilising and securing Rome's hegemony. The navy was there to secure and police SLOCS (core to the Empire's trade), to reinforce and supply legions deployed all over the Empire, and to deter enemies (Bloom 2019; de Souza 2001, 85). The Roman Empire was no seapower but an uncontested naval hegemon, which translated into the unchallenged control of *Mare Nostrum* and an enduring continental Empire.

For the Greeks as well as the Romans the sea was instrumental in empire building, not only as C.S. Gray said 'for the efficient running and defense of [the] empire' (1992, 117) but also from an ideational perspective. The Aegean Sea for the Greeks and then the whole Mediterranean Sea for the Romans contributed to the networking of their respective empires from an economic, political, and cultural perspective even more than a military one. It is interesting to note the difference between the Roman Empire grounded on land and those polities termed thalassocracies, such as the Phoenician networks of merchant cities (circa 1000 BCE), whose supremacy, similar to Venice or the Hanseatic League later in the medieval era, did not rest on the control of the hinterland and thus cannot be considered a form of pre-modern or modern empire.

In the pre-modern era, seapower was not limited to naval power, and the non-military dimension of seapower was more relevant than the purely naval one. The power of the near-mythical Minoans in Crete or the Phoenician network of trading cities, which can be considered the first thalassocracies, rested on seafaring prowess and its resulting commercial dominance. They did not face naval competitors, so command of the sea was not central to their political project. It is thus an example of seapower driven and sustained by trade. Early thalassocracies' interests were challenged on land, not at sea. Mastering the seas allowed commerce to thrive but also travelling and thus disseminating knowledge and ideas. Dominant civilisations at that time and in some regions (like the Greeks until the second century BCE and then the Romans) could colonise other territories, trade to their advantage, and diffuse their culture and eventually their norms and values.

A case in point is the Roman Empire, which has traditionally been described as 'continental' and hostile to maritime endeavours. Actually, since the First Punic War, Rome understood not only the importance of mastering naval warfare but also that maritime trade and power projection throughout the Mediterranean would serve their imperial ambitions (Paine 2013, 119–36). In other words, Rome's turn to the sea was linked to its ever-expanding ambitions and its global, Mediterranean outlook. Thus, it comes as no surprise that the Middle Ages did not witness the rise of global, inter-regional seapower politics, since the main characteristic of the period was the 'localisation'/'insularity' of public affairs as opposed to the 'globalisation'/'openness' inherent to the modern era. Nevertheless, for Middle Ages polities that had an interest in the sea (whether due to geography or the existence of a strong maritime culture), seapower, and especially maritime trade, continued to be a determining factor. For example, the 'insularity' of medieval Japan has been deconstructed with the proof that maritime trade flourished throughout the period (Abulafia 2020, 212). The Byzantine Empire, the Venice thalassocracy, and the Hanseatic League illustrate the extent to which the sea still played a crucial role in the societal and political development of some early and late medieval European societies. In other words, the absence of seapower during the medieval era is nothing but a myth that originates in later scholars' emphasis on the 'acceleration' of seapower politics since the Age of Discovery.

The discussion now turns to the three layers of seapower introduced in chapter 3, in order to debate the extent to which the pre-modern characteristics of the era have influenced the elements of seapower, the enactment of seapower, and the outcomes/consequences of seapower. In the pre-modern era, seapower already encompassed the components that are still relevant today: the existence of naval forces able to gain (limited) command of the sea; an economic use of the sea (for fishing, trade, and transportation); maritime traditions and culture; and the sea as a vector of/for ideas and norms. As for the purely material elements, the technological and ensuing tactical and strategic limitations explain the overall preponderance of land power during this period of history. Chester Starr reminds us that 'modern accounts of Athenian history usually fail to stress how remarkable a creation was its naval power, based as it was on fragile fleets of wooden triremes' (1978, 348). The same is true for commercial shipping. Maritime trade existed; it was even crucial in ensuring the success of political projects, most notably the Athenian democracy. For example, the Black Sea grain trade was of uttermost importance to Athens (Paine 2013, 102–3). However, for most, the majority of riches was coming from the land and only a limited portion was transported by sea, which is explained by the precariousness of maritime travel at that time.

The existence of pirates can also explain the reluctance to use sea lanes for transportation, which illustrates the difficulty to control the sea, even in peacetime. Actually, piracy was often tolerated if not encouraged against foreigners (Haywood and Spivak 2012, 24–5), which somewhat resulted in a normalisation of the practice that would persist until the abolition of privateering in the nineteenth century. When Romans realised that piracy was becoming too much of a burden for their economy, they launched a comprehensive eradication campaign led by Pompey that proved efficient but required the occupation of territories where pirates benefited from rear bases. In sum, both at the naval and commercial levels, if limited technological means constitute pre-modern characteristics, then the development of seapower during the pre-modern era was clearly limited by this feature. Operating a ship at sea was far from safe, even in peacetime, and naval weapons had limited reach and effect on the situation on land. Seapower was undoubtedly limited by material realities. However, apart from technological limitations, some decisions with detrimental effects, such as not maintaining a fleet in peacetime, can be attributed to political and ideational considerations.

Turning to the ideational elements of seapower, pre-modern societies are characterised by their reliance on traditions and beliefs for the conduct of politics, or at least by the constant interpenetration between rational decision-making processes and cognitive schemes embedded within popular and religious beliefs. It is interesting to note that according to Herodotus, Themistocles, who had been one of the strongest advocates of developing naval power in Athens, justified his decision to strengthen the navy in view of facing the Persians by interpreting the words of the Delphi Oracle: 'a bulwark of wood at the last Zeus grants to the Trito-born goddess Sole to remain unwasted, which thee and thy children shall profit' (VII.141), meaning ships rather than walls (VII.143–4). Themistocles was a resolute navalist and may even have had personal interests in developing the navy, since his political support came from the plebe who traditionally tended to favour the navy. His use of the Oracle was clever, but it is obvious that decisions to develop naval power in the pre-modern era resulted less from the mythical nature of the sea than from rational strategic reasoning. In other words, the decision to engage the Persian invaders at sea was above all a rational decision, since the Persian superiority on land was beyond question (Tangredi 2013, 15).

That said, Arnaldo Momigliano stresses that 'neither Aristotle nor any other Greek philosopher totally overcame the distrust of the acquisitive instinct and of the plebeian habits which were believed to be peculiar to sailors and maritime cities' (1944, 7). Land-based aristocracy's disdain for the maritime, seafaring, trading class has also been linked to their fear of the connection between maritime culture, naval procurement policies, and political diversity and democracy (Lambert 2018, 21; Paine 2013, 105). This perception of the sea, and especially of sailors, as vector of anti-conservative values and subversive ideas, has been recurrent throughout history, both in Europe and Asia.

The next section discusses the influence of modernity and Renaissance ideas on the cultural dimension of seapower, showing that although the distrust of sailors, mariners, port cities, and the sea in general was still present among European elites, resentment was put aside in the name of rationality (profit). In sum, pre-modern societies, or at least decision-making elites, continued to prioritise social stability over economic power in dealing with the sea. Land people and land affairs allowed a good degree of political, social, and cultural control that maritime activities and people could escape from. Consequently, most rulers were reluctant to promote any form of maritime culture beyond what was deemed absolutely necessary, as illustrated by the Romans' reliance on naval mercenaries discussed above. The pragmatism of rulers regarding seapower can also be found in the ancient and pre-modern Arab world. Ibn Khaldun (1377) makes it clear that although maritime culture was rather alien to the Arabs and their Bedouin identity, when the Calif had enough foresight to understand the importance of seafaring at the geopolitical level, naval power was used successfully against Christians in the contested waters of Middle Ages Mediterranean. So, according to Ibn Khaldun, seapower practice in the Arab world had been a function of conquests as opposed to the trade function prevalent in Europe (Mansouri 2016, 55); it challenged social conventions but was nevertheless an instrument of statecraft (Mufti 2009, 398). All in all throughout the pre-modern era, there are limited written accounts showing rulers' understanding of the leverage of seapower. However, the practice clearly demonstrates rulers' pragmatism towards seafaring and naval power.

Pre-modern societies, especially medieval societies, were characterised by a feudal organisation of the polities, including delegation of responsibilities in terms of security to what we would today call the 'private sector'. In other words, security was decentralised and distributed, and non-state actors could fill in the gap left at sea by the political/public authorities, which did not have either the financial means or the political will to operate as the dominant actor at sea. Pirates and privateers were such actors who could benefit from states' lack of involvement and leverage at sea. Similarly, local authorities could be empowered with maritime security functions. For example, Roskill discusses the role played by the Cinque Ports in the defence of England and the control of trade in the English Channel during the thirteenth century when no 'permanent' navy existed: 'the privileges granted to the Cinque Ports in respect of that trade and of fisheries, and the responsibilities for defence placed upon them in return, made their private navies the backbone of medieval English sea power' (1962, 21).

Even more, N.A.M. Rodger explains that representatives of seaports were regularly summoned to the House of Commons during the thirteenth and fourteenth centuries to advise on naval affairs ([1997] 2004, 124). The competences of the private sector went beyond peacetime activities, since privateers were often involved in the war effort, a practice that continued well into the modern era, until the 1856 Paris Declaration eventually forbade the practice. The absence of a clear distinction between public and private operations, competences, and responsibilities at sea characterises the pre-modern and especially the medieval and early modern eras. Herbert Rosinski explains that the creation of standing navies resulted indeed from the process initiated by rulers all over Europe to consolidate their power by creating a centralised and permanent bureaucracy, including a navy, which goes along with the changes in political systems and the organisation of Europe, from a medieval organisation to a 'purely mechanical balance of physical power' (1977, 122). The importance of nation-states and centralisation processes in explaining the consolidation of navies and the development of seapower is considered in more details in the next section.

Turning to the enactment of seapower, during the pre-modern era this was limited by the means at hand, most notably the obvious technological limitations that made navigation risky, and the cost of operating a navy or a commercial fleet. Naval power was mainly limited to sea fights and the transport of troops since it was not possible to produce further substantial strategic effects from the sea. Therefore, the sea was conceived as a continuation of the land, without a (strategic) dynamics of its own. Naval tactics were conceived as a contribution to *general* strategic objectives rather than to any *naval* strategy. And general strategy was mainly interested in the *land*. For example, Rome's naval campaigns against Carthage during the First Punic War were ultimately about the control of Sicily or even Carthage itself. Pompey's anti-piracy campaign was made successful by the fact that he was granted power over the coastal zone up to fifty miles inland so as to tackle the issue of pirate communities rather than to limit his actions to the destruction of ships. Interestingly, the EU operation Atalanta, tasked with tackling piracy at the Horn of Africa since 2008, has also been authorised since 2012 to operate within Somali coastal territory and internal waters to disrupt pirate supplies/ business model and deny them impunity (Council of the EU 2014).

In the pre-modern era, negotiation with pirates was not uncommon since the eventual goal was to pacify coastal communities rather than to further alienate them. A similar pattern with counter-piracy at the Horn of Africa since 2008 is noteworthy: counter-piracy forces were authorised to operate inland (for example in case of hot pursuit) but it also quickly became clear that pirates were embedded within local communities, which were suffering from deprivation and poverty, hence the importance of the so-called 'comprehensive approach' to security that aims at addressing the root causes of piracy, such as bad governance, poverty, and other forms of criminality.

In another example illustrating the lack of an independent naval strategy, naval battles between Christians and Muslims in the medieval Mediterranean were not about controlling maritime trade, which continued to thrive, but about who would dominate the shores within a broader 'clash of civilizations' (Phillips 2000, 3; de Souza 2001, 74). This is a pre-modern feature of seapower that has never disappeared. Indeed, as Corbett famously reminds us, human beings are land-based people whose political structures are land-based; hence, seapower's final cause is to control the land (Corbett 1911, 15), although to master the sea is to control the land (Gray 1994, 13–14). Thus, the primacy of land considerations in pre-modern strategic thought does not mean that dominant naval Powers of the time did not develop efficient naval tactics or did not understand the importance of winning naval battles. For instance, the battle of Salamis resulted from Athens's realisation of Xerxes's dominant land power and thus Themistocles's strategic decision to take the initiative at sea. In another example, Rome demonstrated advanced naval tactical thought during the First Punic War when they understood that Carthage could only be defeated if its fleet was destroyed, leading to the decision to confront Carthage's navy at sea (Bernstein 1989, 129–30).

The limited strategic effects of naval power in this era shall not, however, hide the importance of pre-modern seapower in general. For example, some Greek thalassocracies demonstrated that the enactment of seapower could be considered the main factor explaining the sustained success story of seafaring societies, which had accumulated many elements of seapower, notably in terms of maritime commerce and culture. The enactment of seapower was also instrumental in empire building, such as in the case of Rome discussed above, via the spreading of values and norms. Maritime transportation also played a key role in cementing China's Middle Empire tribute system, especially during the Ming dynasty (1368–1644). What specifically characterises the enactment of pre-modern seapower is that it was rarely part of pre-modern rulers' regular, business-as-usual policies and activities but rather enacted depending on the context and circumstances, on a 'need to' basis. Pragmatic leaders were not opposed to the use of naval power or the development of a maritime economy, it was just not the preferred or primary tool, or it was not always a readily available tool, or the cost was too high. That said, in certain circumstances seapower was crucial in gaining the upper hand against a competitor, and the success of a few military projects certainly rested on the efficient enactment of seapower.

Yet, the influence seapower has had during the pre-modern era (i.e., its outcomes) remained limited. Naval power in ancient times (e.g., Rome) and Middle Ages (e.g., Byzantine Empire, Venice) has played an important role in support of imperial ambitions and/or defence. But pre-modern seapower in itself has rarely resulted in the emergence of big Powers or in an enduring form of regional dominance, except perhaps in the case of thalassocracies such as Phoenicia and Venice. Even Athens at its apogee was dependent on its land allies, and was eventually defeated by a land Power, namely Sparta. That said, seapower played a role in Rome's fight against Carthage for the domination of the Mediterranean and has been instrumental in securing Rome's control of the Mediterranean. Although Rome's victory in the Second Punic War was secured on land and not at sea, the fact that Carthage had previously lost sea control facilitated Rome's victory over Hannibal's forces, which could not be reinforced by sea (Bernstein 1989, 130). However, to say that seapower has been *decisive* in Rome's overall ascendancy in the ancient world is a step too far. For its part, Carthage's seapower mentality was no match for the Roman martial machine.

In sum, the limited outcomes/consequences of seapower cannot be separated from the lack of material elements of seapower noted above. States exercised their power mainly on land since this is where they could fully enact it. For example, blockades could be tactically effective but to enact long-term strategic effects they needed to be complemented by land operations. Thus, in a form of vicious circle, the sea did not represent the major source of states' power since states' attention was mainly focused on land, and states' attention was mainly focused on land since the sea was not seen as a 'natural' place to enact power. A lack of maritime culture among many elites, if not a plain disdain for seafaring people and culture, further contributed to this process. For example, both Byzantine and Arab elites were dependant on maritime trade and naval power in their struggle for domination of the Mediterranean, but this did not prevent them from showing an appreciation of mariners, which was at best lukewarm and mostly hostile (Paine 2013, 215–19).

Technological limitations are the main pre-modern features that impacted seapower in this era. States and other political entities were still in the process of trying to master the sea. Advantages and opportunities linked to seapower were known and not overlooked, such as fishing, commerce, naval battles, communication, logistics, and even empire building, but the limitations in terms of material elements of seapower recurrently constrained the enactment of seapower and thus its consequences/effects as well as states' willingness to invest more into their mastering of the maritime domain. In other words, political elites' uncomfortable relationship with the sea (most notably as a vector for democratic and/or foreign ideas) is but one of the explanatory factors for the limited impact of seapower in the pre-modern era, though most definitely not the main one. Material elements (or rather the lack thereof) were the main explanatory factors, and pre-modern characteristics such as the importance of traditions and beliefs in decision-making have not had much of a limiting impact on seapower (see table 4.1).

Table 4.1
The layers of pre-modern seapower

Layers of analysis	Pre-modern features
Elements of seapower	• Limited material means, maritime know-how, and technology • Social and political interactions principally limited to the land • Maritime trade as a driver for seapower • Limited ideational inclination towards the sea and seapower (lack of maritime culture within the elites)
Enactment of seapower	• Rarely part of the regular policies, but enacted depending on the context and circumstances, on a 'need to' basis (pragmatism) • Not the preferred tool and not always a readily available tool, or too high a cost • Delegation of responsibility to the 'private sector' • Naval functions included logistics, blockade, naval battle, anti-piracy, trade protection, raiding
Consequences of seapower	• Limited strategic effects of naval power • Not resulting in enduring forms of dominance, (some exceptions like thalassocracies), but often one of the explanatory factors for hegemony (e.g., Rome)

Pre-modern seapower is the story of two spaces. There is the land, the realm of the living (a place of human experience) where societies are organised within political structures. And there is the sea, a wide and wild space lying mainly outside the realm of human existence, and beyond the control of political rulers. That said, it is important to acknowledge that some traditional societies beyond Europe, without developing seapower, were very much linked to the sea and had developed a maritime identity since Antiquity. For example, Polynesian islanders mastered seafaring long before their European pre-modern counterparts. In addition, their life, culture, and political organisation were deeply linked to the sea (Abulafia 2020, 3–39). Although these societies were indeed more 'maritime' than ancient Egypt, Greece, or Rome, they did not develop and enact seapower. For them, the sea was prominent culturally and as a source of livelihood, but it was not a source of political and military power. It must also be noted that seafaring has had an instrumental role in the diffusion of ideas and religions beyond and outside imperial projects. For example, seafaring played a role, albeit probably not decisive, in diffusing Buddhism from the Indian sub-continent to East Asia (de Souza 2001, 127–32).

In the pre-modern era, the land and the sea coexisted, but social and political interactions were largely limited to the land. Pre-modern seapower was a pragmatic form that combined circumstantial naval power with seafaring. Most rulers understood the importance of the sea in peace as in war and were ready to enact it. But, due to technological limitations and elites' usual distrust of the sea (not least since seapower politics were linked to more participatory political systems), seapower was often limited to circumstantial naval power, with navies built on purpose, when needed, and abandoned thereafter, except for the Roman Empire whose navy contributed to securing its long-term hegemony. As soon as it became possible to command the sea in a more efficient way, states and non-state actors started to exploit all the possibilities offered by mastering the sea, most notably resources exploitation, transportation, and military expeditions. Whereas this started during the pre-modern era, the technological, societal, and political transformations that marked the end of the Middle Ages would boost the development of seapower to an extent not seen before.

INTO THE MODERN AGE:
SEAPOWER AND STATE BUILDING

Whereas pre-modern characteristics had influenced the relevance and leverage of seapower only to a limited extent, entering the modernity era would prove to impact seapower in various ways, most notably at the technological, economic, and ideational levels. In turn, seapower itself would be instrumental in the transition to modernity and contribute to the development and consolidation of the (modern) legal, economic, political, and social structures still dominant in the twenty-first century.

First, scientific and technological innovations associated with modernity had tactical, operational, strategic, and political implications. Nautical developments, in particular regarding sailing, and scientific advances made it possible to navigate for longer periods of time without having to call at a port for replenishment, further from the coasts, and relatively more safely with less dependence on the weather compared to the galley era. Therefore, sustained presence at sea, reach, and speed all increased. New technological developments also allowed ships and fleets to execute more complex manoeuvres. Likewise, new types of weaponry enabled navies to do more damage and at a longer range. Consequently, naval power became more important for the conduct of war, since it became possible for navies to properly 'generate strategic effects' (Gray 1992, 136) from the sea. For example, during the Dutch Revolt in the sixteenth century, England managed to prevent Spain from supplying its army fighting in the Netherlands by sea, which had an impact on the hostilities on land.

While the early modern era corresponds to the evolution from galley to sail, the industrial revolution of the nineteenth century induced another move from sail to steam, with all that this entailed in terms of improved manoeuvre, endurance, and reach, let alone new weapon systems also developed in this era. In other words, the modern era is characterised by two radical rounds of technological evolutions in naval/maritime terms. Both have changed the face of seapower in similar ways, albeit not at the same pace. The transition to sail occurred at a time when political modernisation was in its infancy, whereas the transition to steam occurred when modern nation-states were already consolidated and ready to unleash their maritime power over the seven seas.

The importance of technological developments for naval power has been recognised by nineteenth- and twentieth-century commentators. For example, Colomb explains that 'if the sea was to be controlled, it was absolutely necessary that the ships assuming to control should be able to maintain their position at sea continuously' (1899, 5), a condition that was, according to him, met in Britain only since the Elizabethan era (i.e., at the beginning of the modern era). Referring to the nineteenth century, Grivel goes as far as saying that 'perhaps nowhere else than in naval equipment have modern science progresses in the past 40 years [i.e., 1830–70, equivalent to the second phase of the British industrial revolution] engendered such a radical revolution' (1869, 3). This perspective is corroborated by Roskill's point that 'in the next two decades [following the Napoleonic War] technological developments began to influence the instruments of war very profoundly' (1962, 89). Roskill backed his point with a quotation from Lord Palmerston who, in 1859, said that 'steam has bridged the Channel' (94), implying that the Royal Navy might not be able to defend Britain against an invasion by controlling and interdicting the English Channel.

However, Brodie makes it clear that although inventions in naval warfare, weapons, cladding, ship propulsion, and so forth can have revolutionary impacts on tactics and strategy, they do not affect 'the purpose of naval warfare' and the 'basic process by which those purposes are achieved' ([1943] 1969, 4). Brodie is right to stress that 'changes in naval materiel have not been such as to affect fundamentally the relationship of sea power to land power' (447) in what he calls the machine age, broadly from the nineteenth century onward. However, the changes that occurred at the beginning of the Age of Discovery (mainly the evolution from galley to sail but also the development of new weapons, navigation instruments such as the sextant, etc.) have significantly impacted the leverage of seapower, paving the way for modern nation-states to dominate the international system and the world. From a local/regional and time-limited endeavour, naval power in particular and seapower in general, became global and sustainable over longer periods of time. This all happened at a time when world politics became truly global in nature.

Understood as a sum of elements and as the consequence of its enactment, seapower is both a source and an outcome of the industrial revolution. Indeed, while technological advances boosted naval power, Friedman reminds us that 'in the late 18th century the Admiralty was the largest industrial organization in the country, and its efforts probably helped touch off the Industrial Revolution' (2007, 45) – at least the second one, not the pre-industrial revolution of the sixteenth and seventeenth centuries. In sum, the mutually beneficial relationship between seapower and the technological and industrial features of modernity became obvious: technological inventions were instrumental in facilitating seapower; and seapower (or the need to develop it) incentivised industrial investments and innovations. Similarly, Rosinski explains that overseas commercial activities and colonisation were made possible thanks to naval forces, but the riches coming from overseas economic sources via trade and colonial tribute have also been instrumental in maintaining and developing standing navies, especially during wartime (1977, 122).

In Tangredi's words, 'sea power is a facilitator of economic power, and the quest for economic power is, in turn, a motivator for the development of sea power' (2002, 23). This notion fits with Campling and Colás's claim that 'from its inception in the "long" sixteen century, capitalism has found in the sea a vital conduit for long distance trade ... and the place from which to embark on colonial ventures critical to its own existence' (2021, 2). The reciprocal link becomes apparent between seapower and the development of an imperial system at the global level as much as state building at the domestic level (see figure 4.1). It is important to understand the development of

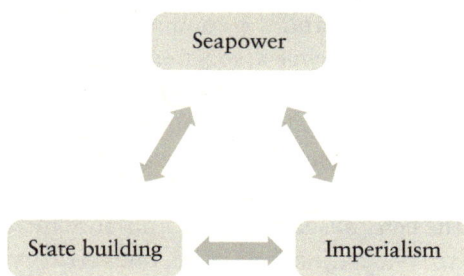

Figure 4.1 Mutually beneficial relationship between seapower, imperialism, and state building

seapower as both a cause and a consequence of the changing economic and political context. On the one hand, mastering the seas became a reality following state centralisation, on the other it was a necessity since profiting from the benefits of trade (and the accumulation of riches from the colonies) required exploiting the sea as an inexpensive means of transportation.

From an ideational perspective, exploration during the Age of Discovery bestowed tremendous importance upon the sea, not only as a medium for transportation and trade but also as a symbol of power and liberty for those commanding it (i.e., a form of extrinsic power), since they could control and 'roll back' the new frontier (Germond 2010). Spanish extrinsic power in the sixteenth and early seventeenth centuries depended on the perception of its unlimited wealth coming from its empire but also from the perception of the Spanish colonial systems' invulnerability to European contenders. Thus, Francis Drake's 1585 successful expedition to the Caribbean and the sacking of Santo Domingo, Cartagena, and Panama not only engendered material and financial losses for Spain but, according to Richmond, more importantly produced effects 'on the minds of the people of Spain and of Europe. Spain's credit was weakened' (1946, 10). Rodger describes a "psychological shock" and "horror" in Spain as well as fear in Spain's allies ([1997] 2004, 250, 253). This is not anecdotal; indeed, in terms of the ideational dimension of seapower, this demonstrates the effect modernity has had on the perception of seapower. While extrinsic power in pre-modern societies was rarely dependent on naval power in particular and on a maritime empire in general, the development of nation-states and colonial empires in the modern era directed attention towards the sea in general and the command of SLOCs in particular. Since then, the extrinsic power associated with navies has continued to be closely associated with states' power.

This process cannot be separated from state building that was taking place all over Europe since the Renaissance. Indeed, navies became associated with modern states and state power since they also became part of the centralised structure and bureaucracy of the state. In other words, to 'one nation, one state, one territory' one could add 'one navy', because navies symbolised states' leverage beyond their external boundaries. Navies in particular and seapower in general have thus become constituents of the nationalist narrative, eventually ending up in Mahan's style of navalism, where 'a navy became, for new nations, the visible symbol of modernization' (Connery 2001, 183), an indicator of progress. Thus, Japan at the end of the nineteenth century was considered successful in modernising quickly by adopting a European/US model (both in terms of order of battle *and* doctrine) whose symbol was the victory against the Russians in 1905 and especially the victorious naval battle of Tsushima.

In contrast, due to Qing China's reluctance to adopt the European model, especially at the doctrinal level, it was not in a position to resist either European imperialism or even Japanese assaults. This shows that to be considered as 'modern' from a naval perspective, technology in itself does not suffice if not backed by a 'modern' doctrine. In other words, as the Japanese/Chinese case demonstrates, in the modern era, it was one thing for navies to adopt the modern technologies available at that time, but the most important factor was how these technologies would be applied (i.e., the conduct of naval warfare) and, above all, states' acknowledgement that the leverage of seapower (not merely naval power) could not be overlooked anymore if they wanted to compete with the dominant Powers of the time. This is an intellectual and doctrinal process that, despite Admiral Gorshkov's best effort in the 1970s, has never really occurred in Russia.

Even though in practice this had been the case since Antiquity or even the Bronze Age, seapower started to be more closely associated with trade values, principles, and policies following the development of mercantile capitalism, which itself proceeds from the conditions offered by the newly 'globalised' world order following the Age of Discovery. Seapower is intrinsically linked to the existence of a class of merchants and entrepreneurs authorised or even encouraged by their states to engage in commerce, including overseas. This seems to be a prerequisite for the development of efficient seapower. Whether those values have to be associated with liberal values is discussed below. Already Ancient Greek scholars opposed militaristic, authoritarian Sparta with democratic, dynamic, and seafaring Athens (Lambert 2010, 84; see also above). During the Elizabethan era, exploration and maritime trade were mainly motivated by financial gains and consequently attracted this dynamic class of merchants ready to apply new thinking and new means available at that time to the maritime domain. The Renaissance unleashed this class of merchants and seafarers, whose involvement at sea was motivated by profit rather than glory or faith. That this civilian dimension of seapower developed parallel with the departure from the obscurantist impulses of the Middle Ages shall not come as a surprise. However, in Ancient Greece or Rome this class already existed but was then mainly limited in their activities and power by the state of technology and the political elites' aversion towards, or at least neglect of, the sea.

It is also important to avoid falling into the trap of opposing modern, liberal, sea-oriented nation-states with pre-modern, authoritarian, land-oriented ones, which, although relevant to some extent, constitutes some form of historical generalisation and neglects the successes of thalassocracies such as Athens or Venice. Additionally, it would be a mistake to consider the medieval era devoid of sea travel and maritime trade. On the contrary, the Middle Ages, with its decentralised structure of political power, enabled merchants and seafarers to create networks outside and beyond political structures. The case of the Hanseatic League with its non-hierarchical network of merchants and trading cities is well documented: kings, territories, land ownership, and religions mattered less than money, profit, flexibility, and the sea (Pye 2015). Civilian networks with a global maritime outlook also developed in the Mediterranean and Atlantic during the early modern era (Curto and Molho 2002) (e.g., Genoa).

In Europe, tensions and wars between the main Powers (notably England, France, the Netherlands, the Holy Roman Empire states, Portugal, and Spain) were quasi-permanent, which resulted in the main geostrategic focus being on the land. However, the Age of Discovery coupled with the development of mercantile capitalism generated interest in the 'unknown' or 'unchartered' world, including from a geostrategic perspective. In Europe, states' territories became mutually exclusive culminating in the principles reassessed at the Peace of Westphalia (seventeenth century), such as states' sovereignty and non-interference in other states' domestic affairs. However, 'problems arose with common spaces between states, such as waterways and oceans (as for example in the short-lived papal division of the world and the Atlantic Ocean between Spain and Portugal)' (Anderson 1996, 144). In other words, the sea became the medium for overseas colonisation (i.e., the struggle for so-called 'empty' space outside Europe), but it also became apparent that SLOCs had to be shared and the high seas would become either a 'great common' or a permanently contested space. The latter apparently contradicted states' interest in maintaining unrestricted access to the 'great void'.

These two characteristics remain pertinent today. In the international law of the seas, we can trace back to Grotius's principle of *mare liberum*, that was devised as a way to prevent any territorialisation of the sea by superior naval Powers (e.g., Britain, Portugal, or Spain) at the expense of smaller Powers (such as the United Provinces) and that predates the concept of global commons, which emphasises the fact that the sea must be free for all to use and exploit/protect (Brito Vieira 2003; Germond 2022a). This 'modern juridico-military ordering of the sea' both results from and facilitates European capitalist endeavours (Campling and Colás 2021, 70). In sum, seapower was meant to allow modern states to make up most of their control of SLOCs both from an economic and a military perspective, each of them linked to the building of colonial empires, or in Frederick J. Turner's ([1920] 1996) words the rolling back of the final frontier. Modernity understood as the affirmation of European nation-states is thus strongly linked to seapower politics (including the push for freedom of the seas), since the geopolitical status quo imposed by the Westphalian principles could easily be challenged overseas, as long as the seas and the SLOCs remain free to use. In turn, the colonial system, which depended on the mastering of the seas, also helped stabilise and consolidate the nation-states in Europe.

The Age of Discovery marks the beginning of the globalisation process at a planet-level, which has had economic, political, and ideational consequences still found in today's (hyper)globalisation process. From the perspective of seapower, the sea began to be regarded as one, if not the main, source of states' (economic) power. This vision became prominent within the major (maritime) Powers, notably Spain, Portugal, the Netherlands, then England, but even continental Powers such as Russia started to pay attention to the sea. Indeed, Peter the Great created the regular Imperial Russian Navy in

1696, following his understanding that naval power was a necessary condition if Russia wanted the upper hand against the Ottoman Empire in the Black Sea region (Kipp 2009). This decision was instrumental in taking the fortress of Azov. Peter the Great also wanted to obtain control of the Baltic Sea, which demonstrates that he understood the importance of seapower in a more holistic way (i.e., the access to SLOCs and the importance of maritime trade). However, Russia never developed a proper maritime culture, although ironically, Peter the Great's vision was to transform Russia, to modernise the country following the example of Western Europeans, notably in terms of seafaring and commerce.

Modernisation and seapower went hand in hand. Another example illustrates the interrelationship. Rolf Hobson and Tom Kristiansen (2012) explain that in the eighteenth and nineteenth centuries, medium and even small European Powers (such as Scandinavian states) maintained very respectable navies that could somewhat protect their maritime trade interests and give them a voice during maritime law and law of the war at sea conferences. This is all the more remarkable when just four hundred years before, Norway and Denmark were subjugated by the forces of the Hanseatic merchants, demonstrating the extent of changes that occurred both from a naval, political, and ideational perspective.

Imperial China during the Qing dynasty (1636/1644–1912) has been presented as a counter-example. The central government did not acknowledge the importance of seapower in the same way as their European counterparts, the development of naval power was not prioritised, and maritime trade, although not negligible, was somehow disregarded. The myth in presenting Imperial China as a non-maritime Power shall nonetheless be qualified: seapower was instrumental in securing the Ming dynasty's leadership in Asia in the fifteenth century, demonstrating China's superiority (de Souza 2001, 96), and the sea has never ceased to play an important role in terms of coastal defence and from an economic, trade perspective (Lo 2012). However, the source of Imperial China's power derived principally from non-maritime elements and from its ability to secure its land borders, which explains the Qing dynasty's inability to comprehend seapower in its Western, Mahanian conception.

The case of Imperial China during the Qing dynasty reveals the importance of the ideational dimension of seapower discussed above. Most European countries (and to a limited extent the US since the late nineteenth century) have developed some sort of a maritime culture or identity. The dominant continental culture of Germany and Austria-Hungary and the lack of maritime culture in Russia should not hide the fact that most of Europe and North America have been characterised by a seapower culture (or at least a maritime, seafaring mentality) during the entire modern era. If some nations, notably England, have developed a stronger maritime identity fostered by enlightened rulers (Lambert 2018), a maritime outlook permeated many modern European states.

A whole discursive universe was constructed around the sea, which, in the collective imaginaries, began to be assimilated with national strength, prestige, progress, and successful capitalism. The sea has been conceived as a global commons that states and commercial actors should be free to use for travel and transportation. In legal terms, this is underpinned by the *mare liberum* principle, proposed by Grotius in the seventeenth century, implemented de facto throughout the modern era, and eventually crystalised in the 1982 UNCLOS. From a political economy perspective, this is what Steinberg calls a 'spatial ideology at the service of the Capital (2001, 165) and Connery calls the 'bourgeois idealization of sea power' (1994, 40). As such, the ocean is constructed as an empty space/void conquered and put at the service of both capitalism and militarism (Steinberg 1999a, 417). Samuel Baker explains that 'romantic-period writers [shared] a renewed appreciation of the ocean as a geopolitical domain ruled by British naval heroism' (2010, 1). In other words, literary and other artistic creations contributing to the 'maritime-imperial ideology' (3) have facilitated British naval mastery. Similarly, Lambert (2018) emphasises sea states' rulers' efforts to promote maritime culture and identity, including via art, architecture, and literature, based on the understanding that maritime culture and affinity with the ocean are not natural elements of one's national identity and thus need to be nurtured. In turn, the Royal Navy became more than a symbol of national identity; it contributed to shaping the representation of British society and Empire (Leggett 2011).

In sum, the myth of seapower – although the term was not yet employed – developed well before Mahan's writings. It is linked to modern nation-state building and mercantile and then commercial capitalism. Despite the realities of maritime trade competition and intra-European wars, seapower developed into a myth, based on the (sometimes exaggerated) perception of seapower as an enabler of national security and economic wealth as well as on the idealised image of the sea and its link to liberty as a value. For instance, Rodger (2004, 173–4) traces the myth of English seapower back to the Elizabethan era, when people and politicians started to associate seapower with liberty, financial gains, and Protestantism. The discrepancies between the facts and practice of English seapower and the way it was collectively imagined are explained by the lack of reliable knowledge as well as the persistence of cognitive representations that contributed to the reproduction of the myth across generations of British public opinion.

That England's ruling class understood the need to foster seapower in order to rise beyond the crowd of European monarchies certainly played a role. If we recall the importance of maritime culture in fostering seapower (something already considered by decision makers and thinkers in the pre-modern era, notably in Ancient Greece), Queen Elizabeth I 'certainly showed foresight in fostering the expansion of the sea-faring section of her people' (Roskill 1962, 31). Yet, this made her 'necessarily dependent on that small group of merchants, ship-owners, sea commanders and investors' (Rodger [1997] 2004, 343). In other words, the very fact that European leaders realised and accepted the link between seapower and wealth is sufficient to explain the variation in policies (and perhaps in outcomes) between European and non-European Powers, such as Imperial China's central leadership of the Qing dynasty in the modern era.

Already at the end of the eighteenth century, philosopher Johann Herder linked the (supposed) dominance of European culture with seapower, or at least with the geographical determinants of seapower: 'had the east of Asia possessed an earlier commerce, and a Mediterranean Sea, which its present situation has denied; the whole current of cultivation would have been altered. It flowed westwards; because eastwards it was unable to flow, or to spread' (1803, 119). Thus, it appears that the myth of seapower, the development of a maritime culture, the actual elements of seapower, and the progress of the modern states have mutually reinforced each other over the course of modern Europe's history (see figure 4.2). The myth of seapower has contributed to developing a strong maritime culture throughout the continent, and beyond the major colonial Powers that were Portugal, the Netherlands, Spain, and then France and England. The presence of this maritime culture is instrumental in explaining the success of seapower politics, at least to some extent, and the development and stabilisation of modern nation-states. In turn, modernity, the reality of the nation-state system, and the practice of seapower that are mutually reinforcing help explain the enduring myth of seapower across the modern era.

In practice, the contribution of seapower, or rather seapower politics, to state building can be traced back to Ancient Greece. Kyriazis and Zouboulakis (2004) explain that Themistocles's introduction of 'naval law' to fund the building of triremes and thus face the Persian threat eventually contributed to the stability of the political system and to the fostering of social justice in Athens by granting poor citizens political rights in exchange for serving within the navy: 'the Naval Law and the subsequent naval service revolutionized Athenian society, bringing about general equality in all aspects of its citizens' lives, abolishing the legal and civil differences between rich and poor, and transforming Athens into the most authentic democracy known at that time' (120–1).

One of the reasons why the development of seapower can have such tremendous impacts on other political and societal processes is found in the capital-intensive nature of anything 'maritime', let alone 'naval'. The building of a navy, or of a substantial merchant fleet, consumes considerable material but also financial resources. Moreover, to operate a fleet on a sustainable basis puts constant pressure on any state's finances. As discussed above, this was a reason why Sparta neglected its navy following its victory over Athens, with all that this entails. More recently, the rapid modernisation of the Chinese Navy in the late twentieth and early twenty-first centuries went hand in hand with China's sustained economic growth for about three decades. In sum, decisions to allocate resources to the development of seapower are likely to impact states' structures and societies beyond the 'naval' or 'commercial shipping' functional areas, for they are not banal budgetary decisions; their repercussions can be significant and long-lasting. On the other hand, such impacts can result from the consequences of having developed seapower rather than the actions that are necessary to develop seapower in the first instance (see below).

The acceleration of the development of seapower and the consolidation of nation-states are two parallel and interrelated processes that, broadly speaking, started in Europe at the end of the Middle Ages. The need to develop standing fleets resulted from rulers' need to 'build state' via central bureaucracies; in other words (1) to operate a standing navy to control one's maritime domain and respond to enemies' attacks without having to rely on private or devolved stakeholders, and (2) to benefit from the advantage seapower brings, especially its commercial dimension, in terms of riches. Rulers able to make the most of the riches coming from the sea, not least a result of the technology available, were obviously in a better position to consolidate the structure of the state. However, the need to deploy public power on the sea also pushed rulers to establish institutionalised and permanent navies, which became part of the bureaucratic structure of the state. Standing navies became a permanent tool at rulers' disposal rather than one that had to be 'called up' in case of emergency (Till 2022, 14). In turn, funding these new bureaucracies and operating the fleet (which is capital and technology intensive) required resource extraction and a further centralisation of the state.

The mutually reinforcing link between seapower and state building is thus obvious. But as Jan Glete discusses, for a navy to be efficient it also needs the support of the elites and those having their say in maritime affairs (2000, 64), mainly maritime entrepreneurs engaged in maritime trade activities. This was all the more important when the ruler, as in the Netherlands, 'tried to tax the seagoing activities of his subjects in order to fund his maritime policy', which obliged him 'to attune his maritime policy to the maritime interests of his subjects' (Sicking 2004, 4). It thus appears that modern state building and seapower have been inextricably linked (see figure 4.2). For rulers, naval power, in the form of 'permanent' navies, was, on the one hand, part of the process consisting of consolidating the state's central power by developing an instrument capable of defending against invasions, blockades, and projecting power, but also justifying taxes and increasing their central power at the domestic level (Glete 2000, 68). On the other hand, maritime trade was part of the mercantile project consisting of accumulating enough resources to consolidate states' structures and military forces as well as to face potential enemies in case of war, which required the protection of private assets at sea.

Seapower and state formation are interlinked, but the strength of this relationship remains difficult to assess. Rodger reminds us that states and their level of centralisation differed greatly (2012, 17), and it would be wrong to reduce the diverse processes that have led to states developing seapower to just one aspect (i.e. state building). For instance in the sixteenth century, 'the relative efficiency of England's permanent naval administration ... contrasted with heroic improvisation in Spain'. England's success depended on both a strong 'political

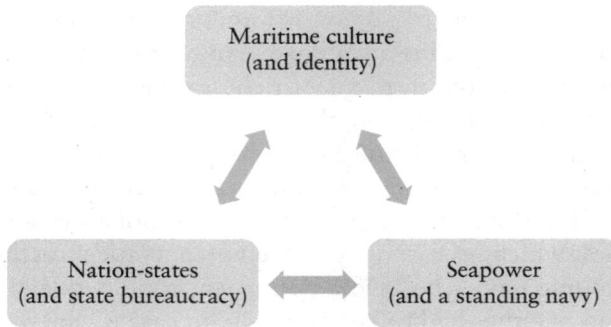

Figure 4.2 Mutually beneficial relationship between maritime culture, seapower, and nation-states

commitment and administrative sophistication' (Rodger [1997] 2004, 340, 430). To fully understand the role of seapower and modern state building one has to question whether following a seapower rather than a land power path has resulted in a different form of consolidated state. Kyriazis argues that 'the choice of seapower by a state leads to a different regime than the choice of land military power, because sustainable seapower necessitates a wide alliance of interests, which brings with it more democratic values, develops more efficient and complex forms of organizations, requires the acquisition and diffusion of new knowledge and expertise, which brings with it institutional change and economic growth' (2006, 71). In other words, if economic growth is taken as an indicator of success for state formation, a seapower policy is supposed to favour it by offering more possibilities for a 'wide alliance of interests' and 'more representative political institutions' (77). For example, England's evolution into a seapower state required a sustained financial and procurement strategy for which the king had to compromise with parliament meaning that the parliament began to take responsibilities in naval affairs (Rodger [1997] 2004).

Just as for state building, the relationship between seapower and liberalism is bidirectional (cf. figure 4.3). On the one hand, the development of seapower within the context of modernity has been favoured by rulers' decisions to adopt more liberal policies in terms of openness to trade, the class of entrepreneurs, capitalism, the world, and ultimately the sea. On the other hand, the development of

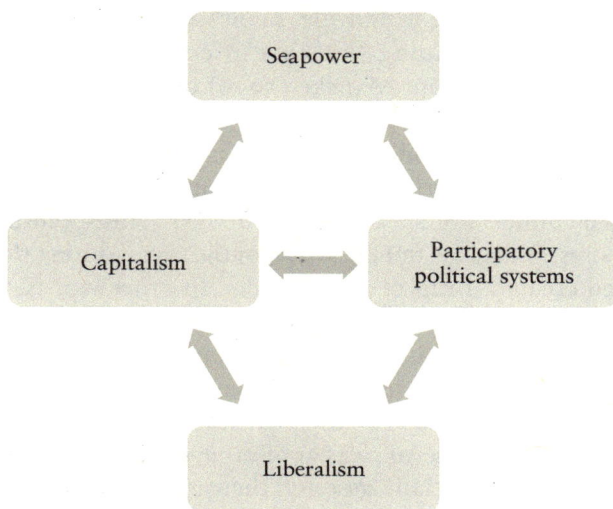

Figure 4.3 Seapower and liberalism

seapower has directly and/or indirectly resulted in the consolidation of liberal principles and even democratic ones via the need to foster inclusive political systems to co-opt political and economic elites into seapower projects (Kyriazis 2006; Kyriazis and Zouboulakis 2004; Lambert 2018).

It is important not to overemphasise an organic link between seapower and democracy though (Till 2022). For example, the current modernisation of China's Navy and the strength of its civilian seapower are directly linked to the country's overall economic performance, which originates in the liberal globalised market economy that China has embraced since the 1980s. However, the Chinese state remains illiberal, and we can doubt that the current seapower politics of China will eventually result in a spread of liberal values within China. China's openness to maritime trade and initiatives, such as the Maritime Silk Road/Belt and Road Initiative, point towards Beijing's contribution to the stabilisation of the global liberal order. However, the commercial tensions with the US as well as the geopolitical tensions around Taiwan, the South China Sea, and beyond remind us of the fragility of such an endeavour and demonstrate that China's seapower politics is also embedded within political realism and China's aspirations as a world leader.

As mentioned above, in Europe, seapower has been instrumental not only in state building but also in colonial empire building (see figure 4.1). Elizabeth Mancke (1999) discusses the inextricable link between the development of seapower and the formation of colonial empires. According to her, 'the long apprenticeship in mastering oceanic space contributed to the ability of Europeans to build land-based empires in Asia and Africa in the nineteen century' (225). She also stresses that the militarisation of the ocean during the modern era helped create a form of global order. In other words, seapower has not only been an instrument of European imperialism (since control of the oceans was key to empire building), but it can also be considered the cradle for global governance.

Indeed, clashing interests on the high seas necessitated the elaboration of diplomatic and legal rules applicable beyond Europe. Whereas Portugal and Spain initially asserted their right to claim sovereignty over the oceans (*mare clausum*), the view defended by the Dutch, English, and French that the seas shall not fall under the sovereignty of any particular state (*mare liberum*) became dominant, and there appeared a need to define 'the terms of interaction in this nonstate arena' (232). Regulating state and state-sponsored activities beyond the geographical boundary of Europe and without imposing rules and laws (contrary to what was done vis-à-vis pre-colonial American, Asian, and African polities) was something rather new as a concept and a practice. It certainly contributed to strengthening the habit of developing a corpus of more widely accepted and acceptable rules through treaties and other less formal agreements (customary public international law), and thus constitutes a form of proto-global governance that has continued to play in favour of the dominant sea Powers (Kraska 2009).

According to Steinberg, representing the sea as an empty space has 'served to support and constitute a system of power/knowledge that has maintained the systematic colonization, exploitation, and domination of lands lying beyond the ocean's vast expanse' (2001, 38). Early global sea-borne empires, such as the Portuguese and Dutch in the Indian Ocean and Southeast Asia in the sixteenth and seventeenth centuries, were not in a position to control the land or impose European settlements on land, and thus were not interested in reforming/modernising 'political rule or social structures' (Münkler 2007, 50). Their power rested on their ability to control the SLOCs to and from Europe. Thus claiming that the Indian Ocean was a *mare clausum* was directed against European competitors not local authorities. The aim was to establish and operationalise a lucrative trade monopoly. In sum, Jeremy Black reminds us that 'what made Europe distinctive in world history was its ability to use the oceans in order to create the first trading systems and empires able to span the world' (2004, 1).

Colonial empires in the nineteenth century were supported by a narrative consisting in justifying colonisation through a so-called 'civilizing mission'. However, colonial Powers were not interested in modernising political and social life in the colonies. In sum, the intimate link between seapower and colonisation in the modern era shall not support the erroneous view that it has helped spread modernity to the colonised world in any positive way. Seapower that was instrumental in allowing economic and political modernity to flourish in Europe mainly resulted in economic (and political) exploitation overseas. European seapower is also inextricably linked to slave trade, with European nations benefiting from the lucrative triangular trade and navies protecting this 'legitimate' business (Spence 2015, 196) until its prohibition in 1807.

The *Pax Britannica* from 1815 to 1914 illustrates modern seapower. At the same time as the Royal Navy ruled the waves, colonial empires thrived, privateering faded, and nation-states in Europe consolidated around the principles of the Westphalian order and the so-called 'Concert of Europe'. Whereas the expression 'silent service' is now reserved for the submarine branch of the navy, it was traditionally employed to characterise the Royal Navy of the nineteenth century, playing a crucial role in defence of the *Pax Britannica* but without much publicity (Corbett and Hodges 1916, 20; W.C. Wood 1919, 109). However, modern seapower is intimately linked to balance of power; it fits with the realist, zero-sum game approach discussed in chapter 2. British dominance had increasingly been contested, and an important element of this contestation was naval power. Whereas France and its naval thinkers were rather proponents of the *guerre de course* (cf. chapter 1), growing tensions at the end of the nineteenth century, both on the continent and in the colonies, as well as the unification of Germany, created further incentives and opportunities to challenge British rule. And indeed, naval arms races between competing Powers ahead of World War I and then World War II were instrumental in explaining the cause, conduct, and outcome of the two global conflicts.

Eventually, the beginning of a new cycle of hegemony (with the *Pax Americana*) and the inception of the post-modern era coincides with Paul Kennedy's *Victory at Sea*, which he describes as a 'seismic shift' in balance of power leading to the replacement, since 1945, of the Old World by the 'new' one (2022, under preface). The Cold War era strategic environment was framed and constrained by the imperatives of nuclear deterrence whose maritime dimension quickly became central, since the ultimate guarantor of nuclear deterrence is the second-strike capability offered by strategic submarines. Modern, realist considerations were prominent and as a result, seapower during the Cold War was often reduced to naval considerations and balance of power (e.g., preparing for a potential 'decisive' naval battle in the High North, protecting one's strategic submarines and chasing those of the enemy, coercive forms of naval diplomacy in the developing South). Ironically, the West's eventual preponderance in the Cold War is as strongly related to military/naval dominance as to its control of the global supply chain compared to the Soviet's increasingly suffocating economy that was unable to sustain the arms race whose naval dimension was not negligible.

SEAPOWER IN NON-EUROPEAN SETTINGS

Despite efforts to develop scholarship that accounts for the role of the *fait maritime* in the history of polities and civilisations from Antiquity to the contemporary era (e.g., Abulafia 2019; Paine 2013; de Souza 2001), 'there remain major asymmetries in this perspective, with the greatest focus still placed on the Mediterranean cultures', which are primarily due to the geographical imbalance in written sources (Arnaud 2017, 7). However, in the very case of seapower, whereas access to primary sources for ancient and medieval European history is less of an obstacle, the paucity of period writings accounting for the practice of seapower by Europeans is as remarkable as in other geographical areas. Another similarity between the maritime historiography of European and non-European societies is that existing literature on the pre-modern and medieval eras focuses more on maritime culture and less on naval warfare. Naval power becomes more central to scholarship focusing on the early modern, modern, and contemporary eras, which follows trends in the practice of seapower (and for that matter naval power) both in Europe and in other geographical areas. It is thus important to clarify the significant role seapower played in non-European pre-modern and medieval settings.

First, at the ideational level, the limited written accounts of non-European seapower thought mirrors the European case. Indeed, pre-modern European seapower thought has also been limited. And the perception of a vibrant seapower scholarship in Europe is based on the over-emphasis put on Ancient Greek thought, in particular Herodotus and Thucydides. Whereas Ancient Greece produced some key philosophic-political texts accounting for the importance of seapower, Roman authors who have mentioned the sea have done so in a descriptive, factual way, and medieval political writings in Europe were not focused on seapower (except somewhat in the case of the role sea transport played in the context of the Crusades).

Thus, there is a clear gap between the paucity of European seapower thought (at least before the Renaissance, cf. chapter 1) and the perception of seapower as an inherently European concept and practice. This is because seapower scholarship has emerged and diffused since the nineteenth century in Europe and the US. Consequently, seapower scholarship has been dominated by Europeans since Europe de facto dominated the world, and this domination had been the result of Europe's mastering the seas since 1500. Therefore, Greek thought, considered the cradle for European political thought in general and seapower in particular, was put on a pedestal. This has resulted in a systematic lack of attention paid to non-European seapower thought. Yet, relevant elements although limited and fragmented, are found in key non-European texts, from the ancient Hindu's *Manusmriti* to Ibn Khaldun's *Muqaddimah* (1377).

Second, China, India, and the Arab Caliphates were continental powers by their size, their reliance on agriculture, and a landowning-based social and political system. Due to their geographical position, they had to deal with critical continental threats, often on more than one front. This had pushed them away from a seapower orientation but not from developing maritime power, although none of these three continental pre-modern Powers can be said to have developed or sustained a maritime mindset. Asian continental Powers were simply *less* reliant on maritime economy for state building. The organic relationship between maritime trade, naval power, and state building that characterises modernisation in Europe was not as prominent in Asia. That said, maritime culture was not inexistent. Elites were averse towards the sea for fear of the subversive values associated with trade and voyages, but this is not different from the European pre-modern mentality. For example, in China, the Song navy played an important role in deterring the Mongols and thus delaying the fall of the dynasty;

the Yuan navy was a central element of the recurring plans to invade Japan; and the Ming used their maritime dominance to exercise soft power in order to secure and expand their tributary system. In India, the Chola Empire developed strong maritime power capabilities able to contest sea control in waters as far away from India as modern-day Sumatra (Rehman 2017; Sivasundaram 2018; Tagliacozzo 2018).

Yet, continental polities are less likely to sustain a fleet over longer periods of time due to the cost of such an endeavour and long-term land-based threats resulting in land-oriented strategic imperatives. Thus, one of the main explanatory factors for the decline of maritime power in these polities before 1500 was the need to focus primarily on land borders. The Mongols posed a threat to China, India, and the Caliphates at different scales and at different times but nonetheless acute enough to deserve full attention and to instil in the longer term a continental mindset resulting, over time, in neglect of the importance of seapower. Still, it is important to recognise that these three Powers exerted seapower in a way that was crucial to their continental hegemony in some time-limited eras (e.g., the Cholas in India, the Ming in China, and the Caliphate in the Mediterranean).

Third, medieval and early modern thalassocracies, such as Srivijaya and Majapahit in today's Indonesia, were highly dependent on seafaring and the securing of sea routes for communication and trade but also political control over vassals and eventually defence against external threats. The sea has been instrumental to their enduring regional dominance over rather long periods of time in a way similarly experienced by Phoenicia, Athens, or Venice, frequently used as key examples of European seapower states. These examples demonstrate the persisting bias in the literature towards European seapower.

SEAPOWER AS MODERNITY?

As this chapter shows, pre-modern seapower constituted a form of unachieved or underachieved seapower, explained by the fact that seapower could only truly thrive in a modern technological, economic, political, and ideological context. Pre-modern societies' seafaring prowess and the role played by naval power in the ascendancy of Greek thalassocracies or even Rome shall not hide the limited technological means available and elites' disdain for the sea that characterised most of the pre-modern era. That said, most of the elements of seapower that became prominent during the modern era (from warships to maritime trade and from naval tactics to maritime culture) were present in the pre-modern era, albeit rarely all of them together, and most of them in an attuned form. Consequently, both the enactment and the consequences of pre-modern seapower were constrained.

Modern seapower cannot only be conceived as an outcome of modernity, because it is also a cause of it, or at least a major contributing factor. Seapower epitomises modernity; by essence it is modern, if not synonymous with modernity. Indeed, the term itself was coined by Mahan in the late nineteenth century to account for, and advocate, the modern reality that consisted in power maximisation politics by nation-states in a globalised economy. Seapower was then instrumental, not only in the form of naval power but also more generally as an enabler of colonialism and capitalism, and thus as a direct and indirect contributor to modern nation-state building. This is not dissimilar to Modelski and Thompson's demonstration that 'a rise to global status is negatively related to pre-modern political organisation and positively correlated with nation-statehood' (1988, 136).

However, contrary to Colomb's argument mentioned above, modernity was not a condition for seapower to develop but merely a catalyst. Some important characteristics of the modern era, such as technological advances, belief in technology, constriction of time-space, a growing (albeit limited) openness to the outside world, and the importance of liberty as a value (favouring trade via entrepreneurship), have all impacted on the development and enactment of seapower (cf. table 4.2). The development of seapower, in turn, has had tremendous impacts on the processes occurring at the level of colonial empires, (nation-)states, the corporate sector, and societies, via sometimes contradictory endeavours and processes such as explorations, trade, exploitation, colonialism, the contribution to Europeans' material power basis and institutional stability, the advancement of a culture of openness to the world, the need to accommodate participatory political systems, and the establishment of international law rules (see figure 4.4).

The mutually reinforcing connection between seapower and modernity has been cemented in the collective imaginaries – as illustrated by romantic writers' and artists' literary and visual productions – allowing the myth of seapower to flourish. In turn, this ideational element must be taken into account when assessing the societal (and governmental) support for seapower politics, what Mahan refers to

Table 4.2
The layers of modern seapower

Layers of analysis	Modern features
Elements of seapower	• Technological breakthroughs (platforms, weapons, navigation) enabling navies to deliver strategic effects • Openness to the sea linked to capitalism and secularism • Technology from the industrial revolution allowed seapower to develop, but the need to develop seapower also incentivised technological/industrial developments. • Maritime culture and identity as enabler of seapower politics
Enactment of seapower	• Reciprocal links between the need to develop seapower to consolidate nation-states and the positive impact of nation-states on the development of seapower • Reciprocal link between the need to develop seapower to accumulate riches (e.g., from colonial empires) and the possibility to develop seapower from growing economic power and states' bureaucratisation
Consequences of seapower	• Consolidation of nation-states in Europe • Colonial system • Liberalism • Cradle for global governance

as the character of the people and of the government. In addition to the myth embedded in the modern notion of seapower, modernity allowed rationality – in particular the quest for economic profit – to take over other principles as the dominant explanatory factor in decision-making processes, thus allowing seapower to flourish in Europe, despite the enduring distrust for the sea and 'sea people' (seafarers, mariners, fisher-folks) among many ruling elites. The example of Qing China shows how important this element of modernity is when it comes to explaining the development (or not) of seapower. Conversely, this specific condition for the development of seapower illustrates the central importance of the ideational dimension of modernity. In other words, despite the indisputable importance of the technological dimension of modernity in elucidating the rise of modern seapower, the ideational dimension shall not be underestimated.

Seapower epitomises modernity since it has been instrumental in the process of consolidation of nation-states, the increased (free) flow of capital, and the spread of European values and norms. That said, post-modern features of seapower could also be found during the modern era. For example, the Grotian concept of *mare liberum* (which eventually resulted in the adoption of UNCLOS in the late twentieth century)

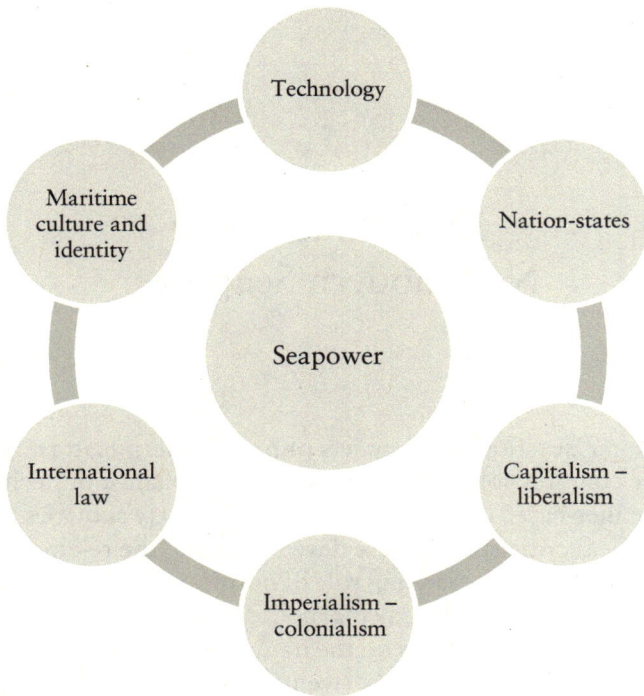

Figure 4.4 Seapower as modernity

illustrates post-modern features framing the modern maritime order: the high seas are not susceptible to ownership and thus represent something post-modern by essence. Already in the medieval, early modern era, the Hanseatic League revealed some post-modern characteristics of seapower: the Hanse was indeed a loose network of merchants and cities whose main driver for regulating activities, policing the sea, and thus challenging established, land-based political structures, was profit maximisation. As such, it prefigured corporate seapower (see chapter 6). Its preferred and most efficient means of pressure was commercial bargaining more than military power, although the Hanse could exercise forms of naval power, such as blockading, when needed. In sum, the inception of post-modern features started well before the twentieth century. The next chapters discuss the challenge these features posed to modern seapower, leading to further transformations of the concept and practice of seapower.

5

Post-modern and
Neo-modern Seapower

This chapter questions the impacts of post-modern features, such as a further compression of time-space; a deep reliance on technology and computer-based communication for day-to-day activities (and the philosophical criticisms of these developments); the re-emergence of non-state actors; the expanding role of norms, values, and non-realist objectives in IR (e.g., environmental politics); and the increasing power of supranational institutions on the nature and practice of seapower. In the late twentieth and early twenty-first centuries, naval power understood in its traditional acceptation continues to play a central role (i.e., securing and exercising command of the sea). However, beyond naval considerations, post- and neo-modern features of seapower have developed alongside more traditional ones. Hence, this chapter deconstructs the practice of maritime security and ocean governance to illustrate that deterritorialised practices, such as the projection of norms and security, are complemented with practices of control and territorialisation. Indeed, the process of deterritorialisation of security is challenged by a process of (re-)territorialisation of the sea that has initiated a move towards a neo-modern form of seapower, which demonstrates the existence of enduring permanencies when it comes to seapower – most notably in relation to the stability of the global order that serves maritime nations' interests as well as those of their allies. This paves the way for chapter 6, which further discusses the collective and civilian dimensions of seapower that are not only modifying the balance of power at sea but also impacting on the very concept of seapower.

SEAPOWER IN A
DETERRITORIALISED WORLD

Deterritorialisation as a process is post-modern since it goes against the modern diplomatic and international law principles devised at the time of the Peace of Westphalia, which grant established borders a quasi-permanent status and stress the centrality of the principle of non-interference in other states' domestic affairs. In the modern era, colonisation and especially war amongst Europeans have recurrently contradicted these principles. However, colonisation was then justified with the concept of *terra nullius*. The act of colonising was not perceived as a violation of the Westphalian principles, since in the eyes of the colonial Powers the colonised territories (and populations) were regarded as belonging to 'nobody' and thus outside the realm of Westphalia as an order. War (in Europe) did contradict the Westphalian principles, but this was meant to be the exception, recognised as a voluntary violation of the principles, not rejection of them or a contestation of their legitimacy.

From a realist perspective, war implies a state of exception and thus the conduct of war entails violating borders, and the outcome of war justifies border modifications. For example, in 2023, Putin's Russia considers that Ukraine must now account for the so-called *realities* on the field resulting from Russia's war of aggression that ignores international law principles. In the twenty-first century, such occurrences, reminiscent of the modern era, are rare. Yet, interventions in the name of values and principles, such as the 'responsibility to protect'; policing activities abroad; projecting security and security norms; and controlling human activities beyond one's own external boundary, or the boundary of one's regional organisation, such as the EU, imply a form of deterritorialisation of security: a rejection of the quasi-sacralised status of borders. In other words, whereas the 'abroad' space is still considered legally outside one's zone of influence, this is not the case from a functional perspective, that is, states perform security and governance functions beyond their external boundaries, and in narratives, they construct this practice as legitimate (as a form of governance), although jurists and international law scholars may debate the extent to which this contradicts the spirit if not the letter of the Westphalian principles.

The deterritorialisation of security refers to the supposed growing obsolescence of borders and legally defined territories when it comes to scholars' understanding of and practitioners' dealing with current (real or perceived) threats to international organisations, states, societies, individuals, and the environment. This presupposes that someone's security depends on the security – or the securing – of others, or that obtaining security 'inside'/'home' is contingent on securing the 'outside'/'abroad'. Threats originate and proliferate 'elsewhere', often far away from one's own territory, but eventually impact 'us', since they are not static and localised but ubiquitous. They are not limited to foreign states and their military forces but encompass a wide range of infra-military threats and non-state actors, such as pirates, transnational criminals, terrorists, and illegal fishers, who operate beyond and across borders without much consideration for sovereignty and public international law. In fact, criminal actors take advantage of the lack of coordination between states, the overlapping of jurisdictions, and the discrepancies between legal systems to perform illegal activities. They are versatile and multifaceted, and threats can mutate and merge. For example, a rise in illegal fishing by foreign, extra-regional fleets can lead to an increase in piratical activities, as was the case at the Horn of Africa at the end of the 2000s.

To face these deterritorialised threats, state actors are increasingly engaged in power and norms projection beyond their external boundaries to tackle the threats where and when they materialise, as far away from home as possible and as soon as possible (Germond 2015). This further contributes to the deterritorialisation process, since state actors are voluntarily operating, materially or normatively, beyond their external boundaries, thus eroding the foundations and stability of the old Westphalian principles of sovereignty and non-interference in other states' domestic affairs. Post-modern features also include further international cooperation in the field of defence and security, with a bigger role played by international organisations and non-state actors. The latter can be both protagonists (e.g., private security companies, NGOs) and antagonists (e.g., terrorist organisations, pirates).

Finally, technological changes are happening at a faster pace, and these impact on maritime strategy and operations. For example, progress with the speed of communication (both physical and digital/virtual) has contributed to further time-space compression, which impacts the battlefield. Technological breakthroughs in the field of information, computing, cyber technologies, and artificial intelligence have created both opportunities and challenges. In fact, in the post-modern era, 'one of the most difficult and fundamental questions for naval leaders is how to deal with this type of change' (Hattendorf 2000, 253). Due to the length of naval procurement cycles, technological opportunities must be identified and applied to weapon systems and platforms in a timely manner. Whereas new information and cyber technologies can be implemented rather quickly 'over-the-air', their translation into new operational doctrines and tactics can take much longer. In the context of network-centric warfare and effect-based operations, where speed, quantity, and quality of information are crucial, outer space and cyberspace have become prominent. These two battlefields are extremely technology driven. Furthermore, cyber operations can take place in the grey zone, which contributes to blurring the boundaries between 'regular' (acceptable) power politics and warfare (cf. below).

The sea is prone to the proliferation of illegal activities, since it is a wide space, largely under-policed, difficult to monitor, and even more challenging for state forces and agencies to control and patrol. Controlling ocean space cannot be achieved permanently and globally, even in today's highly technological world. Indeed, whereas surveillance technologies allow developing a more comprehensive and accurate 'global picture' of human activities and flows at sea (in other words 'global maritime domain awareness'), the maritime domain still cannot be occupied, as by nature, the sea 'is not susceptible of ownership' (Corbett 1911, 93). As the site of piracy, drug and people smuggling, arms trafficking, illegal fishing, pollution, the ocean space might well be 'the biggest crime scene in the world' (Stavridis 2017, 274). A way to respond to this challenge has been to control the flows at the entry and exit points on land, mainly in ports. This implies focusing on the flows and nodes rather than on space and networks. Despite the obstacles towards efficiently controlling the maritime space, states include geographically distant maritime regions in their security perimeter, for transnational threats need to be tackled beyond one's external boundary.

Controlling the sea far away from home has strategic and security value. It allows projecting power and forces overseas in a traditional, modern way. But in a more post-modern way, it also represents a means to expand one's zone of control and competencies beyond one's external boundary, which can be considered a form of post-modern deterritorialisation (from a functional, not so much from a jurisdictional, perspective). That said, global ocean governance (including maritime security) is an increasingly cooperative process, with state and non-state actors engaged in vertical and horizontal integration and cooperation. The less 'military and strategic' the issue to tackle, the more likely it is that state actors will engage in cooperative behaviours and practices (including with non-state actors), since the complexity of ocean governance is acknowledged as is the need to adopt comprehensive and integrated approaches (cf. below). The fluidity of the legal framework offered by UNCLOS and other instruments of the current ocean governance regime further facilitates extra-jurisdictional constabulary operations.

In response to the changing nature of security threats and actors at sea (as well as the evolution of the concept of security), innovative scholarly debates focusing on maritime security and 'blue crime' have emerged. The object of study has moved from national security to environmental, economic, and human security. The transnational, multi-space, and multi-stakeholder dimensions of maritime security are central to the analysis of the phenomenon (Bueger 2015; Bueger and Edmunds 2017, 2020, 2021; Bueger, Edmunds, and Ryan 2019). This new strand in the literature, although not focused on the concept of seapower itself, has largely contributed to the field by highlighting the complexity of maritime security (and by extension security, defence, governance, and prosperity at sea), and the process of ordering and reordering taking place at sea in the twenty-first century. Interestingly, Rear Admiral Eccles already emphasised in the 1970s the importance of the oceans within the ecosystem upon which humanity's survival depends and the need to account for the environmental dimension of sea control (1979, 204–5).

In sum, in a deterritorialised world, post-modern characteristics are to be found in both the final cause of seapower (i.e., the stability and security of the global maritime order) and the actors of seapower (i.e., states, international organisations, and non-state actors). States still use the sea as a medium for interventions abroad (i.e., traditional naval projection operations in a post-modern context) or for soft power projection (e.g., forward presence), but resources are also increasingly devoted to the enforcement of norms and the exercise of (legitimate) public violence at sea beyond states' territorial and jurisdictional waters (i.e., maritime security and global ocean governance practices). Non-state stakeholders, from shipping companies and maritime insurances to fisher-folks to private security companies, play an important role in this post-modern organisation of the global maritime order (cf. chapter 6). The example of the Hanseatic League shows that such practices are not without historical precedents, but in the modern era, states' activities beyond their external boundaries were limited and restrained except in case of war. The deterritorialisation of security has challenged this Westphalian practice. Yet, this has not fundamentally altered the nature of seapower. Indeed, seapower is still about exercising command of the sea in order to achieve economic, political, or security objectives on land; and maritime preponderance, which includes controlling the global maritime order in peacetime, still contributes to global leadership.

Naval Power in a Post-Modern World

Navies have been involved in power and forces projection since the ancient times (cf. chapter 4). For example, the Roman Republic used the navy to project troops onto the North African territories of Carthage, and the Roman Empire used its navy to supply and flank legions spread all over the empire. Modern navies were then used to win wars and sustain empires. What has changed in the post-modern era is that (besides wars of aggression) states intervene in other states' domestic affairs under the rubric of human rights protection or other norms and in the name of internal and/or global security, which no longer fits with the modern conception of security/defence and bears post-modern characteristics outside the realm of political realism. A case in point is the academic debate on the expansion of the security agenda, which has evolved from territorial defence and national security to a broader and wider conception that considers other layers of security, such as individual, human, societal, regional, global, and environmental security (Buzan, Wæver, and de Wilde 1997; Fierke 2007; Krause and Williams 1996). The evolution of the concept of security towards a 'projection of security' agenda in the 1990s and 2000s was closely linked to the preponderance of Western nations from a military and 'global leadership' perspective.

Both the aim, or final cause, of Western-led projection operations (i.e., global liberal order, value change, or human rights protection) and the way they are conducted (i.e., minimal casualties, minimal collateral damage) have been labelled post-modern to account for the fact that even though they were still 'a continuation of politics by other means', they were no longer constrained or guided by a modern system of thought. Obviously, beyond the academic debate, the boundary between a pre-modern, modern, and post-modern practice is open to debate. For example, to tackle piracy in the Mediterranean the Romans needed to project power and forces, and even to occupy coastal territories, and the final aim of Pompey's campaign was the internal security of the Roman Republic. The aim of post–Cold War Western military interventions has not been territorial acquisitions but rather the imposition of values and norms as well as the promotion of a stable liberal world order. This is what constitutes the main difference between modern and post-modern interventions. The goal of territorial acquisitions and increased sovereignty has been replaced by the goal of stability through norm projection and regime change, which nevertheless sometimes requires the use of force at high intensity, including naval power and forces projection.

The sea has been instrumental in the post–Cold War foreign intervention operations notably in terms of sealift and power projection: Gulf (1991), Kosovo (1999), Afghanistan (2001–02), Iraq (2003), and Libya (2011) to name but the most substantial ones. Navies have contributed to the deployment of air assets (including for surveillance, reconnaissance, air combat, close-air support, and strategic bombardments). They have also heavily contributed to the logistics (transport of material and supplies), especially during the Gulf and Iraq wars. Accordingly, in Western states' narrative, the ocean tends to be represented as a 'great void' (Steinberg 2001) that contributes to Western navies' flexibility and versatility to project power and forces where and when needed. In addition to the freedom of manoeuvre granted by the sea, navies indeed enjoy legal advantages, that is, they can operate close to other states' territorial waters without breaching international law, and political advantages, that is, they can either remain discreet, off the media coverage, or on the contrary be ostentatious in demonstrating their military might by deploying substantial assets and publicising it (Germond 2015). With shrinking military budgets following the end of the Cold War and the politics of 'peace dividends', navies have had to do more with less, which has incentivised the development of naval multilateralism (Hattendorf 2000, 233; Germond 2008).

Western maritime doctrine and naval warfare have also been impacted by post-modern political considerations, such as minimising casualties both within one's own armed forces and within the enemy's population (all the more since the 'enemy' is the regime, not the population). This cannot be separated from the aim of the above-mentioned operations (i.e., human rights, regime change). Indeed, it is crucial to get popular support at home by reducing the risk of casualties and in the target country by avoiding collateral damage. Technological developments in the field of surveillance, communication, and target acquisition have contributed to making these political objectives achievable. Navies have been early adopters and proponents of the new information technologies due to an inherent need for integrating data and the command-and-control system within a multidimensional space and at a global level.

Network-centric warfare means that combat is not centred on a platform (e.g., warships) but rather on a system of land, sea, air, and outer space platforms and sensors that enables improving domain awareness, command-and-control, as well as target acquisition. In other words, improvements in sensor, communication, and computer-based analysis technologies (including AI) have enabled the networking of information (i.e., increased quantity and quality of information and its fast and continuous sharing) as well as platforms. This results in an integrated but decentralised C4ISTAR system (command, control, communications, computers, intelligence, surveillance, target acquisition and reconnaissance) and an improved 'common operational picture'. This eventually improves combat efficiency (speed and accuracy) and enables conducting effect-based operations (e.g., strikes that will have a disproportionate effect on the enemy command-and-control structure and paralyze its decision-making cycle). Such a doctrine relies on recent and still-evolving technologies and on the mastering of outer space and cyberspace. Whereas it is possible to identify their impact on naval warfare, it is too early to conclude about their broader impact on seapower beyond the fact that the elements and enactment of seapower are increasingly linked to outer space and cyberspace. This fits with Modelski and Thompson's suggestion that the centrality of seapower (and of who controls the sea) might eventually be replaced by outer 'space power' (1988, 144–6).

Luttwak (1974), Bull (1976a), Booth (1979, 1985), and Cable (1983; 1985) emphasise the importance of naval diplomacy and the role played by naval forces as an instrument of state power. Given the importance of soft, extrinsic power as well as deterrence, it is not surprising that naval power still contributes to states' prestige in the twenty-first century: from China's commissioning of its first aircraft carrier in 2012 (i.e., the ultimate symbol of naval power since World War II), to Peru's maintaining in service what remained of the last operational battle cruiser until 2017 (*Almirante Grau*), to Ukraine's sinking of the Russian cruiser (and Black Sea flagship) *Moskva* in 2022. This is another feature of post-modern seapower that is not new but whose importance has grown, along with the contribution of soft power and public diplomacy to deterrence and suasion strategies. Prepositioning of forces has replaced 'gunboat diplomacy', but naval diplomacy in the form of port visits, coalition building, and freedom of navigation operations continues to play an important role in stabilising the global maritime order (Le Mière 2014; Patalano 2022). In sum, whereas naval positioning and fleet-in-being have existed as a practice (and as principles of maritime strategy) well before the rise of the post-modern world (Taylor 2017), today's emphasis on the symbolic naval functions, such as ostentatious presence or humanitarian assistance, highlights the importance of extrinsic power in its very post-modern garment. Similar to power and forces projection, the enactment of soft seapower can also eventually result in a more stable liberal world order.

This extrinsic dimension of seapower is not limited to big navies; it is also important for so-called small navies. Although their material contribution to projection operations remains limited for obvious reasons, the symbolic effort is nonetheless relevant. For example, Canada stated that its navy's ability to participate in coalition operations is crucial to 'express solidarity with our friends' (RCN 2017, 13). Participating in such operations also offers individual navies the opportunity to 'learn by doing' and to be among those that are 'setting up the rules of the game'. Consequently, it is not surprising to find that participating in coalition operations has become a key performance indicator of some small navies. This is obviously not without risk. Indeed, small navies may bandwagon with more powerful ones and eventually be dragged into operations that have been designed by, and are largely conducted in the interest of, other states (Germond 2019). There is also a risk of overspecialization, as illustrated by the Baltic States navies' focus on mine warfare/mine counter-measures. If specialization is achieved at the expense of other crucial functions of the navy this strategy may not be sustainable in the mid to long term.

Since the end of the Cold War, navies have been increasingly involved in (peacetime) constabulary tasks. This can represent a quarter of big navies' activities and easily increase to three-quarters or more in the case of small navies. This has implied a greater involvement of military (naval) forces in the day-to-day running of security, which is a direct result of the expansion of the security agenda and the emphasis on so-called new threats as well as the comprehensive approach to security that integrates various levels of interventions, from long-term development aid and security sector reform activities that address the root causes of poverty, resentment, or bad governance, to police/military operations that respond to crises in the short term. Naval forces have to deal with non-state and non-military actors, including terrorists, smugglers, human traffickers, pirates, and illegal fishers; they have to collaborate with police forces and legal officers. Three decades ago, navies were not always well prepared and willing to contribute to maritime security operations and thus to the third side of Booth's triangle (e.g., d'Oléon 1996, 143), but their constabulary function has now been normalised. However, traditional, modern, war-fighting navies may still be less adapted than coastguards when it comes to 'enforcing good order at sea in peacetime' (Bateman 2007, 112).

Navies are not always well prepared for these new sets of tasks, for example, there may be a lack of relevant legal training or the absence of established rules of engagement and procedures for arrest and detention. In some countries naval personnel have no police power, which adds complexities when navies are engaged in multi-stakeholder operations. The involvement of navies in day-to-day security and policing activities, including within states' territorial waters, is a post-modern function. Navies stop being states' instruments during war (i.e., in exceptional circumstances), to become part of their daily governance effort both within and beyond territorial and jurisdictional waters. This can be perceived negatively by the public or create political controversies, such as with HM Government's decision to employ the Royal Navy to manage the issue of migrants crossing the English Channel on small boats (House of Commons, Defence Committee 2022).

Yet, if governmental actors do not devote enough resources to ocean governance, private actors can step in, such as Search and Rescue (SAR) vessels chartered by NGOs in the Mediterranean to rescue migrants (Cusumano 2017). It is also noteworthy that small navies in general (and non-European small navies in Asia, Africa, and South America in particular) have always been limited by the means at disposal and have thus (traditionally) been more focused on constabulary missions (Germond 2014; Morris 1987). This function has been reinforced in the past decades because of the need to exercise sovereign rights in EEZs, whether to address maritime crime, protect one's economic rights, or deny other states' claims.

Well aware of the need to account for the actual evolutions taking place within societies, states, and the international system, Geoffrey Till (2007) introduced the conceptual distinction between modern and post-modern navies. According to him, 'modern' navies seek to maximise power and overpower their competitors; they thus correspond to a very 'realist' understanding of world politics, where the main variable to take into account is balance of power. Post-modern navies appreciate that the defence of their maritime interests and securing the global commons can only be achieved within multilateral frameworks (e.g., 1000-ship navy, Global Maritime Partnership, NATO); they respond to a more 'liberal' vision of the management of global problems whereby relative gains matter more than absolute gains.

This echoes Pugh's (1996) argument that navies have entered a 'post-Mahanist world' and adapted their role and practice accordingly, whether naval bureaucracies like it or not. If post-modern seapower is about the stabilisation of the liberal world order, then there is a collective form of seapower in the post-modern world, which chapter 6 examines. In short, seapower can be enacted in a joint way, and the benefits of its enactment can be shared and are not mutually exclusive. Furthermore, a variety of actors (states, shipping companies, local communities) benefit, albeit not equally, from this enactment and its outcomes in the form of the stability of the maritime order (Germond 2019).

That said, it is still debatable whether the liberal model followed by so-called post-modern navies applies only to like-minded navies within the Western world or can be endorsed by non-Western navies as well. China, for example, has cooperated with Western navies at the Horn of Africa in counter-piracy operations. This can be considered a liberal application of seapower: defending the global commons, which is in the interests of China as a member of the global liberal order benefiting from the free flow of goods. However, China remains primarily outside, or at the edge, of the Western, US-led maritime collaborative framework (Sadler 2023). Here, the role played by security communities is crucial. Indeed, despite some convergent security interests, neither China nor the West perceives each other as belonging to the same security community. This does not prevent China's navy from adopting a more post-modern outlook as illustrated by the establishment in 2017 of a naval base in Djibouti that can be instrumental in the development of China's prepositioning capacity. But this forward naval presence at the Horn of Africa can be interpreted either as Beijing's willingness to contribute its share of policing the oceans or, more likely, as a 'realist' move towards balancing India and the West in the Indian Ocean.

This debate can only be made with reference to the notion of dominance linked to seapower. As discussed in previous chapters, seapower across history has traditionally served European and liberal Powers more than others, and seapower is inextricably linked to liberalism. States that do not share the same view regarding the global liberal order are thus less likely to adhere to the Western notion of seapower, and may rather oppose the deterritorialised element of it, which can be regarded as a way for the West to control the world via the control of the maritime domain, notably SLOCs and the global supply chain. For example, Zhang Wenmu claims that 'a traditional Western notion of sea power is the ability to control the sea, while China's concept of sea power is a marriage of the notion of equal sea rights and sea power. In the latter, the application of power on the seas cannot exceed the former but rather should serve the aim and scope of a nation's sea rights' (2006, 23). In practice, China's Belt and Road Initiative as well as its assertive practice in the South China Sea demonstrate projection ambitions not dissimilar to those of its Western counterparts, albeit unlikely compatible with them. How this has initiated a neo-modern turn in naval policies is discussed below.

For their part, India's and Brazil's emerging regional seapower politics are less likely to clash with Western interests at sea (G. Kennedy and de Sousa Moreira 2022). That said, India and Brazil need to affirm regional preponderance in their respective 'maritime backyard' (Germond 2015, 30–1). For India, the challenge is to control the Indian Ocean where the US Navy stills rules the waves and China grows its ability to project power in the area. Brazil's maritime aspirations cannot be dissociated from the often-forgotten importance of the South-Atlantic sea routes. For them, seapower is firmly grounded in neo-modern considerations (cf. below).

Finally, another post-modern feature of naval affairs relates to navies' involvement in the battle of ideas, or what is now called public diplomacy: navies have to 'sell' their missions and strategy to a wide range of internal and external stakeholders. For example, discussing the case of NATO's maritime strategy, Smith-Windsor (2009, 8) suggests four categories of stakeholders that need to be rallied: NATO sailors (who must adhere to the strategy), other allied services (which should not think they are marginalised), Allied public opinion, and the wider international community (public diplomacy). Delivering maritime/naval concepts or defence white papers then becomes an exercise in public relations. Security is a complex concept that is evidently understood as more than assuring states' survival; official narratives are also complex, and the very exercise of writing security strategy documents has become post-modern in that the target audience was not previously taken into account in the formulation of naval policies, whereas public opinion home and abroad cannot be overlooked in today's world of hyper-communication.

Table 5.1 shows that all three categories of naval missions have integrated post-modern features. However, the outcome is still aligned with classical seapower, that is, maritime preponderance and control of the global maritime domain as a key instrument for global leadership. It is then not surprising that leadership challengers, such as China, attempt to rival Western seapower while, in narrative, claim that they propose an alternative world order.

Global Ocean Governance in a Deterritorialised World

There has been a diversification of maritime stakeholders and activities, from Greenpeace activists to mass maritime tourism and from deep-sea mining to migration on small boats. Additionally, traditional sectors such as the fishing and shipping industries have witnessed tremendous changes in terms of business models, operating structures, scope, and governance. Ocean governance as a concept or a practice is multifaceted. The term 'ocean' refers to the maritime domain/space, the marine environment and marine ecosystems, and to some extent coastal areas, but it may also refer to the agents operating within those spaces, ranging from fish stocks to fisher-folks and from smugglers to naval forces. The term 'governance' refers to a complex process of interactive and multi-stakeholder decision-making and policy implementation/management.

Ocean governance aims at stewarding marine resources and controlling flows and human activities at (and from) the sea, including in ports and littoral regions and across various dimensions (environment, economy, security) and jurisdictions. It is a complex process of interactive decision-making and policy implementation at the global level that involves formal and informal mechanisms (regimes and norms) and governmental and non-governmental actors. It must be understood

Table 5.1
Post-modern naval missions

Missions	Post-modern features
Military	Projection operations in line with projection of security, norms, values, and stability of the global liberal order rather than territorial wars
Diplomatic	Public diplomacy, demonstration of extrinsic power for deterrence or persuasion
Constabulary	Policing and governing the sea to manage so-called new threats (trafficking, piracy, illegal fishing) and stabilise the liberal maritime order

as legislative, executive, and to some extent judicial, both in its intent and scope. Indeed, governance is first about making policy decisions at the political and strategic planning levels, but then it is about implementing and applying them at management level, including control, enforcement, repression, and justice. At sea, this conceptual and practical complexity results in a mix of actors and dimensions of governance, a phenomenon only reinforced by the globalisation of issues and actors in the absence of a world government adds to this complexity. This is especially true for managing the oceans and their inherent transboundary issues, including maritime crime.

Although water connects almost everything, the sea is shared between numerous states and thus split between various jurisdictions. At first glance, UNCLOS gives the appearance of a clear legal separation between sovereignties and more specifically defined areas, such as territorial waters, EEZs, and continental shelves. However, due to the intrinsic characteristics of the maritime space (liquidity and fluidity), there is no physically demarcated boundary at sea. Sovereignty is contestable, jurisdictions overlap, and responsibilities clash. This engenders difficulties for state actors that want to regulate, govern, secure, manage, or steward the sea. This also offers opportunities for criminal non-state actors who can use legal disparities and jurisdictional 'fuzziness' to their own advantage.

Various actors and stakeholders are involved at different levels of ocean governance, namely states, including their naval forces and other agencies; international organisations and regional institutions, such as the EU; and a vast variety of economic and other private stakeholders, such as shipping companies, fishing industries, environmentalists, and coastal communities. Those actors have different and sometimes competing responsibilities, interests, objectives, capabilities, *modus operandi*, and allegiances, which may or may not clash. It is important to differentiate between actors whose main aim is to use the sea (e.g., for profit, pleasure, or livelihood) and those whose main aim is to 'regulate/manage' the activities at/from the sea. For coastal communities the sea does not only represent a source of revenue and livelihood but also it is strongly linked to their own identity and sense of place. Practically, this diversity of stakeholders represents a serious challenge for planning and coordinating policies and activities in an efficient way, all the more since those actors' agency is constrained by the nature of the milieu in which they operate as well as the transboundary nature of their activities. Chapter 6 further discusses the importance of the public-private partnership in terms of maritime security.

Ocean governance is multidimensional as it tackles environmental, economic, social, and security issues. It ranges from marine environment protection and fisheries monitoring to maritime economic growth to counter-immigration and counter-trafficking. The security dimension tends to be neglected by some stakeholders whose interests lie in economic growth and environmental protection. However, political actors have recognised that economic growth cannot be sustained if security does not prevail in the maritime domain; in other words, as former EU commissioner Maria Damanaki (2014) stressed, security is a crucial prerequisite for investments and growth in the maritime domain/sector. As for coastal communities, societal security plays an important role, since ocean governance policies may impact on their sense of place, in addition to potential infringement on their means of livelihood resulting from dispossession, depletion, and pollution.

Maritime spatiality, whose characteristics proceed from the liquid and fluid nature of the ocean (Steinberg and Peters 2015), constrains the agency of various stakeholders as well as the efficiency of governance and policies. The maritime milieu is uninhabitable and cannot be occupied in a traditional sense (Corbett 1911). As mentioned above, it is thus generally more difficult to monitor and regulate despite the low density of human agents compared to the land. In spatial planning terms, it is not always easy to draw clear boundaries between spaces, places, and sites of ocean governance. And the common-sense distinction between land and sea is far too restrictive. Where the sea stops and the land starts is not the shore but the coast, which is a frontier zone rather than a border.

Several attributes of ocean governance bear post-modern characteristics. First of all, ocean governance implies a conceptualisation of
security beyond the traditional modern acceptation. Maritime economic objectives (profit), marine environment protection (ecology),
maritime security (governing human activities at/from the sea), as well
as social well-being cannot be separated. Indeed, it is hard to imagine
a profitable 'blue economy' if the marine environment has been dam-
aged and resources depleted or if local communities are alienated. It
is equally hard to imagine maritime economic growth in the absence
of security in the maritime domain, since investors are likely to be
reluctant to commit, and economic actors will account for the cost
engendered by any form of insecurity, as illustrated by the insurance
premiums that shipping companies have to pay when transiting via
pirate-infested or war-torn regions. Maritime security also includes
the protection of the marine environment and ecosystems, as well as
energy security, which is an economic concern too. The environment
cannot be protected if economic, security, and community actors are
not part of the process. In fact, ocean governance epitomises the post-
modern, comprehensive conception of security in its broadened and
deepened acceptation.

Second, ocean governance is a multi-stakeholder approach that is
post-modern in that it goes beyond the states. Ocean governance
is characterised by the fragmentation of actors and the multiplicity of
competent authorities, resulting in a complex regime. At a national
level, this remains manageable but at a global level, the multiplicity of
actors, processes, interests, norms, and responsibilities make it even
more complex. To address this governance challenge, multiple actors
have integrated both horizontally and vertically. The horizontal integration consists in fostering cooperation between similar types of actors
operating at the same level of governance, for instance, governments
or coastguards working together, like-minded marine NGOs collaborating, or corporate maritime actors within a sector of the economy
coordinating their activities and aligning their objectives. The vertical
integration consists in fostering cooperation between actors operating
at different levels of governance, for example, governments and their
agencies consulting with shipping companies or environmental NGOs
collaborating with fishing industries. Inter-agencies' cooperation may
take place between various governmental agencies without moving
to the next stage of integration (i.e., with non-governmental stakeholders) and without moving to the level of international cooperation

(i.e., with other states' agencies). Also noteworthy is the growing role of non-state actors as substitutes for states (not unlike the situation during Middle Ages), for example, environmental NGOs involved in the daily practice of marine environment protection or SAR services delivered to maritime migrants.

Finally, the very existence of ocean governance processes highlights the conflicting nature of the Westphalian system in the maritime milieu. Indeed, ocean space is characterised by a high degree of inter-connectedness among both issues and actors. Thus, responses and remedies to problems are also, logically, interconnected. However, global interests continue to clash with individual actors' interests. The proliferation of international cooperation forums bringing stake-holders together at a regional level (e.g., EU, Arctic Council, Council of the Baltic Sea States, Association of Southeast Asian Nations) and an international level (e.g., International Maritime Organization [IMO]) along with an extensive scope of integrated processes ranging from marine protected areas (MPAs) to ecosystem-based management to maritime security cooperation have contributed to the mitigation of those discrepancies through the development of a global ocean governance regime. However, this liberal process continues to be bal-anced by more realist considerations, including geopolitical ones. States continue to somewhat privilege forums, policies, and actions that are primarily in their own interest and to avoid engaging in coop-eration considered detrimental to their own interest. Morality also plays an important role. For instance, following Russia's invasion of Ukraine, science cooperation and polar research with institutions supporting or supported by Putin's regime ceases being politically (or even morally) acceptable for Western states.

Tanaka (2004, 2008) discusses the differences between a zonal and an integrated approach to ocean governance. The zonal approach is reminiscent of the international law of the sea traditions that have favoured the creation of fixed legal boundaries at sea, but it does not account well for the fluid nature of the oceans and the resulting inad-equacy of fixed jurisdictions and too rigid mechanisms. Indeed, traditional Westphalian zonal approaches tackle regional/local issues in accordance with the national interest of concerned states and possibly national stakeholders (e.g., national fishing industry). However, this may not be representative of the actual situation where transboundary issues arise in a fluid environment. The example of fish stocks shows that not only do 'fish cross UNCLOS boundaries' but also illegal, unregulated, and unreported fishing (IUUF) is a transnational activity, and the impact of climate change on fish stocks is not constrained by jurisdictional considerations. Although the need to act globally is acknowledged, the national interest of various states and national stakeholders does not always align with global interests, which results in inefficient forms of cooperation.

Even when actors agree on the need to cooperate, they may disagree on the method. Post-modern governance questions the over-reliance on traditional international law and Westphalian principles as the preferred framework for cooperation, since it results in too rigid policies that may not always be adapted to the realities of ocean governance due to the nature of the maritime milieu and the transboundary characteristics of marine and maritime issues. In the late twentieth and early twenty-first centuries, the EU has demonstrated that a sufficient degree of willingness to integrate approaches as well as a sense of common interests that transcends sovereignties can result in an integrated approach to ocean governance. Approaches have also been functional (i.e., limited to a particular policy area such as fisheries policy), which reduces complexity but at the expense of a truly integrated approach to transboundary and multi-level issues. In the field of environment protection and resource management, MPAs offer the possibility to transcend boundaries, but the integration remains limited to a particular space and a particular domain (i.e., environment/resource protection).

In sum, post-modernity has impacted seapower via deterritorialisation processes that have influenced the elements, enactment, and consequences of seapower. Threats, actors, and governance mechanisms are increasingly global in nature, scope, and reach. International organisations as well as corporate and NGO stakeholders have increased their leverage at sea. Post-modernity has brought forward the liberalist approach to seapower, whereby the final cause of seapower remains the stabilisation of the global, liberal world order. Naval forces have been instrumental in contributing to post-modern, supranational forms of interventions as well as in policing activities beyond territorial waters. Yet, environmental protection, food security, resource management, and more broadly, ocean resilience in the era of climate change means that maritime security functions have gained in importance, as has the non-military, transnational dimension of ocean governance. Ironically, this has paved the way for neo-modern forms of maritime territorialisation.

THE RE-TERRITORIALISATION OF THE SEA AND NEO-MODERN SEAPOWER

This section illustrates that the post-modern process of deterritorialisation has been complemented with a neo-modern process of territorialisation, whereby states maintain or even increase their control over maritime spaces. This translates into a neo-modern form of ocean governance as well as a return to naval power politics.

From a Void to a Grid: The Territorialisation of the Sea

The characteristics of ocean space (global, fluid, hard to monitor) and the consensus around the principle of the free seas (*mare liberum*), have been key to seapower politics, enabling empires and nation-states to thrive and wars to be won. It has also facilitated the proliferation of criminal and unregulated activities, while controlling non-state actors operating at or from the sea and stewarding marine resources have usually been more arduous and challenging than the equivalent on land. Freedom of the seas remains the guiding principle of ocean governance, but it is challenged by states' growing desire 'to control more of the ocean' (Bosco 2022, 10) in order to maintain control, regulate or prevent the free flow of goods and people, police human activities at or from the sea, and promote a sustainable use of marine resources, especially in light of the increasing issues of pollution and the effects of climate change on marine ecosystems.

To project their sovereignty and control over maritime spaces, states and international organisations have introduced 'new patterns of territorial organisation with which to formalise [their] political and economic control' (Suarez de Vivero, Rodríguez Mateos, and Florido del Corral 2009, 628). To better monitor, control, police, manage, exploit, or protect ocean space, states have initiated a process of territorialisation of the sea that translates into extended national jurisdictions over maritime areas (EEZs and continental shelves) as well as transboundary ocean governance mechanisms and initiatives, such as marine spatial planning, zonation, MPAs, maritime surveillance, and police operations. This has resulted in 'a new sea-based territoriality' (Suarez de Vivero and Rodríguez Mateos 2014, 62). In other words, governance practices that were usually found on land have been transposed to the maritime domain (Germond-Duret 2022), resulting in a form of 'terraqueous territoriality' (Campling and Colás 2018, 776), which has opened the way to a neo-modern form of seapower.

From a void that we could (in theory) travel freely, the ocean has become a regulated grid. This territorialisation practice is a neo-modern form of control over ocean space. But still, this occurs in parallel with the recurring trend consisting in representing the ocean as a void. In fact, as Deleuze and Guattari (1988) explain, the sea is both a 'smooth' space (i.e., resisting regulation) and a 'striated' space. This contradiction results from, or mirrors, the synergistic processes of post-modern capitalism (Steinberg 1999a, 1999b, 2001), deterritorialisation of security that is post-modern since it challenges the principles of the Westphalian order, and neo-modern maritime security practices by states and international organisations resulting from the need to tackle threats as far away from home as possible and to secure the maritime domain in order to enable economic activities.

UNCLOS – the result of a compromise between the interests of big maritime nations in favour of limiting areas under exclusive national sovereignty (not least in order to maintain the right of 'innocent passage' of warships close to shore) and developing states (and non-maritime nations) that wanted to extend their sovereignty over as much of the sea as possible for economic and defence reasons – has facilitated this process of striation. For example, within the EEZs, states have both rights and duties, such as managing fish stocks in a reasonable but also an economically efficient way, that require, or justify, more control. There is also an increasing number of claims to extend sovereignty and control (e.g., over continental shelves), and UNCLOS forms of legal sovereign titles over maritime areas have been complemented by further processes of territorialisation, such as MPAS, zonation, and security corridors. This is what Campling and Colás call a 'parcelisation of the sea' (2021, 4). In addition, more states, such as China and Russia, are trying to forbid benign military activities in zones they claim to be under their exclusive jurisdiction, further infringing on the UNCLOS regime (Bosco 2022, 11), threatening to close some seas (Hendrix 2020, 46–53), and contesting the maritime rules-based order (Sadler 2023).

Environmental protection, a post-modern feature of world politics, has been a motor of the regulation and thus territorialisation of the sea. This is what Steinberg describes as 'the stewardship of the ocean' (2001, 177). Indeed, although the aim of environmental protection at first appears not framed with geopolitical interests, 'economic expecta-tions for marine basins are beginning to acquire a dimension that turns the latter into crucial pieces on the geopolitical chessboard' (Suarez de Vivero and Rodríguez Mateos 2017, 26). Stewarding the ocean is not restricted to marine environment and resources protection. It includes other economic and security considerations: food security (fisheries protection); energy security (protection of offshore installations, transit routes, SLOCs, undersea infrastructures); marine safety; and SAR. Whereas stewarding the oceans concerns the management of marine resources, ocean governance and maritime security are concerned with the management and control of human activities at sea. This necessi-tates global maritime awareness and thus maritime surveillance. Data can then be used for other types of security activities, including, counter-trafficking, counter-piracy, and counterterrorism. Eventually, under the banner of ocean governance, states and international organ-isations can effectively increase their control over the maritime domain, which constitutes a neo-modern form of territorialisation of the sea.

However, the sea has kept its physical attributes and still cannot be occupied and controlled like land spaces, and states remain willing to maintain the principles of freedom of the seas that is in their interests (and that of the system). The result is that 'the sea has not become the land, but an order at sea has developed, which combines all of the above in a neo-modern form of governance of a non-territorializable space, non-zero-sum space, compromising between *mare liberum* and total security' (Germond 2022, 53). Since ocean governance and maritime security norms must be implemented at sea, the naval mis-sions usually considered as post-modern (e.g. constabulary missions) are in fact becoming neo-modern, since it is about controlling space beyond one's external boundary and territorial waters and projecting normative power within and beyond one's jurisdictional waters.

In the twenty-first century, maritime security tasks are only to a limited extent carried out by naval forces, and states' instruments at sea are not limited to naval forces. In other words, public but non-military agencies are part of the maritime security apparatus: coastguards, branches of the police forces or customs, environmental agencies, legal inspectors, and advisers are mandated to regulate human activities at and/or from the sea and in ports. Crucially, this shows that post-modern threats, such as deliberate pollution or IUUF do not necessarily require the day-to-day involvement of the military. Once established, regulations are applied by most stakeholders which self-regulate their activities, either because they believe in the norm that is relevant to their business activities or because they fear potential penalties. This also contributes to the transformation of the maritime space into a land-like territory in terms of public power forms of control. Indeed, the sea, like the land, is now part of states' territory (albeit sometimes not legally but functionally), and thus does not belong to the realm of the exceptional. In other words, so long as only naval forces could legitimately and practically represent the state at sea, the maritime domain had kept a separate geopolitical nature, differing from land territories on which states' control is permanent and total. The importance played by non-military agencies in regulating the sea shows that the maritime space has acquired 'normal' bureaucratic characteristics. This normality, however, implies the logic of territorialisation discussed above. Indeed, as long as only naval forces could govern maritime affairs, states could 'only' control s l o c s in a bid to monitor and control flows, whereas neo-modern forms of striation enable states to monitor and control extended spaces/areas.

Naval Neo-modernity
(with Post-Modern Characteristics)

The post–Cold War era has witnessed a reduction in the number of ships in the post-Soviet and Western world (along with a reduction in operational capabilities and readiness in the Russian case that has become apparent in 2022/23). A similar intrinsic power decline can be witnessed in the majority of African countries and several South American ones. This has been widely documented in the literature, the causes ranging from budgetary restrictions and the search for 'peace dividends' to the versatility of new platforms and weapon systems. In peacetime, budgetary decisions regarding naval procurement are linked to considerations of domestic politics (P. Kennedy and Wilson 2022). The politics of 'peace dividends' is reminiscent of the old habit consisting of neglecting the fleet following a decisive victory (e.g., Sparta). It is also more generally linked to post–Cold War sea blindness (Bueger and Edmunds 2017).

When facing budgetary restrictions, naval planners are left with two broad options: either to overspecialise (e.g., mine counter-measures, amphibious capabilities, riverine forces) and rely on multilateral naval cooperation entirely (post-modern option), or to still aim at a 'balanced fleet' albeit one reduced in size, which is likely to have reduced capabilities in several areas in addition to issues of warship availability. In the West, the policy of decommissioning a large quantity of platforms and replacing them with a limited number of new warships fitted with state-of-the-art systems and weapons has been criticised as preventing Western navies from deploying enough assets wherever needed, since ships (even those benefiting from the most advanced technologies) cannot be at two different places at the same time (Till 2022, 242; Stavridis 2017). For example, in the UK, with the commissioning of the new HM Queen Elizabeth class aircraft carriers, the impact of the prioritisation of carrier battlegroups on other components of the navy has raised questions as to whether this was reinforcing the 'frigate gap', a lack of platforms to carry out missions at the lower end of the spectrum (House of Commons, Defence Committee 2021). Yet, commissioning state-of-the-art warships can only be afforded if one reduces the number of active ships in the fleet. Large but unsophisticated navies are vulnerable in the face of more technologically advanced opponents or those with anti-access/area denial (A2/AD) capabilities, even rudimentary ones, as demonstrated by the collapse of the Russian surface Black Sea Fleet in 2022–23. In sum, whereas Western navies are constantly adding new, sophisticated technologies to their arsenal, they have experienced a steady decline in the number of available ships since the end of the Cold War.

However, this trend is found almost nowhere in Austral, South, South-East, and East Asia. Naval build-ups (if not naval arms races) have been taking place, in Australia, China, India, Japan, South Korea, and Singapore to name but the most striking examples. The process is almost generalised in the Indo-Pacific region. Even the Philippines is considering acquiring submarine capabilities to deter China in the contested waters of the South China Sea. This is what Paul Kennedy, in the introduction to the 2017 re-edition of his *Rise and Fall of British Naval Mastery*, identifies as a 'new age of navalism' in the East that goes hand in hand with the substantial and fast economic growth in the region. Various factors explain this trend: regional instabilities and competitions between states; open conflicts or tensions regarding sovereignty over portions of the sea and/or islets (e.g., Paracel, Spratly, Diaoyu/Senkaku); general power politics and geostrategic competition (notably China versus India); the need to police the sea against ever-more sophisticated criminals; and the desire to use the sea as a medium for power projection and global leadership (e.g., China's Belt and Road Initiative).

Many of these motivations fall under the 'modern' umbrella because they are linked to core national security interests around sovereignty, geopolitics, and power maximisation. The territorial dimension of the process is also clear: sovereignty over maritime territories is contested, which implies the development of naval capabilities to claim and coerce, or deter and protect. Yet, UNCLOS has given more sovereign rights to many small or medium Powers which have needed to develop a 'green water' navy able to operate credibly in support of political and legal claims. These new medium-sized navies can rely on support from land-based assets to increase their control of coastal waters and beyond (Hattendorf 2000, 259–60). For instance, China has prioritised A2/AD capabilities to deny potential enemies from using the sea as an entryway for power projection into China's territory (or claimed territories), including maritime areas under China's sovereignty (or claimed to be, notably in the South China Sea). The aim is to contest the West's ability to intervene worldwide using naval forces as a vector of seapower. Ukraine has recently shown, with its success against Russia's surface naval forces, the extent to which naval units were at the mercy of land-based weapons and inexpensive maritime drones. The US/Western navies' long-term commitment to maintaining their naval dominance is likely to be key to the future leadership of the international order (Hendrix 2020; Maurer 2022, 235–6).

Non-European Western states in Asia such as Japan, South Korea, and Australia have followed a similar path, although their neo-modern orientation became clear slightly earlier than that of European and US navies and has been even more pronounced due to acute tensions and arms race in the region, most notably the rising competition with China (Gresh 2020). The 2021 AUKUS partnership demonstrates Australia's need to bolster its naval capabilities in light of China's increasing assertiveness but also that the UK has cleverly managed to outsource its security in the Indo-Pacific in the long term to a trusted partner while cementing US support.

Labelling these developments as nothing more than traditional modern naval politics would miss two important elements. First, the ultimate motivation explaining current naval arms races is to be found in both modern *and* post-modern considerations; indeed sovereignty claims and territorial defence are intimately linked to energy security and prestige (e.g., 'rewriting' history in the case of China's 'rejuvenation' narrative). It is thus less of a return to modern power politics and more of an ongoing move towards neo-modern seapower, that is, transcending modern and post-modern features.

Second, the practice of naval power politics in Asia, notably in the South China Sea, corresponds to the above discussed practices of territorialisation of the sea, albeit to fulfil national objectives rather than ocean governance ones. Thus, labelling this trend as neo-modern allows considering the post-modern elements of the process along with the modern ones. This also applies to similar practices outside Asia. For example, the two UK carrier battlegroups serve both modern and post-modern objectives: responding to potential aggressors (e.g., Russia) and promoting the interests and ambitions of Britain globally (HM Government 2021). In sum, neo-navalism mirrors the realisation of the importance of seapower for global leadership. Navalism was, in the late nineteenth early twentieth centuries, the way contenders to British rules decided to challenge London. It is thus not surprising that at the dawn of a global leadership challenge, navalism is again becoming a dominant feature of IR and states competition.

In the twenty-first century, despite the advances of post-modernity, navies remain central elements of seapower and play a crucial role in global ocean governance. In other words, the nature of the maritime domain makes them an enduring vector of seapower, but the nature of their involvement has occurred in accordance with changes in missions and contexts. The end of the Cold War has not rendered modern naval missions obsolete, but they have become less central due to the reduced likeliness of blue water war-fighting. This was especially true for the Western navies, which, at the beginning of the post–Cold War era benefited from an uncontested, global command of the sea. Then, post-modern missions, such as power projection in the context of foreign interventions, became prominent in Western navies. Dominant navies have contributed to power and forces projection and ultimately to regime change (e.g., in Iraq and Libya). Moreover, as Patalano (2022) shows, since 'order' is not a simple function of hierarchical power anymore (e.g., naval order of battle) but is contingent to ocean governance, then there is a continuum between war-fighting and maritime security missions.

Since the mid-2000s, China's rise and Russia's revival, including their power politics practice (e.g., Georgia, Ukraine, Syria, South China Sea, Taiwan, East China Sea) has placed modern naval missions back on Western navies' agendas. Command of the sea cannot be presumed as granted anymore, especially in some regional seas. As for China and Russia, securing regional sea control would be crucial in case of a conflict with the West. This trend is likely to result in naval procurement programmes that account for both the need to obtain command of the sea in highly contested areas and the vulnerability of warships to land-based assets.

In peacetime, control of the maritime domain, maritime security operations, and ocean governance practices have led naval missions to adhere to a post-modern agenda, that is, fighting criminal actors and promoting free trade and the blue economy. However, the need for governance has also fostered a neo-modern agenda for naval missions. The sea is a grid, a striated space that needs to be controlled, monitored, and secured. Whenever possible it is done in cooperation with like-minded allies or partners, including non-state stakeholders (cf. chapter 6). But when national objectives clash (for example due to diverging opinions and interests regarding sovereignty over certain maritime spaces, such as with China in the South China Sea or Russia in the Arctic), then modern considerations around the concept of a zero-sum game reappear at the expense of the liberal reinvention of modernity. In other words, modern, post-modern, and neo-modern features of seapower coexist.

Grey Zone Activities
in the Maritime Domain

Grey zone activities epitomise the blending of post-modern and neo-modern forms of power politics at sea, which demonstrates the hybridity of seapower. The grey zone is not a geographically defined area but rather a political and legal realm where the boundaries are blurred between state and non-state actors, between war and peace, and between legal and illegal activities. Hybrid warfare and operations in the 'sub-threshold battlefield' follow a set of criteria that differentiate them from business-as-usual political and diplomatic activities as well as from well-marked war operations. Whereas the literature has traced hybrid warfare and grey zone tactics to more traditional covert operations, propaganda, and sabotage, the following (often post-modern) characteristics apply to them in the twenty-first century. First, in terms of attribution, the traceability of the perpetrator/aggressor is more arduous, and responsibility is less obvious both legally and politically. It might even be challenging to define 'what is peaceful and what is hostile' (Beckett 2021), or in other words what constitutes an aggression and what constitutes an acceptable level of political, diplomatic, or economic opposition. In practice, perpetrators usually deny their responsibility and use propaganda and disinformation tactics to accuse their opponent of attacks that are not explicitly or clearly attributable.

Second, the intended target of an operation in the grey zone is not always well defined. It can be a state or a group of states, but it could also be a vaguer, broader, and global entity. For example, sabotage of critical infrastructures (such as undersea cables) can be directed against the stability of the international order, affecting whole populations, economic security, and even democratic principles by generating confusion and resentment. Third, hybrid warfare is by nature not (or not exclusively) dependent on military means. The military component can be limited or altogether absent. Assets employed are often unconventional, making the most of civilian capabilities. It ranges from cyber-attacks to lawfares to disinformation.

Fourth, hybrid warfare is asymmetrical in that with limited means and resources aggressors can produce disproportionate damages, including immaterial ones, such as elections meddling. Finally, grey zone operations are often characterised by their impunity. Indeed, because of the doubts and ambiguity about the intended target, the aggressor, the legality, or jurisdiction it is more difficult to react and punish the perpetrator. Additionally, to avoid unwanted escalation, states might be reluctant to claim that their jurisdiction has been attacked, which then furthers impunity (Raine 2019).

The sea is a geophysical and geopolitical space particularly appropriate to grey zone tactics, since its political, legal, and material characteristics facilitate hybrid warfare and at the same time render responses more difficult. First, the principle of *mare liberum* and the characterisation of the sea as a global commons (*res communis*) results in a legal regime that grants state and non-state actors ample freedom to operate at sea. Outside jurisdictions (e.g., on the high seas) or when jurisdictions overlap or are thinly defined (e.g., undersea infrastructures), liabilities and responsibilities are difficult to trace and/or to assert. Moreover, when something 'belongs to nobody' or to everybody, it is more difficult to generate a response to a hostile act, since someone has to take responsibility for responding to the aggression whereas jurisdiction might not be clearly established. Second, the sea is a wide, wild space, which is difficult to monitor and much less controlled than the land and thus prone to covert and hybrid activities.

The recent sabotage of the Nord Stream pipelines in the Baltic Sea has highlighted the vulnerability of all undersea assets but most notably internet cables and energy pipelines and connectors. It has also highlighted the above-mentioned difficulties in terms of attributing responsibilities and responding to the *fait accompli*.

Another development with grey zone activities at sea is the use of civilian assets to achieve national objectives. This is not new either. For example, the Soviet fishing fleet was known for its contribution to intelligence gathering. China has started to develop a 'lawfare' method whereby the interests of the national fishing industry are aligned with national objectives, such as the occupation of islands in the South China Sea. This involves backing and protecting Chinese boats fishing in contested waters with either civilian coastguard vessels or even naval units. This leads to a 'fish, protect, contest, and occupy' strategy (Dupont and Baker 2014, 87). In other words, what starts with fishing considerations ends up with legal claims or *fait accompli* over contested territories. Although China can visibly manipulate civilian actors into contributing to Chinese Communist Party's objectives, the use of civilian seapower is very complex: Chinese fishermen have their own agenda (i.e., profit making), but they can benefit from the protection of their state in a very competitive area where resources are somewhat scarce. When they get involved in a zero-sum game with other regional countries' fishing fleets, the Chinese fishermen may then benefit from the support of their powerful state agencies. The Chinese government for its part does not only protect national fishermen's rights and interests, but also fishing actors legitimise China's neo-modern power projection (in the form of ocean governance and control) into the South China Sea. This further contributes to both the practice of control over the South China Sea and the narrative of presenting the region as being under Beijing's sovereignty and in need of further control. Practice and narrative are mutually reinforcing, and civilian assets and corporate interests contribute to the national interest agenda.

Thus, grey zone tactics are a product of the deterritorialisation of security but can also reinforce processes of control and re-territorialisation at the intersection between peace and war. This exemplifies the versatility of seapower as an instrument of power politics at the level of its elements (using or targeting civilian assets), enactment (ambiguous responsibility, impunity), and consequences (systemic stability versus disruption of the system).

MORE THAN POST-MODERN SEAPOWER?

The post-modern era has witnessed the transformation of the practice if not the nature of seapower: the non-naval dimension of seapower has grown in the context of global ocean governance and maritime security, and different practices of control of the maritime domain have appeared, moving beyond SLOCs protection towards ocean striation and the territorialisation of the sea. The post-modern world order bears its own characteristics along with remaining modern and emerging neo-modern ones. Thus, seapower has become something more than post-modern resulting from the assemblage of territorial and non-territorial forms of governance and the performance of expanded security and defence tasks.

The evolution of seapower from pre-modern to modern to post-modern to neo-modern has not been as linear as it might first appear. As table 5.2 shows, not only roots of modern/post-modern/neo-modern seapower have to be found in pre-modern/modern/post-modern seapower but also there are permanent, or at least recurring, features of seapower that somewhat transcend any artificially defined historical eras. In fact, the nature of seapower remains almost unchanged: seapower is about the control of the global maritime domain, and maritime preponderance facilitates global leadership. Obtaining and exercising command of the sea (in wartime) and controlling the global supply chain in peacetime has been complemented by ocean governance and maritime security practices: a form of post-/neo-modern sea(power).

As Steinberg explains (referring to Paul Virilio and Foucault), the sea has this dual identity: on the one hand, as claimed by Virilio, the incorporation of the marine domain within the controlled perpetual motion of capitalism and statist militarism represents a victory for modernity' (1999b, 369). On the other hand, as claimed by Foucault, the sea is a domain that resists state control. In turn, this results in a need for control and striation. Freedom of the seas cohabits with forms of territorialisation, although, overall, 'the exercise of seapower still rests on the sustained consensus around *mare liberum*' (Germond 2022, 48). Seapower combines modern and post-modern characteristics, which have merged into neo-modern practices of territorialisation and control beyond traditional, modern, power, and forces projection. At first glance, state actors appear to have kept the monopoly on the legitimate use of violence at sea (using their navy or

Table 5.2
The layers of post- and neo-modern seapower

Layers of analysis	Post- and neo-modern features
Elements of seapower	• Technological breakthroughs (outer space, information/ communication, cyber, AI, automation) • Civilian assets (both public and private) • Traditional naval power
Enactment of seapower	• Power projection (deterritorialisation of security) • Extrinsic (soft) power • Ocean governance and maritime security (including forms of reterritorialisation) • Collective and civilian seapower (see chapter 6) • Grey zone activities • Neo-modern navalism/naval power enacted in a neo-modern way
Consequences of seapower	• Stabilisation of the liberal world order or disruption thereof • Territorialisation of the sea

non-naval state agencies). Chapter 6 illustrates that non-state actors gain in importance, and states make the most of civilian seapower to promote their own interest via civilian stakeholders.

At a higher level of geostrategic analysis, neo-modern seapower and the renewed navalism in Asia raise the question of whether, as Modelski and Thompson (1988) indicate, we might witness the inception of a new cycle in world politics with China (and more generally Asia) becoming the dominant actor, but not necessarily as a result of a global war. If this is true, shifts in seapower might still constitute a necessary condition for this new cycle to emerge.

Solidaristic and Civilian Seapower

Post-modern and neo-modern characteristics of IR and security in the twenty-first century have given birth to two complementary forms of seapower: collective (or solidaristic) seapower, whereby like-minded nations with compatible maritime interests and values cooperate to maintain the stability of the global maritime order and defend broader liberal values; and civilian seapower, whereby non-state actors participate in the defence of these objectives (in particular the stability of the global supply chain) while also benefiting from the maritime order (which is core to the global value chain).

SOLIDARISTIC SEAPOWER[1]

The concept of an 'international society of states' (or just 'international society') originates in the ideas and writings of Martin Wight and Hedley Bull (fathers of what will come to be known as the English School of IR). Since the late 1950s, they rejected the 'either realist or liberalist' framing of IR as a discipline (Buzan 2004; Bull 1976a). While acknowledging the role played by both power politics and interdependence in explaining international politics, they rather emphasised on the rationality of states as the main explanatory factor for the relative degree of stability that has characterised IR in the post-war era (Bull 1977, 51–2). In line with the Grotian tradition of 'rationalism', the English School rejects deterministic explanations: the international system is anarchical (since there is no supranational government) but sovereign states (which are equal in rights, not in power) constitute a 'society' of states. This explains that there is a good degree of order and little interstate violence despite the anarchical nature of the international system. Violence may be endemic to the anarchical system (wars happen after all), but the rationality of actors largely limits the occurrence of violence. States have very different conceptions of 'justice' and competing foreign policy objectives but being and thinking 'the same' is not a necessary condition for coexistence and for the international society to exists. Indeed, since states' interest is to maintain some degree of order and civility among themselves (and to bring stability to their relations), they share a common interest in restraining the use of force, in regulating IR, and in abiding (most of the time) by international law, so coexistence is made possible.

Depending on the depth of the objectives and values shared, there is a spectrum from a pluralistic to a solidaristic international society (Buzan 2004, 49). A pluralistic society is the minimalist version described by Hedley Bull: members share the desire to maintain order among themselves but actively cultivate their differences; states have to agree on some basic common rules, institutional procedures, and behaviour (mainly non-aggression and diplomatic rules); and they have to abide by what has been agreed. Rules are thus respected like 'roads rules', based on the principle of reciprocity: it does not cost much to respect them, but the collective gain is substantial. A solidaristic society is the maximalist version: members share more objectives than simply the desire to maintain order and are ready to act upon (or enforce) the objectives they share (even at a cost). Members of a solidaristic society share values and identities (e.g., the Western conception of human rights). Their working together and sharing both objectives and values in turn means that members of a solidaristic international society have a bigger common interest in maintaining these mutually profitable arrangements and thus, since the existence of the international society shall never be taken as granted, it is rational for its members to work towards maintaining, and perhaps strengthening, the international society, even when upholding rules generates a cost.

At a *global* level, the conditions for a solidaristic society to emerge have not yet been met. However, Barry Buzan claims that the concept of international society shall not only be applied globally (as Bull envisaged), but also it is meaningful at other *sub-global* or regional levels (2004, 16–18, 47). This is where a limited version of a solidaristic international society, in terms of membership or geographical scope, can emerge. Solidarism can be more pronounced at the regional level due to the sharing of more objectives, values, and institutions (Stivachtis 2015). Indeed, traditional English School scholars have

almost exclusively focused on human rights as the pinnacle of solidaristic shared values, whereas economic solidarism explains the
emergence of sub-regional solidaristic societies such as the EU (Buzan
2004, 19). Similarly, there are solidaristic security values, which are
found at a sub-global level, and a version of collective security can be
found in security communities like NATO (149).

Western nations consciously share common interests and values
beyond coexistence, a sense of common belonging, and of being bound
by a common set of rules that are reinforced by deep economic interdependence and shared institutional frameworks. Although English
School scholars interested in the sub-global level of analysis of the
international society preferred to focus on regional societies (e.g.,
Europe) rather than trans-regional societies, the 'Western community
serves as the most obvious candidate for a subglobal international
society' (Stivachtis 2014, 117). Additionally, the West also champions
the core rules of the international society in a proactive way (including
their enforcement) in opposition to those who violate them, even at a
cost (e.g., current sanctions against Russia and assistance to Ukraine).
The West does not only form a self-contained solidaristic society of
states, but also it proactively promotes its core norms within and
beyond its polities. The extent to which this contributes to 'solidaris-
ing' the whole of the international society is open to debate (Ahrens
and Diez 2015).

The concept of a solidaristic society is thus useful as an alternative
characterisation of the West beyond its liberal nature and also as a
tool to understand how the West operates in the current era of growing authoritarianism and challenges to core values of the international
society. This concept applies to the maritime order. At the global level,
the pluralistic society at sea is at the minimalist end of the spectrum
with states sharing minimal, self-preserving objectives around freedom
of navigation and economic interests. However, at a sub-global level,
there is a solidaristic society of maritime nations, which are bound by
common maritime interests, values, and cooperative mechanisms.

The Pluralistic Maritime Order

The principle of freedom of the seas has been developed and implemented in support of maritime trade. In fact, within the Westphalian
system, it was in nation-states' best interest to adhere to the norms of
the free sea (cf. chapter 4). Thus, the maritime domain was not to be

divided into zones of exclusive sovereignty but was to remain a free space, a global lane of communication enabling the free flow of warships, goods, and capital (Connery 1995; Steinberg 1999a). This denotes a self-preserving, mutually beneficial arrangement for trade and power projection that has been the basis of the pluralistic society at sea, within which maritime and continental states alike share the common objective to maintain some degree of order at sea, notably freedom of navigation as well as maritime safety and security, which are in their economic interest. Coexistence at sea is self-centred in that members of the pluralistic society contribute to a stable maritime world order insofar as it does not contradict their national interest.

Within a pluralistic society, to facilitate relations in a mutually beneficial way, technical coexistence requires states to agree on a set of technical rules and institutions (e.g., Universal Postal Union, International Civil Aviation Organization). Coexistence at sea has necessitated agreement on common standards concerning navigation, communication, safety, as well as on the relevant legal frameworks. Today, UNCLOS is accepted as the 'constitutive instrument' that 'outlines the rights and obligations of States' (Beckman and Sun 2017, 201). When it comes to regulating international shipping, the IMO plays a leading role in developing international rules and accepted standards for maritime security, safety, and marine environment protection.

The pluralistic society comprises of states as different as the US and the UK at one end of the spectrum and China at the other end. They all benefit from freedom of navigation in their own way. Within a pluralistic society, it is in all members' interest to keep the established, mutually beneficial arrangements. However, norms and institutions tend to serve the interests of dominant actors within the international society (cf. chapter 4). The contemporary, law-based international maritime order is a creation of the dominant sea Powers that continues to work in the best interest of maritime nations, although it practically serves the interests of all actors benefiting from a global ocean that remains free and safe for trade, communication and (sustainable) exploitation of resources.

The core principles of the pluralistic society at sea (i.e., freedom of navigation and law of the sea) have recently been challenged by traditional land Powers that contest the status quo (revisionism). For example, China's narrative claims that freedom of the seas is used by Western actors as a pretext for dominance, as in the South China Sea (Bosco 2022, 244). The invasion of Ukraine highlights Russia's very limited acceptance of the pluralist norms. It has been argued that Russia has never really been more than an 'entrant' into the society of states (Neumann 2011). Russia posits that the non-intervention norm and the agreed rules of the pluralistic society do not apply to its neighbourhood (Kaczmarska 2015), which includes the Black Sea that Russia has a 'primal' need to dominate (Stavridis 2017, 157). States that violate core principles of the international society (e.g., *jus ad bellum* and *jus in bello*) put themselves outside the international society and consider themselves not bound by its norms.

Reciprocally, members of the society are likely to consider that such states are excluded from the society (Buzan 1993, 349). This can result in communication breakdown or the end of institutional cooperation. For example, in reaction to the invasion of Ukraine, the members of the Arctic Council decided to suspend high-level talks and activities with Russia, de facto putting the work of the council on hold. When a 'minor' actor remains outside the international society (e.g., North Korea), the implications for the society itself are limited; however, when a 'major' player like Russia in effect exits the society, the consequences can be substantial. For example, in the High North, the risk is that Russia might intensify its engagement with non-Western, non-Arctic states, such as China and India; the pausing of the Arctic Council might also jeopardise the safeguards against the Chinese fishing fleet endeavours in the region (Buchanan 2022) and put at risk sustainable development efforts in the High North (Germond 2023b).

In another example, to assert its claims over contested areas in the South China Sea, 'China takes international law seriously, but wishes to remake certain elements'. In particular, China advances the argument that 'the extent of a state's maritime domain should principally be a question of sovereign decision informed by national economic and security needs, subject only to broad constraints of reasonableness and neighbourly accommodation' (Guilfoyle 2019, 1017). In practice, China has applied a grey zone strategy in a bid to modify the status quo without crossing the threshold of wartime operations and risking escalation: claims over fisheries rights; citizen protection; the use of paramilitary, police, and naval forces; and broader geopolitical claims are interlinked and coordinated, with one reinforcing the need and justification for the other (Patalano 2018; see also chapter 5). In other words, China claims to use its seapower in support of the global maritime order, and it clearly has interests in maintaining the stability of the global supply chain due to its position as the main manufacturing nation. However, China 'will also want to fashion what exactly that order is' (P. Kennedy 2017, xxxv), which is not what the dominant maritime nations of the West want. These examples highlight the fragility (or in Bull's words, the thinness) of the pluralistic society at sea.

The Solidaristic Society of Maritime Nations and Collective Seapower

At a sub-global level, a group of like-minded states, conscious of their similarities and common interests, constitute a solidaristic society of maritime nations, within which the depth of the objectives they share is greater (see fig. 6.1). Members, whose security and prosperity strongly depend on the sea, uphold freedom of navigation, contribute to maritime security and ocean governance, and work towards a 'resilient ocean'. They are also united by their sharing of core maritime traditions and values. And they are ready to proactively defend these to address challenges to the stability of the global maritime order, which indeed serves their interest first, but more generally is understood as benefiting stakeholders of the global liberal order.

Members of the solidaristic society of maritime nations, on a spectrum from core maritime states such as the UK and Denmark to the US, Canada, or Australia, share a century-long history of cooperative behaviour without major ideological or geopolitical insurmountable divergencies (neither on land nor at sea), except in the case of Imperial Japan in the first half of the twentieth century. Like-minded maritime nations share similar defence, security, foreign policy, and economic objectives. They share a common desire to uphold freedom of navigation but also a feeling of a common membership to a society of nations that shares values such as freedom, free trade, human rights, and political accountability. As discussed in chapter 3, scholars of seapower have traditionally linked maritime cultures and identities to trade values (Till 2004, 22) or even liberal, democratic values (Lambert 2018) and the 'free society' (Eccles 1979). Maritime values have traditionally been linked to the interests and attributes of the dominant sea Powers (as opposed to the more authoritarian and mercantilist land Powers), which have proactively nourished their maritime identity. In turn, the maritime culture or outlook that is part of the

Shared values and identity
• Trade and liberal values
• Maritime culture and identity

Shared objectives
• Freedom of navigation
• Maritime security
• Resilient ocean

Shared norms and mechanisms
• UNCLOS
• Ocean governance
• Collective seapower

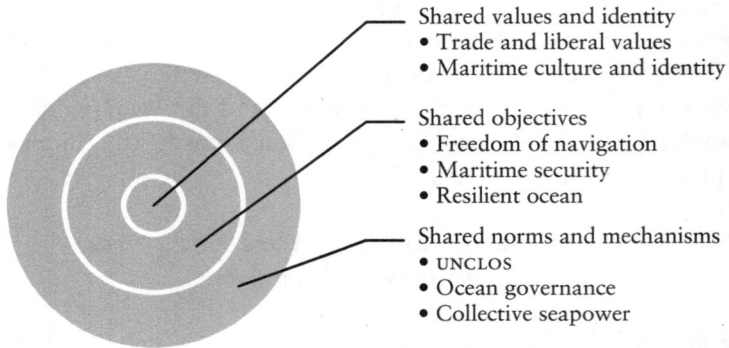

Figure 6.1 The solidaristic society of maritime nations
Source: Adapted from Germond (2022a).

necessary conditions for seapower to flourish has facilitated progressist political systems (albeit not in a way that has prevented slave trade, colonisation, and other wrongdoings). This explains why the sea and seafaring values have historically been represented more negatively by authoritarian rulers (e.g., China's Qing dynasty), who have been suspicious of maritime stakeholders and the values they vehiculate (Quilley 2014).

Today, the solidaristic society of maritime nations roughly equates with 'the West'. Seapower identity 'has become a collective Western possession rather than the sole preserve of individual states' (Lambert 2018, 323, 325; Lambert 2017, 13). The US still enjoys an overwhelming naval dominance and uses it to secure their worldwide interests and their control of the global supply chain. Lesser allies and partners usefully contribute to Western maritime dominance. Japan, the UK, France, and even South Korea have significant naval forces, and the number of warships that maritime nations can muster still matters. Despite being net contributors, they benefit from the status quo at sea guaranteed by the US without having to overspend on their navies. However, their ability to operate independently of a US-led coalition is limited (e.g., for the UK, France) or inexistent for most (P. Kennedy 2017, xxviii–xxix).

As discussed throughout this book, the current norms and institutions of the global maritime order tend to serve the interests of maritime nations and, according to Campling and Colás (2021), even those of capitalism. Modelski and Thompson stress that, in history, dominant post-global war alliances have always had a naval centrality, from the 'division of the world' between Spain and Portugal in 1494 to the US-UK 'special relationship' (1988, 23) to which we can indeed add NATO. However, the recent rise of illiberalism and revisionism at sea (e.g., Russia breaking the rules in Ukraine and the Black Sea, and China challenging the rules in the South China Sea) has led members of the solidaristic society of maritime nations to proactively uphold current norms and assure the perennity of the global maritime order. Within a solidaristic society, members collaborate to develop common strategies for addressing issues within the international society. For maritime nations, one of these mechanisms of solidarity is a collective seapower strategy.

As discussed in chapters 2 and 5, because of the narrow emphasis traditionally put on the balance of *naval* power, modern, Mahanian seapower has usually been considered in *relative* terms within a zero-sum international system. However, within a solidaristic society of maritime nations, seapower shall be understood in *absolute* terms, with members sharing (in a non-mutually exclusive way) the objectives, means, and benefits of the joint enactment of seapower when it comes to upholding freedom of navigation, maritime security (securing the maritime domain), and governing the oceans and its resources (i.e., 'ordering ocean space') (Germond 2022a, 54; Germond 2019).

Solidaristic seapower has two main characteristics. First, it is less state-centric, less naval, and more civilian: from international shipping companies to fishing communities, private/civilian stakeholders from various sectors (security, economy, NGOs) and with various levels of power have a role to play in stabilising the maritime order and upholding its norms. For example, in reaction to the invasion of Ukraine, J. Overton argues that the old concept of a '1000-ship Navy' (Mullen 2006) has been put in practice, not as 'a collection of primarily nation-state naval capabilities used against non-state actors and natural disasters [but] a collection of mostly interagency, non-naval, and sometimes non-state capabilities, using diplomatic and economic power, and even guerrilla tactics, against a nation state's (Russia's) elements of maritime and national power' (Overton 2022). There is a substantial civilian dimension to collective seapower discussed in the section below. The role of the private sector in contributing to securing the objectives of the solidaristic society of maritime nations fits with Buzan's argument that transnational forces are instrumental in cementing a solidaristic society (Buzan 2004, 197–8).

Second, solidaristic seapower is more collective: within the solidaristic society of maritime nations, the burden and the benefits of collective seapower are shared among members (and private stakeholders when relevant), but not all will benefit and contribute equally. Eventually what matters is that they all benefit in their own way from the overall stability of the maritime order: 'structures, policies and objectives are collective; expected gains/benefits are absolute, shared between actors and not relative. [As such] collective seapower fits with the description of the sea as a non-zero-sum space' (Germond 2022a, 54). Collective seapower is not just a post–Cold War phenomenon. Ideas akin to it have been suggested, albeit mainly as a way to secure Britain's interests via naval cooperation in light of the growing threat posed by continental Powers at the turn of the twentieth century. Take for example Sir Julian Corbett's 'collective security system of independent states linked by the sea and their sea power in a network of strategic alignments' (Halewood 2021, 572), or in other words 'Sea Commonwealth' (Lambert 2017). Another example arises with Sir Halford Mackinder's suggestion that 'the British Navy shall have expanded into the Navy of the Britains' (Halewood 2021, 565), and cooperation between 'insular' nations was critical to a peaceful world order. Post-modern and neo-modern features of the world order (cf. chapter 5) have increased both the need for and the means of maritime cooperation between like-minded maritime states. The rise of China as a global contender and Russia's revisionism mirror challenges to the *Pax Britannica* at the end of the nineteenth century.

Navies of the solidaristic society of maritime nations share missions, resources, as well as intelligence and information to achieve their common goal. Working together, sharing the burden of stabilising the global maritime order, is key to Western navies (Hattendorf 2011, 315). A relatively high degree of trust exists, and the feeling of a common belonging is strong. This inter-state/-national cooperation has been reinforced by the strong connection between sailors, mariners, and seafarers. Already in the nineteenth century, Grivel talked about 'brother nations' at sea (1869, 7). This accounts for the cultural affinities of maritime nations but also for the solidarity and feeling of a common belonging between sailors originating in the characteristics of the naval profession and the nature of the maritime milieu with its many dangers and privations.

This solidarity transcends political and ideological boundaries, although particularly true of Western (and now in particular NATO) nations. Admiral Sir George Zambellas, the then First Sea Lord, praised the existence of an 'international brotherhood of the sea' (2014, 69) that facilitates naval cooperation between like-minded nations. Elsewhere he also specified that 'deep down – as a maritime family – we are all supported by the same water and driven by the same current' (2013, 30). This aligns with Hattendorf's point that as a result of 'centuries of shared naval tradition … natural ties … exist among sailors around the world' (2000, 255), which facilitates all sorts of multinational operations.

Collective seapower materialises at various levels. At the ideational level, there is not only an acceptation but also a strong belief in the principle of the 'free sea' and a common desire to uphold relevant norms, which derives from strategic considerations, but also from what Lambert calls the 'soul of seapower', that is, maritime values linked to progressive forms of political organisations (Lambert 2018, 2). The collective dimension of this endeavour is also endorsed. At the narrative level, maritime values and related norms, including freedom of the seas, are promoted. The importance of the sea for security and prosperity is emphasised and related to the need to stabilise the maritime order and uphold relevant norms. The narrative promotes collaborative processes to achieve maritime objectives. A prime example is the vision exposed in HM Government's 2021 *Integrated Review* and its accompanying Command paper. At the political level, budgetary decisions are made, and necessary actions are taken to play one's part in the defence of the society of maritime nations, in line with the above value and narrative. At the strategic level, members of the solidaristic society of maritime nations oppose, in a coordinated way, those who do not share these values and undermine the principles of the free sea. They are ready to antagonise those actors opposing such principles.

At the operational level, this translates into confidence-building measures with allies and partners, joint exercises, and multilateral operations. In the current context, the deployment of naval assets in defence of freedom of the seas is paramount, and as demonstrated by the maiden voyage of carrier strike group CSG21, led by HMS *Queen Elizabeth*, the symbolic and operational value of this deployment rests on the number of visits and join exercises/operations with partners and allies as diverse as Ukraine, Oman, India, Singapore, Japan, and South Korea. Exercising seapower is not limited to naval operations though. It is about using the leverage of one's maritime dominance to achieve one's goals. For example, the US, the UK, European countries, and others banning Russian ships (flagged/owned/operated) from their ports.

Finally, at the institutional level, maritime nations work to cement global institutional mechanisms (e.g., the UNCLOS regime) that are pillars of the global maritime order. They also endeavour to develop sub-global mechanisms that enable more solidarism. Whereas NATO is an enduring example of a solidaristic, mainly Western, regional institution, the recent AUKUS partnership between Australia, the UK, and the US demonstrates the importance of developing a complex network of institutional mechanisms that bring together like-minded maritime nations, strengthen commonalities, and offer economies of scale. Collaborative processes do not need to be state-centric, and institutional cooperation can be loose with actors of civilian seapower contributing to the common effort (e.g., major shipping companies suspending their operations to and from Russia in the wake of its illegal invasion of Ukraine).

CIVILIAN SEAPOWER[2]

The civilian dimension of seapower has played a crucial role since the pre-modern era, from the Phoenician thalassocracy to the Hanseatic League whose power relied mainly on maritime trade dominance to the role played by Roman sea merchants and Venetian maritime entrepreneurs in the success story of their respective polities. Seafaring has enabled contacts between civilisations since the ancient times with an overlapping of 'trade, the projection of political power and the diffusion of ideologies and cultures' (de Souza 2001, 199). This section discusses the nature of civilian seapower as a private-public relationship mainly in the post-modern era. Despite its origin in ancient times, the relevance of civilian seapower in the twenty-first century demonstrates that the boundary between the modern, post-modern, and neo-modern forms of seapower is becoming very thin in the case of its civilian dimension.

Scholars interested in seapower have primarily focused their attention on naval power and thus on the role of navies as vectors of seapower (see chapter 1). That said, most of the classical writers since Mahan have acknowledged, or even emphasised, the determinant role played by the commercial or economic use of the sea. In other words, the interplay between the navy and the merchant marine or between naval and economic power has widely been discussed in the literature.

For example, Till (2022) devotes one chapter of his *How to Grow a Navy* to the importance of the civilian sector, which he titles "All of One Maritime Company" to account for the holistic nature of any maritime endeavour. This 'company' consists of the shipbuilding industry, the shipping industry, and the fishing industry.

However, by framing their analysis within strategic studies or military history, classical authors have mainly attached these considerations to naval power. The primary role of the navy is to secure and exercise command of the sea as well as protect SLOCs during war and police the oceans in peacetime; maritime trade and the maritime economy are crucial to create a sustainable basis for the development of states' power in general and the navy in particular. A rare exception is Steinberg (2001) who deconstructs the representation of 'ocean space' as a form of power-knowledge matrix, emphasising the importance of the capitalist agents and not so much states and their naval forces. Lambert (2018) highlights the cultural and ideational determinants of seapower and, as such, demonstrates that civilian actors and interests have played a crucial role in the development and maintenance of seapower.

The minimal account of the non-naval dimension of seapower is illustrated by the quasi-absence of the expression 'civilian seapower' from the academic literature. Indeed, as of June 2023, Google Scholar has only three mentions of 'civilian seapower' (in three of my most recent publications) and three references to 'civilian sea power'. Tritten (1989, 17) acknowledges the enduring importance of the 'interrelationship between civilian sea power and the Navy'. W.S. Chan (2020) coins the concept during his PhD studies at Lancaster University under my supervision (2014–19). And G. Chan (2020, 15) uses the expression to describe China's current advances as a maritime trading nation.

Civilian power is a concept that has become prominent since the 1970s, mainly to account for the international actorness, and foreign policy, of the EU (e.g., Orbie 2006) and to some extent Germany and Japan (Maull 1990). Civilian power is characterised by a (mostly) non-militarised foreign policy, the normative and ideational intents of the foreign policy in question, and a focus on actors' economic means, the role played by non-state actors, and the interdependent nature of the international system. Thus, civilian seapower is a form of material and ideational power enacted by state or non-state actors at or from the sea, which does not (necessarily) imply the use or presence of military/naval assets or structures.

The civilian dimension of seapower can be reduced to three main elements. First, naval power depends on sea-borne trade and vice versa. Second, states can make the most of the maritime civilian assets at their disposal or under their control (including public and private assets) to increase their leverage, their control over the oceans, and fulfil their various objectives. This comprises the cultural and normative dimension of seapower, including the ability to influence the structure and functioning of polities and societies as well as the spread of ideas and ideologies. And third, corporate maritime actors are a depository of civilian seapower; they can indeed utilise their maritime assets to develop or increase their own power and leverage over world politics and economy via their organic relationships with states. States are becoming more reliant on them to fulfil global objectives such as the stability of the global, maritime, liberal world order. Civilian seapower is not separated from, or in competition with, naval power; it is simultaneously dependent on and contributing to it.

The Merchant Marine

As classical writers have widely discussed, naval power is organically related to civilian assets. Mahan argues that the seas, 'a wide common', represent a big lane of communication, 'a great highway' ([1890] 2007, 25) vital for trade. Trade, in turn, is vital for nations' wealth, including as a prerequisite for developing naval power. Classical proponents or scholars of seapower have all stressed the importance of the commercial shipping element of seapower. Colomb (1899, 9) posits that 'abundant sea-borne commerce' is instrumental for naval power; it is a precondition to develop proper naval power. Gray explains that land or continental Powers, such as Germany or Russia, can eventually develop naval power if they devote enough resources to it, but the difference between a naval Power and a sea Power is the latter's dependence on SLOCs for its 'economic well-being' (1992, 6). In other words, the relationship between seapower and sea-borne trade explains why modern navies have been tasked with the protection of merchant ships and thus SLOCs or with the acquisition of command of the sea in relevant areas.

For Corbett, the aim of naval warfare is to control communications 'for *commercial* or military purposes' (1911, 94), given that, in his view, national strategy shall integrate naval, economic, legal, and cultural elements (Lambert 2017, 3). In other words, the aim of naval warfare, and thus by extension the aim of seapower, is to enable the merchant marine to operate in the interest of the state. The merchant marine is a constituent of states' seapower and as such must be protected by naval power, which itself derives from the wealth that sea-borne trade generates or helps sustain.

In the modern era, nations' wealth via sea-borne commerce was dependent on ships flying their flag, thus the role of the merchant marine was obvious in terms of intrinsic economic power. In the words of Gretton, 'the transport element is an indispensable part of sea power' (1965, 22). Merchant shipping is crucial in peacetime and perhaps even more in wartime, since communications must not be interrupted (Richmond 1934, 38ff.). Even landlocked Switzerland recognised the crucial role played by an independent merchant marine during World War II and consequently established the Swiss High Sea Fleet in order to increase national independence in light of the challenges facing the global supply chain. In today's globalised world order, the ownership of ships and, perhaps even more importantly, the ownership of the goods/cargo being transported and where they originate play a bigger role than the nationality of the ships' flag.

However, the proliferation of flags of convenience and the reliance of (Western) big Powers on foreign-flagged ships and open registers bears some strategic risks. In case of war, relying on ships flying another nation's flag creates vulnerabilities in terms of supply, logistics, and access to resources. At the end of the 1980s, Grove had already noted that 'something has clearly gone wrong with the Mahanian paradigm' (1990, 4) in reference to the fact that big naval Powers, including the two superpowers at the time, did not have large enough merchant fleets to sustain their strategic dominance. Grove actually devotes an entire chapter of his *Future of Sea Power* to the economic dimension of seapower. In the twenty-first century, given the rising East-West tensions and considering China's strength in regard to civilian seapower, Western lack of commitment to their flagged commercial sector is striking. This illustrates decision makers' sea blindness as well as the power of economic agency (and actors) in a globalised, liberal world order.

In the twenty-first century, the upsurge of piracy in Southeast Asia, the Horn of Africa, and the Gulf of Guinea has required peacetime actions to protect maritime shipping far away from one's territorial waters. High-profile counter-piracy coalition operations under the aegis of NATO or the EU, as well as the involvement of non-Western Powers such as India and China at the Horn of Africa, reflect this strategic imperative. However, with the drastic reduction in the number of platforms within Western navies, the viability of navies as protector of commercial shipping in peacetime has been put in doubt (e.g., Willett 2011, 34). A cheaper way to protect one's merchant shipping (in contrast to protecting transit areas) without having to deploy naval assets is to offer vessel protection detachments (VPDs) (i.e. place military personnel aboard ships). There is a risk of confusion between national and private commercial interests, which may drag one or the other stakeholders into actions that they do not back or that are not in their best interest (Brown 2012). Also, since many ships are registered under flags of convenience, these countries have neither the interest nor the means to offer VPDs.

Alternatively, commercial actors have relied on private security companies to ensure the protection of their ships and personnel. This practice has increased since the outburst of piracy at the Horn of Africa in 2007–08. Indeed, many flag states do not want to engage their armed forces in the business of ship protection and have thus enabled the flourishing of private maritime security companies, since they became the only viable solution at the disposal of shipping companies. The use of private security guards on-board ships transiting via dangerous areas demonstrates the limits of states' support to their merchant marine – both their willingness and capability.

Private security guards or even military personnel on-board commercial ships illustrate the fact that due to the geographical and legal nature of the global commons, privateering has not totally disappeared from the seas. Indeed, as Mabee (2009) notes, today's practice reflects historical privateering in that there are 'similarities of service between professional armed forces, the professional nature of the activity, and due to the profit-oriented nature of violent enterprise' (152). Given the rise of piracy within the context of post-modern globalisation and neo-modern control of the maritime domain, states need to find solutions to problems they do not have the financial, material, and eventually political will to solve themselves. This is akin to the situation before the consolidation of nation-states, when it was the norm for monarchs to delegate security functions to private stakeholders, since they did not have the necessary funds to maintain standing navies (cf. chapter 4).

Private-Public Partnerships

The relationship between private maritime assets and states' power goes beyond the merchant marine's role. The essence of civilian seapower is a form of power not directly enacted by public actors and state agencies. States can control or influence civilian private agents, but they are not the principal agency of civilian seapower. However, states can make the most of civilian seapower assets, either by indirectly controlling them or by benefiting from their very own existence and agency. Civilian seapower can support 'hard security' objectives. As shown below, the relationship between state actors and private actors within the context of civilian seapower is reciprocal. Both stakeholders have interests they will defend, and both can gain from cooperating with each other. This may result in positive outcomes for both or with one set of actors gaining more than the other. The involvement of states in private maritime endeavours and vice versa might also create challenges for one or the other set of actors.

Private maritime actors include fishing fleets, shipping companies, shipbuilding industry, maritime insurances, extracting industry, port authorities, and so on. Tritten (1989) stresses the importance of civilian assets and ventures, such as merchant marine and shipbuilding industrial complex for states and navies: 'Civilian merchant seamen constituted a reserve pool of manpower which the Royal Navy expected to tap when needed. This interrelationship between civilian sea power and the Navy remains valid today' (16–17). As discussed in chapter 4, since the ancient times, the civilian maritime sector has been instrumental in providing crucial resources and know-how to states and monarchs in case of war as well as in developing and sustaining a maritime culture. Tritten (1989) notes that despite recent examples such as the Falklands War, when civilian assets were crucial (i.e., many ships reallocated from commercial service, improvisation of flight decks, civilian crew retained), there is a tendency to forget the crucial role played by the civilian maritime sector.

Post-modern features of the globalised world, such as the proliferation of criminal non-state actors engendering neo-modern attempts to control or even territorialise the maritime domain, induce the need for states to coordinate with non-state actors. Governing, or controlling, the maritime domain under one's jurisdiction, or beyond, is a form of seapower, albeit one which goes beyond states' agency. In addition to states' neo-modern practice of control via non-military assets (discussed in chapter 5), the complexity of ocean governance, including the fact that managing human activities in the maritime domain goes much beyond maritime security, implies that a substantial amount of non-state/private stakeholders are also part of the process consisting in controlling/regulating the sea.

Non-state actors are involved in day-to-day ocean governance, which is crucial in terms of maritime security: shipping companies, port authorities, fishing fleets, marine environment NGOs, science consultants, and coastal communities are all part of the complex process of global ocean governance discussed in chapter 5. Self-regulation, good practice and codes of conduct, and the use of private security companies all illustrate the importance of the civilian and corporate sector in a post-modern maritime environment. Civilian actors can also substitute for states' inaction. In addition to the above-mentioned case of private security companies as an alternative to VPDs, there are also instances of environmental or human rights NGOs operating at sea in a private capacity to address issues that states are reluctant or unable to deal with, respectively resource overexploitation and SAR.

The civilian dimension of seapower is also linked to the post-modern collective nature of seapower discussed above. Indeed, to project and maintain order and stability within and from the maritime domain, civilian stakeholders must be involved, since they are often key to the implementation of security policies. For example, non-naval elements of the EU's seapower are equally if not more important as naval ones and have practical impacts in terms of projection of security beyond the EU's external boundary for maritime safety, fisheries policy, immigration, and pollution (Germond 2015), that is, post and neo-modern forms of control over maritime spaces. The 2022 UK *National Strategy for Maritime Security* states that 'protecting shipping lanes and upholding freedom of navigation ... involves collaboration with the shipping industry' (HM Government 2022, 16). The US initiative to develop a so-called Global Maritime Partnership is a good example. Rahman (2008) stresses that 'one of the truly innovative aspects of the proposed global maritime security network ... is its intention to incorporate into the network not only the assets of navies and other government agencies but also those of the private sector – the international maritime industry' (4).

Again, nurturing public-private maritime partnerships is not a new practice. For instance, representatives of seaports were regularly summoned to the House of Commons during the thirteenth and fourteenth centuries to advise on naval affairs (Rodger [1997] 2004, 124). Yet, Rahman (2008) makes the important point that in a technology-driven maritime operating environment, state actors increasingly rely on private stakeholders as a key source of intelligence and knowledge: 'shipping companies have been invited to contribute as part of the global sensor grid, feeding information from their ships' automatic identification systems into the overall MDA picture ... Perhaps the most important sources of data are generated by non-military means, such as the commercial and customs information concerning ships, cargoes and crews' (16, 30). This dependence on the commercial sector is all the more important for navies that rely on a constant flow of information and communication via satellites, especially for surveillance and target acquisition, already noticed by Friedman (2000, 307–9), but also more generally for MDA. In case of war this dependence can become critical. For example, Ukraine has been provided crucial communication assets by the US corporation SpaceX in the form of Starlink satellite internet terminals.

The Ukraine war further illustrates the importance of civilian seapower in relation to the collective form of seapower discussed in the previous section. The opposition to Putin's war of aggression is multifaceted, with three main components: political support to Kyiv, weapons supply to Ukrainian forces, and financial and economic sanctions against Russia and Russian interests. Private actors, whose interests align with those of the leading maritime nations, play an important role in the latter. For instance, major shipping companies such as MSC, Maersk, and ONE have exercised important leverage by suspending their operations to and from Russia. Indeed, this has contributed to cutting Russia off the global trading grid.

For their part, Russian maritime assets (i.e., Russian-flagged ships and ships owned or operated by Russian companies) have been banned from entering Western ports, which further isolates Russia from the global shipping lanes. Altogether, the effects on the Russian economy and ability to sustain its war effort further demonstrates the leverage of civilian seapower. This fits with the argument that long wars and strategic confrontations are usually won by coalitions of maritime nations as a result of long-term strategic effects exercised via the control of the global supply chain. The private maritime sector is an important element of this mechanism. In the case of the Russian war in Ukraine, the private sector contributes to the collective effort and complements states whose leverage is limited by the risk of military escalation.

The above discussion of China's use of its civilian maritime sector for the purpose of grey zone activities in the South China Sea further illustrates the added value of public-private partnerships. Indeed, the purpose of operating in the grey zone is to avoid direct encounters and escalation. The private sector offers this option, since in a globalised world order the boundaries between public, state-owned, state-backed, and fully private endeavours are hard to establish. The distinction between civilian and military seapower is blurred. In this case, three different actors play a role: the Chinese private fishing sector, China's paramilitary forces (under civilian administration), and the Chinese Navy. The three actors can synergistically contribute to fostering China's national interest, blurring the distinction between civilian and military seapower.

A consequence of the enactment of civilian seapower is states' ability to exercise economic, political, and cultural influence beyond their external boundaries. Since this influence is performed through civilian means and agency, this process can also originate at the initiative of non-state, private actors. In fact, in liberal societies, civilian seapower usually 'emerges almost haphazardly from the relatively free interplay of individual enterprise reacting to the competitive economic forces within the nation and in world markets' (Eccles 1979, 207). Whereas such initiatives are likely to be directed by the state/government in illiberal countries, private actors (especially large corporations) still play a role in this regard. This enactment of power is a form of soft seapower, since it is a mixture of civilian, normative, and cultural power, which is enacted at, from, or via the sea, but whose consequences are felt on land in terms of power relations and norms.

This process is also reciprocal. Whereas the sea represents an access road for one's own projection of norms and values through commerce and cultural penetration, it is also an entryway into one's own territory (e.g., prohibited items, arms, drugs, terrorists, illegal migrants, and ideas). This dimension was very prominent during the modern era, since maritime transport was the main if not the only means of communication with, and cultural penetration into, distant territories. Chapter 4 highlights the importance of seapower for empire building (including the dissemination of ideas and ideologies) and modern nation-state building. Mariners and port cities were traditionally represented negatively as agents and sites of cultural deviance and impurity (Quilley 2014).

The role of ports as sites of cultural and economic penetration and vectors of cosmopolitanism is particularly salient. Studies have focused on the role of ports as nexuses between various stakeholders across polities (Oliver and Slack 2006) and on how political and cultural influence (and even the performance of states' identity) can be exercised through ports in both directions, that is, hinterland/nation-states to foreland and vice versa (W.S. Chan 2020). Indeed, whereas ports and port cities favour the mixing and spread of cultural values Kokot (2009, 10, quoted in W.S. Chan 2020, 51) recalls that 'port cities have triggered a wide range of imaginations and projections, blending fantasies of freedom and faraway places with images of danger and moral decay'. Bearing in mind the reciprocal relationship in terms of influence as well as the crucial role played by ports, it appears that economic, cultural, and eventually political penetrations are interlinked.

This trend has been constant throughout history in trade-driven societies in Europe and in China (especially during the reign of the Qing dynasty). If this has not prevented European Powers from engaging in flourishing trade and developing seapower, the Qing dynasty's limited though pragmatic endeavours have contributed to its eventual demise. In other words, protection against foreign cultural penetration backlashed on China, since it also prevented acquiring and assimilating crucial knowledge, including military doctrines, training, and structures. Whereas the relationship between economic and cultural penetration during the colonisation era is well documented, including the role of maritime transportation and naval power, such practice in the post-modern era is less obvious. In fact, in the twentieth and twenty-first centuries, the maritime dimension of this link is less visible, since cultural penetration seems to follow the virtual lanes of the internet as much, if not more than, the SLOCs. However, the hinterland-port-SLOC-foreland nexus still plays a role as an enabler of political and cultural influence via economic penetration. The maritime dimension of economic, political, and cultural penetration still constitutes an important feature of civilian seapower.

China's Belt and Road Initiative is a good example of the synergistic link between naval and civilian maritime power. Whereas the belt (or SLOCs) represents the material structure within which the initiative is implemented, the main agents are (beyond the Chinese government and other states) ports, shipping actors, and other investors and local authorities. China's strategy relies on the soft and coercive power deriving from its economic and financial strengths that contribute to Beijing's geopolitical agenda. China's leverage on its civilian maritime sector is facilitated by the nature of the regime: 'China's socialist legacy, augmented by its state-led development model, offers China's leaders significant ability to deploy the state's enormous economic assets to advance their diplomatic agenda' (Reilly 2013, 2). China and Chinese firms have invested in and contributed to developing maritime/port infrastructures along the so-called Maritime Silk Road, most notably in Vietnam, Singapore, Malaysia, Thailand, Myanmar, Pakistan, and Egypt, but also in Israel, Greece, Spain, Italy, and the Netherlands.

The main agents of this 'port diplomacy' (Barston 2014, 77) are private or state-owned and they have allegiance to the government. The convergence of civilian and naval objectives means that the Maritime Silk Road is linked to Beijing's interests in securing a network of bases and friendly ports for its navy from the South China Sea to the Gulf that has been termed a 'String of Pearls' in the West. However, beyond the obvious links between the economic dimension of the Maritime Silk Road and the geostrategic objectives of China, this is first and foremost a civilian initiative. In other words, the Maritime Silk Road initiative is a form of civilian seapower: by dominating the economic (port) actors, China can extend its control of strategically relevant S L O C s in a way that can eventually develop into proper geostrategic/military advantages beyond trade, access to market, and energy security.

Whereas the recent acquisition of a naval facility in Djibouti is indeed instrumental in sustaining the forward deployment of Chinese naval units in the region and beyond, the navy relies on civilian (state-owned and foreign) stakeholders for logistical support along the Maritime Silk Road. This is what commentators have described as 'places' for the logistics of China's navy rather than 'bases' for power projection (e.g., Kostecka 2011). In this regard, civilian seapower works hand in hand with naval power. Whereas China's naval power politics is currently aimed at near seas, civilian maritime assets will, in due time, contribute to both China's overall power on the world stage and to its growing seapower. However, as China becomes more assertive, civilian seapower is likely to fail to contribute to Beijing's political narrative consisting in presenting China as a 'benevolent' global actor.

Corporate Seapower

The civilian dimension of seapower depends on the existence (and in some instances the instrumentalisation) of civilian stakeholders; consequently, it easily becomes bidirectional. The civilian sector can be implicated in policy-making processes regarding ocean governance, via lobbying activities or stakeholder participation. For example, the release of the EU *Integrated Maritime Policy* (Commission 2007) and the *Maritime Security Strategy* (Council of the EU 2014) has followed an intensive process of consultation across countries and maritime stakeholders, which demonstrates a certain degree of bottom-up approach to maritime affairs policy-making within the EU. The 2022 UK *National Strategy for Maritime Security* has also benefited from a comprehensive process of engagement with industry and academic stakeholders (HM Government 2022, 18).

However, civilian stakeholders' participation in ocean governance is biased towards economic actors, such as shipping companies, fishing unions, and the tourism industry. Consequently, for-profit interests may overpower environmental and social concerns. For example, coastal communities have not always welcomed the operationalisation of the concept of Blue Growth/blue economy, claiming that their specific concerns are not sufficiently taken into consideration during participatory processes (e.g., Hadjimichael, Bruggeman, and Lange 2014). Such concerns can include fear of dispossession of vulnerable coastal populations through conservation and development projects, the unsustainable exploitation of natural resources, ocean privatisation, and threat to cultural values (Germond-Duret 2022).

The influence that corporations in general and multinational companies in particular have on states is well documented. The influence can be exercised via instrumental power (i.e. direct lobbying on political actors), influence on the media (Arnold 2003; Mitchell 1997), discursive power, as well as structural power (i.e. norms, regulations, and agenda setting) (Fuchs 2005; Fuchs and Lederer 2007). The container shipping industry is a case in point for corporate seapower. Indeed, it has been empirically demonstrated that it 'operates in an oligopolistic market structure' (Sys 2009, 267). Thus, dominant players within this sector can exercise influence over other economic and public actors, all the more since states and their economies strongly rely on the unimpeded flow of goods along the global supply chain. The business of port infrastructures, and by extension the shipping industry, epitomise 'the imperatives of borderless world visions and calculations' (Sparke et al. 2004, 491).

However, decisions made by companies do have important effects on state actors and societies. This is a sector very much self-regulated. States' authority over this sector has traditionally been weaker than with other cognate sectors, such as air transport (Strange 1976, 358). Moreover, the sector is very much consolidated with less than twenty major operators and a handful of mega-alliances. Thus, multinational corporations are in a position to influence states within forums such as the IMO on decisions regarding sectoral norms and regulations (Hendriksen 2020), for example regarding the use and *modus operandi* of private security forces on-board ships (Gould 2021). Yet, states can in return influence corporations (Fuchs 2005). When corporations gain advantages by influencing public actors, they enter into an organic relationship, which implies that states can also influence them (e.g., to make sure they contribute to state's interests) because corporations have become dependent on their sustained relationship with states. This organic relationship is particularly strong when a corporation is closely linked to a particular state.

A good example is Maersk, which has been the world leading shipping company since 2005 (number two since 2022) and is a dominant player in many trade lanes. Maersk is a mega corporation, whose main activities span various sectors, notably maritime transport, logistics, and energy. In 2017, Maersk revenue was more than $30 billion (Maersk 2018), which, although the relevance of such comparison is limited, is more than the GDP (nominal) of a hundred countries. It also has more employees than many states' bureaucracies. The company is thus well positioned to exercise leverage on public actors.

First, its prestige, soft power, as well as economic leverages grant bargaining power, power to influence decisions by port authorities, and public policy decision makers. For example, the company can use symbolic statements of power (extrinsic power) to influence public actors. In 1998, Maersk sent the then largest container ship (the *Regina Maersk*) touring North American ports in a clear bid to 'send a message to port officials and politicians [stating that] the advent of mega containerships made upgrading of existing port infrastructures necessary' (van Ham and Rijsenbrij 2012, 159). Beyond prestige, Maersk's dominant position within the sector) allows setting up the rules of the game. For example, as of 2007, the company had 'a monopoly position ... at 31 ports' and a 50 per cent share in 62 ports

(Frémont 2007, 438). Secondary ports rely on Maersk's activities, and thus, the company can 'secure its port operations in the long term, with, no doubt, the ability to influence policy within the port as well' (441).

Then, corporate decisions, such as the relocation in 2001 of its transhipment hub away from the Port of Singapore (PSA) to the Port of Tanjung Pelepas in Malaysia was said to have a large impact: first on the sectoral activities, since this 'resulted in a decline of approximately 11% in PSA's overall business' (Bae et al. 2013, 479), but also eventually on the Republic of Singapore itself due to its extreme reliance on PSA for its economy. In turn, this relocation was considered to have positive effects on Malaysia by virtue of an increasing role in the Southeast Asian trans-shipment business.

Second, Maersk is strongly linked to the state of Denmark. The company's headquarters are in Copenhagen, and Denmark is the flag state for many ships they operate. Maersk is in a position to influence decision makers via lobbying and the presence of 'seven executive officers from Mærsk' among Danish 'power elite' (Ellersgaard 2016, 297–9). For example, Denmark's deployment of a frigate to the Gulf of Guinea in 2021 to tackle piracy follows recurring calls for action by Maersk whose activities were impacted (Goldman 2021). But the relationship is reciprocal and organic. In fact, 'there is historically an established line of communication between the [Danish shipping industry and the Danish State]' (Larsen and Nissen 2017, 43).

Denmark, as a small Power, can also benefit from the global corporate power and prestige of Maersk, which increases Copenhagen's influence in the maritime transport governance arena, including its security sector. In the case of the Proliferation Security Initiative that encourages maritime interdiction practices, some participating states 'have served as the de facto leaders ... for important functional issues, for example, Denmark on container shipping issues (leveraging the clout and experience of its corporate national Maersk, the world's largest container shipping line)' (Cooper 2011, 328). Denmark is thus recognised as one of the 'major seafaring nation[s]' (325), which constitutes a form of extrinsic, soft seapower. In turn, the prestige Denmark gains from being recognised as a leading maritime nation helps cement Maersk's own power and influence (something that Swiss-based MSC cannot benefit from). The link is thus clearly organic. Consequently, Denmark seems also in a good position to reciprocally influence Maersk, since the company must maintain this relationship.

TWENTY-FIRST-CENTURY SEAPOWER:
COLLECTIVE AND CIVILIAN

This chapter has delved into two post-modern dimensions of seapower in the twenty-first century: collective and civilian seapower. Whereas the former is a relatively recent feature of seapower, which mirrors the evolution of statecraft and IR in the post-modern, post–World War II era, the latter could already be found at the inception of seapower in ancient times, since the relationship between navy and merchant marine, between military power and economic power, has always been a core feature of seapower.

Within the pluralistic society, there is a common belief in the freedom of the seas and in the need to maintain a reasonable level of order and security in the maritime domain to benefit from the advantages that freedom of the seas grants to states and economic agents. Post-modern seapower is thus inherently liberal, but a form of liberalism that is limited in scope and ambitions and constrained by domestic considerations. Moreover, only solidaristic maritime nations share a common desire to uphold freedom of navigation and to maintain the status quo in the maritime domain, which has been favourable to the West's global leadership. The West dominates the global (liberal) order via its control of the global supply chain and the global reach of its combined navies. Seapower, in its collective form, is thus still the 'higher-order power medium' (Modelski and Thompson 1988, 13), and as such will be key to respond to the coming global leadership challenge.

Civilian seapower embraces various forms, and the distinction between state and non-state actors as well as between military and civilian assets and activities is increasingly blurred. Civilian seapower is an emerging, if not contested, concept though. It refers to the use of private assets by states in view of gaining leverage and pursuing national interests, but it also implies an organic relationship between public and private actors. It can take various forms, ranging from the need to protect the merchant marine, which remains strategically crucial; to cooperation with non-state stakeholders in view of controlling the maritime domain; to exercising soft normative power through civilian stakeholders and ventures. The use of civilian/non-military public assets (e.g., civilian coastguards) is also part of the post- and neo-modern practice of ocean governance. Corporate maritime actors, in turn, can exercise forms of power via lobbying or sectoral self-regulation. At a higher strategic level, civilian seapower can also serve global leadership ambitions. China is a big country with global strategic interests and with one of the fastest growing navies in the world. China increasingly values its civilian seapower and clearly benefits from it beyond the role played by maritime transport and maritime economy. China can use civilian seapower to gain political if not military advantages.

7

Conclusion

The Future of Seapower

The scholarly, some would say artificial, division between pre-modern, modern, post-modern, and neo-modern seapower does not correspond to clearly define historical time frames. When does pre-modern seapower end? At the beginning or at the end of the medieval period? When does post-modern seapower start? In the post-war period or following the end of the Cold War? To further complicate the picture, pre-modern seapower bears the seeds of modern seapower, modern seapower the seeds of post-modern seapower, and post-modern seapower the seeds of neo-modern seapower. Overall, the study of the evolution of the concept and practice of seapower across historical eras has shown that seapower – and especially its three layers: elements, enactment, and outcomes – demonstrates timeless characteristics. This concluding chapter first looks at the specific features of seapower that are closely linked to each specific eras, and then highlights the major continuities and changes that explain the centrality of seapower when it comes to cycles of global dominance. The book concludes with suggestions for the next steps for seapower studies, most notably the need to decolonise the field.

The sea played an important role in the pre-modern era whether during peacetime seafaring or wartime naval operations. Some pre-modern polities thrived via civilian seapower (e.g., Phoenicia, the Hanseatic League) or via a mix of naval power and maritime commerce (e.g., Carthage, Venice, but also Aksum and Sri Vijaya). However, pre-modern seapower was restricted by the means and technology at disposal as well as by the lack of maritime culture within the elites, resulting in a limited ideational inclination towards the sea and seapower. Whereas seafaring was well developed within the boundaries of existing knowledge (e.g., cartography and navigation) and of what was technically possible to achieve at the time, seapower was rarely part of rulers' regular policies. The sea was best left to merchants, as exemplified by the mostly civilian dimension of the Phoenician thalassocracy, and seapower was rather enacted in a pragmatic way depending on the context and circumstances – on a 'need to' basis. It was rarely the preferred tool at rulers' disposal and strategic effects were usually limited. When enacted, the final cause of pre-modern seapower was to control the land rather than any long-term strategic goal of commanding the sea. That said, pre-modern seapower bore some features of modern seapower, most notably an embryonic contribution to empire building via physical means (i.e., transportation, military might, wartime supply, communication) and ideational means via the spread of values, ideas, and religions. Although rarely remembered as such, not least because few contemporaries wrote about it, the Roman Empire is the prime example of successful use of pragmatic seapower contributing to Rome's enduring dominance.

Modern seapower mirrors technological breakthroughs (e.g., sail and then steam propulsion, ship cladding, fleet reach and range, accuracy and power of embarked weapons, navigation aids), allowing navies to produce strategic effects but also merchant fleets to travel the seven seas and contribute to a large extent to the global value chain. At the cognitive level, more openness to the sea was linked to mercantile (and then commercial) capitalism and secularism that favoured rational (often profit-driven) decision-making. There was a reciprocal link between the need to develop seapower to consolidate nation-states and the role nation-states played in facilitating the development of seapower. Modern seapower contributed to the consolidation of nation-states in Europe; the development of colonial systems of exploitation; the flow of capital, values, and norms; but was also a cradle for global (ocean) governance and an engine for the development of more inclusive political systems in Europe. In other words, exploitation of SLOCs as a means to commerce and to project power and forces was complemented by the recognition of the specific nature of the sea that requires specific rules (*mare liberum*) or specific practices that have served dominant Powers and their interests. Whereas this practice was an obvious characteristic of the nineteenth century (*Pax Britannica*), modern seapower still permeates the twentieth and twenty-first centuries, for the final cause of modern seapower revolves around hegemonism, defence/security, and wealth.

The interconnections between post and neo-modern seapower are even stronger. Under the banner of ocean governance and maritime security, seapower contributes to modern forms of military power (traditional power and forces projection); post-modern forms of military power (e.g., counterterrorism, counter-immigration); post-modern forms of political and economic power (e.g., extrinsic soft power, civilian seapower, stabilisation of the liberal world order); and neo-modern practices consisting in the territorialisation of the sea, marine resource grabbing, and assertive foreign policies (e.g., territorial claims). As such, the current era sees a form of merging of all features of seapower.

The final cause of post-modern seapower revolves around security and wealth and the stability of the liberal international order that serves both economic and dominant political interests. However, the final cause of neo-modern seapower is to control the sea to extend states' functional power and reach if not their jurisdiction and sovereignty. Whereas neo-modern seapower and the practice of territorialising the sea also contribute to the stability of the global maritime order, other forms of neo-modern seapower politics (such as China's assertiveness in the South China Sea) result in renewed confrontations between states and the creation of spheres of influence, not unlike what happened at the end of the nineteenth century, when seapower politics contributed to confrontational dynamics that eventually led to the outbreak of World War I.

Solidaristic and civilian seapower demonstrate the current merging of seapower features beyond the modern/post-modern/neo-modern categories. The ongoing merging of modern and post-modern features into a form of neo-modern seapower follows the intensification of the interpenetration between the material, ideational, military, and civilian dimensions of seapower. Thus, seapower must be understood for what it is: a way for some actors – not limited to states – to control other actors or processes and, more generally, to control the destiny of the world. Seapower has been a central feature and component of IR since Antiquity. The analysis of its evolution, as a concept and a practice, throughout the pre-modern, modern, and post-/neo-modern eras has shown both continuities and changes (cf. table 7.1).

The elements of seapower have been present since ancient times, although first in an attuned way and rarely all together at the same time. Seafaring, and thus the commercial dimension of seapower, has always been prominent. When commerce protection was less crucial

Table 7.1
The evolution of seapower

	Pre-modern seapower	Modern seapower	Post-modern seapower	Neo-modern seapower
Elements and forms of seapower	• Civilian maritime sector • Naval forces • Limited endorsement of maritime culture	• Naval power assets • Merchant marine • Naval bureaucracy and maritime industry • Awareness of the link between seapower and dominance • Openness to the sea linked to capitalism and secularism	• Civilian • Collective	• Naval power • Police forces • Lawfare • Civilian assets
Practice/ enactment of seapower	• Seafaring, trade • Naval battles • Support for land forces • Flow of ideas • Enacted on a 'need to' basis (pragmatism) • Limited strategic effects	• Flow of goods and capital, transportation of riches • Naval power projection (with strategic effects) • Spread ideas • Consolidate nations-states and colonial empires	• Ocean governance, maritime security, and policing • Spread of values • Projection of security	• Territorialisation of the sea • Neo-navalism • Expansion of jurisdiction and sovereignty over the sea
Final causes of seapower/ consequences	• Control of the land • Limited contribution to empire building	• Hegemonism • Security • Wealth • Cradle for global ocean governance	• Security • Wealth • Stability of liberal order	• Control • Striation

(either because commerce was not maritime or because threats and disruptions were limited) naval power was less relevant. For example, Phoenician and Greek merchants did not face many threats, since it was, in general, in all stakeholders' interests to let merchants do their business. Naval power was then enacted only in support of overall war efforts (e.g., Athens against Persia or Rome against Carthage).

Piracy, or other punctual threats, were dealt with on an ad hoc basis. This does not mean that naval power was not crucial in wartime but that it rarely needed to be enacted in support of commercial interests. And this does not mean that maritime trade was not important in the pre-modern era. Modern seapower is more deeply linked to, and dependent on, seafaring and maritime trade, but naval power is also more central to the defence of maritime trade in the modern era (not least due to the increased competition at sea made possible by technological developments and fostered by Great Powers rivalry in Europe and then globally in the era of imperialism). With the rise of mercantilist and then commercial capitalism, the globalisation of trade and systems of dominance as well as the inception of colonial empires, seapower gained in importance whether in commercial, military, or ideational terms. This organic relationship between maritime trade and naval power remains central in the post-/neo-modern era, in particular the control of the global supply chain via the control of SLOCs and the global maritime order.

At the ideational level, there has always been an ambivalence towards the perception of the sea. Despite its association with natural beauty, exploration, and a source of riches, the sea has recurringly been either feared (for its inherent dangers) or despised by elites who recognised seafaring's power of disruption as a vector of 'foreign', subversive ideas and values. However, rulers have always demonstrated a high degree of pragmatism, from Ancient Greece to Arab Caliphates of the Middle Ages, and from English monarchs to the Chinese Communist Party in the twenty-first century. In other words, decision makers are rarely totally sea blind. That said, pragmatism and a willingness to use the sea for personal, national, or corporate interests does not mean that an endeavour will be successful. Indeed, Mahan's character of people and government is a necessary element of seapower but not a sufficient one. If other elements are not met or present, seapower or even naval power will not develop, or not to the extent that it will have a determinant role in shaping societies and polities.

The outcomes and consequences of a successful enactment of seapower have also shown impressive regularity throughout eras. Seapower has served those rulers, polities, nations, and states that have mustered its elements and successfully enacted it. Seapower has provided economic and military preponderance. It has enabled control of regional or global systems. Seapower has facilitated the rise to power at regional and then global levels. It has thus been a central feature of global (or before 1500, regional) dominance cycles. Seapower has helped sustain and stabilise orders favourable to dominant Powers of the time, from the *Pax Romana* to the *Pax Britannica* and the *Pax Americana*. This contribution of seapower to global dominance did not start in 1500. The Age of Discovery and then industrial revolutions and the rise of capitalism have only accelerated this feature of international politics.

Despite such continuity, there are also many changes and differences between historical periods and actors. First, the amplitude of dominance generated by seapower was much more limited in the pre-modern era compared to the modern and post-modern eras. This is mainly linked to technological constraints but also to the much-limited impact world trade and the flow of goods and capital had on people, societies, and states in the pre-modern era. Second, with the 'acceleration' since the sixteenth century and the 'great acceleration' (Steffen et al. 2015) of the recent decades, the rapidity of dominance acquisition has changed. However, it is important to note that the change of speed is more noticeable between the pre-modern and modern era than between the modern and the current era. Indeed, China's rising seapower had started to be noticed in the 2000s (and to experts' eyes in the 1980s); the extent to which China will reach a level of challenging power in the coming decades is still debated, but clearly, its potential rise to seapower dominance is not faster than the Spanish, Dutch, British, or US ones in the (modern) past.

There has also been changes in terms of dominant political actors who benefit from seapower, which is obvious given the changes in global leadership that have happened over time. However, this is also about the distribution of power within the international system. There have been periods of regional or global maritime hegemony, such as the Roman Empire's *Mare Nostrum* or Britain's maritime preponderance in the nineteenth century, and periods of balance of seapower, such as during the Middle Ages and, to some extent, during the interwar period. The Cold War period is an interesting case: at first sight there could have been a balance of seapower as there was a global balance of power between the two blocs. However, in practice the control of the global supply chain and the economic-legal order was American/Western, which proved instrumental in 'winning' the Cold War.

The relative importance of the elements of seapower has also fluctuated. In the pre-modern era seafaring was the main driver of seapower whereas during the modern era the naval element had acquired a central position – to the extent that classical seapower scholars tended to equate seapower with naval power (cf. chapter 1). Today, most maritime Powers manage without substantial national merchant fleets, whereas (ironically) the civilian dimension of seapower has grown in importance. Depending on the era, certain maritime stakeholders have accrued importance or been at the forefront of seapower, gaining or losing leverage and centrality.

A case in point is civilian maritime actors: they were prominent during the pre-modern and medieval era (Greek merchants, thalassocracies such as Phoenicia and Venice relying on unimpeded maritime trade, Chinese traders, the Hanseatic network of merchants, pirates and privateers) and then became less relevant following nation-state building, bureaucratic centralisation, and states' monopoly on the legitimate violence at sea in the modern, Westphalian era. That said, economic actors have remained at the forefront of seapower politics throughout the modern era as initiators, facilitators, and beneficiaries. In the current era, civilian seapower actors, the corporate maritime sector, play a crucial role in support of the global maritime order while reciprocally benefiting from its stability.

The ability of rulers and societies to understand and accept that power (and thus security and prosperity) is intrinsically linked to the sea and their own propensity to embrace a maritime mindset have also varied from time to time and from place to place. This is linked to the point above about rulers' pragmatism. However, recognising the importance of the sea and the need to harness seapower has not always been sufficient. For example, since Peter the Great, Russian (autocratic) rulers have demonstrated an understanding of the need to get access to warm waters and the global supply chain and the need to develop a navy to support this cause. However, this has not been sufficient to overcome a deeply embedded continental strategic mindset that has prevented the development of an independent maritime strategy in support of long-term strategic objectives. And the Russian navy has never been more than a complement to the Russian army, as illustrated by its inability to generate strategic effects in the Ukraine war. The Chinese Communist Party's leadership in the twenty-first-century seems to better assimilate the need to develop seapower to position the country to make a bid for global leadership. Indeed, despite its inherent weaknesses in terms of geographical elements (being a large continental state with limited open access to the high seas) and the time it takes to develop material elements of seapower, China is efficiently playing the card of civilian seapower which, some would say, might enable Beijing to claim global leadership without having to resort to a global war.

Finally, in terms of its enactment, whereas maritime trade and naval power have constituted the backbones of seapower since the pre-modern era, recent evolutions consist in the territorialisation of the sea and the more collective, cooperative nature of seapower, which can now be 'shared' within a solidaristic society of maritime nations. It is embedded within the West, led by the US but in no way the pre-serve of Washington. Moreover, the extent to which Beijing adheres to the current global maritime order is debatable, since China actually benefits from the current stability and security of the global supply chains on which the Chinese economic growth is highly dependent.

Mahan and most classical seapower authors have focused on the modern era 'during which commerce and conflict at sea occupied a disproportionately large role in world affairs' (P. Kennedy [1976] 2017, 7). Despite technological changes and other contextual evolutions, classical Mahanian principles still matter (Stavridis 2017, 324). This book's findings concur with Mahan's historical and Modelski and Thompson's quantitative demonstrations of the timelessness of the preponderance of seapower. There is a timeless incentive to go to the sea for economic and military purposes based on rational decision-making processes and resulting in political, military, and strategic advantages discussed throughout this book. However, the analysis of the evolution of seapower through historical eras has also shown how intervening variables play a role as push-and-pull factors: the perception of the sea and the existence of a maritime culture versus the disdain for mariners and for the sea in general as well as the evolution of technology have constituted important pull-and-push factors for seapower. These are subject to change, and thus the cycles of seapower, dominance, and who commands the sea and with which consequences have not been static, despite the timelessness of seapower as a concept and a practice.

Since its popularisation at the end of the nineteenth century, the concept of seapower has been associated with Western political thought and defined in light of Western naval and economic history. Seapower scholarship is overwhelmingly European and Western, and the field has lacked critical, reflective, positional research (de Carvalho and Leira 2022). The concept of seapower has emerged in the academic literature at the end of the nineteenth century, with major authors (all European or American) referring to European practices since the Age of Discovery and to Ancient Greek texts and practice. The association of the concept of seapower within Western political thought and practice has resulted in the following collective imaginaries and academic constructions and misconceptions regarding non-European civilisations and seapower: first that the contribution of non-Europeans to seafaring, naval strategy, and maritime thought has been minimal, and second that maritime identity, seafaring culture, and seapower politics are attributes of European, Western nations and societies.

However, there is non-European, non-Western naval thought that has run parallel with the traditional European one, with non-European texts from Antiquity to the Middle Ages, notably from China, India, Mesopotamia, and the Arab Caliphates. Highlighting the existence of non-European seapower thought that complements the traditional European one further validates Modelski and Thompson's (1988) claim that the link between seapower and global hegemony is timeless and indeed universal but fluctuates according to cycles of dominance. Further research on this topic is required and likely to strengthen seapower scholarship in the twenty-first century.

The framework for analysis this book proposes enables going beyond the rather sterile debate about the timelessness of seapower by emphasising the varying importance of the diverse elements of seapower across historical eras, while recognising continuity in terms of the pragmatic enactment of seapower as well as its outcomes in terms of regional or global dominance. In particular, this allows reflection on these specific periods of global leadership challenge and the role seapower plays in achieving leadership transition, whether peacefully or not. However, more than timeless, it is universal; hence, the many similarities between the European and non-European, the North and South practice and conceptualisation of seapower.

It is finally possible to rephrase the initial definition of seapower at the outset of this book in light of the application of the 'three layers of analysis' framework to the evolution of seapower since ancient times. Seapower is the exercise of power at, from, or towards the sea. The naval and commercial aspects of seapower are but two sides of the same coin, as are its public/state and the private/civilian dimensions. Seapower is characterised by its three layers: constituting elements, enactment, and consequences. Seapower depends on geographical, geopolitical, material, and ideational elements, and consequently, its relative importance fluctuates depending on eras and places. Cultural and political agency is key; seapower is a mindset. However, the preponderance of seapower as a 'social fact' demonstrates a high degree of timelessness and universality regardless of its elements. The pragmatic enactment of seapower by public or private actors, often in a collective, solidaristic, way, spans military, political, economic, legal, and discursive realms. In other words, it permeates all aspects of human, societal, and political life. Its consequences or outcomes can be comprehended in terms of national interests, economic wealth, systemic stability, or global dominance. And this is why seapower scholarship is so important in the twenty-first century; the concept of seapower is instrumental in guiding our understanding of the role that the sea will play in an era of major geopolitical tensions.

The renewed interest in seapower and its associated components and practices is illustrated by the growing number of books devoted to the topic in the very recent years (Bosco 2022; Campling and Colás 2021; de Carvalho and Leira 2022; Gresh 2020; P. Kennedy 2022; G. Kennedy and de Sousa Moreira 2022; Lambert 2018; Sadler 2023; Till 2022). The future of seapower studies is guaranteed. However, seapower studies will also be constrained by the scholarly community's ability to adopt and assimilate a decolonising agenda. The discussions in this book of the organic relationship between seapower, capitalism, state building, imperialism, and colonialism help clear the way for new debates about seapower in a post-/decolonised academic world. Indeed, by accepting that seapower is 'what states make of it' and thus acknowledging the past wrongdoings that seapower has facilitated, we can, as a community of seapower scholars, start looking forward to the future of seapower in the context of the impending global leadership challenge between the progressist forces of maritime nations and those of authoritarianism.

Notes

CHAPTER ONE

1 As a matter of clarification regarding Mahan's military rank, it must
   be noted that he was promoted to rear admiral only after retirement
   following a 1906 Act of Congress 'that advanced all retired navy captains
   who had served during the Civil War', and he nonetheless 'kept the title
   of "captain" as his *nom de plume*' (Crowl 1986, 448).
2 The original work is credited to Sir John Nickolls in the French allegedly
   'translated' version (1754). However, in the English translation of the
   French book (also dated 1754), editors explain the work was originally
   written by an anonymous French civil servant, later recognised as Marquis
   Plumart D'Angeul under the fictitious name of John Nickolls, and the
   original work is indeed in French, although many ideas have been borrowed from Josiah Tucker (1749) (see Higgs 1935, 78–9).

CHAPTER SIX

1 This section is based on and adapted from Basil Germond (2022c).
   My thanks go to the Australian Naval Institute.
2 The expression 'civilian seapower' has been coined during discussions
   with a former PhD student at Lancaster in 2014–19 (see Chan 2020, 165).

References

Abreu de Moura, J.A. 2022. 'Maritime States and the Value of the Sea'. In *Power and the Maritime Domain: A Global Dialogue*, edited by G. Kennedy and W. de Sousa Moreira, 59–72. London: Routledge.

Abulafia, D. 2020. *The Boundless Sea: A Human History of the Oceans*. London: Penguin Books.

Ahrens, B., and T. Diez. 2015. 'Solidarisation and its Limits: The EU and the Transformation of International Society'. *Global Discourse* 5 (3): 341–55.

Anderson, J. 1996. 'The Shifting Stage of Politics: New Medieval and Postmodern Territorialities?' *Environment and Planning I: Society and Space* 14: 133–53.

Arnaud, P. 2017. 'Introduction'. In *The Sea in History: The Ancient World*, edited by P. de Souza and P. Arnaud, 1–7. Woodbridge: Boydell Press.

Arnold, D.G. 2003. 'Libertarian Theories of the Corporation and Global Capitalism'. *Journal of Business Ethics* 48: 155–73.

Bae, M.J., E.P. Chew, L.H. Lee, and A. Zhang. 2013. 'Container Transshipment and Port Competition'. *Maritime Policy & Management* 40 (5): 479–94.

Baker, S. 2010. *Written on the Water: British Romanticism and the Maritime Empire of Culture*. Charlottesville: University of Virginia Press.

Barber, J., and J. Sipos. 2004. 'The Future Maritime Security Environment'. In *The Future of Canada's Maritime Capabilities: The Issues, Challenges and Solutions in a New Security Environment*, edited by R. H. Edwards, 165–75. Halifax: Centre for Foreign Policy Studies, Dalhousie University.

Barston, R.P. 2014. *Modern Diplomacy*. 4th ed. London: Routledge.

Bateman, S. 2007. 'Navies and the Maintenance of Good Order in Peacetime'. In *The Politics of Maritime Power*, edited by A.T.H. Tan, 95–114. London: Routledge.

Bauman, Z. 1987. *Legislators and Interpreters*. Oxford: Blackwell.

– 1992. *Intimations of Postmodernity*. London: Routledge.

Beckett, C. 2021. 'Getting to Grips with Grey Zone Conflict'. *Blog Strategic Command*, MoD, 26 April, https://stratcommand.blog.gov.uk/2021/04/26/getting-to-grips-with-grey-zone-conflict.

Beckman, R., and Z. Sun. 2017. 'The Relationship between UNCLOS and IMO Instruments'. *Asia-Pacific Journal of Ocean Law and Policy* 2 (2): 201–46.

Bernstein, A.H. 1989. 'Maritime Strategy in the Punic Wars'. In *Seapower and Strategy*, edited by C.S. Gray and R.W. Barnett, 100–31. Annapolis: US Naval Institute.

Black, J. 2004. *The British Seaborne Empire*. New Haven: Yale University Press.

Bloom, J.J. 2019. *Rome Rules the Waves: A Naval Staff Appreciation of Ancient Rome's Maritime Strategy 300 BCE–500 CE*. Barnsley: Pen & Sword Military.

Booth, K. 1979. *Navies and Foreign Policy*. New York: Holmes & Meier Publishers.

– 1985. *Law, Force and Diplomacy at Sea*. London: George Allen & Unwin.

Bosco, D. 2022. *The Poseidon Project: The Struggle to Govern the World's Ocean*. Oxford: Oxford University Press.

Boswell, T., and M. Sweat. 1991. 'Hegemony, Long Waves, and Major Wars: A Time Series Analysis of Systemic Dynamics, 1496–1967'. *International Studies Quarterly* 35 (2): 123–49.

Brewster, D. 2017. 'Silk Roads and Strings of Pearls: The Strategic Geography of China's New Pathways in the Indian Ocean'. *Geopolitics* 22 (2): 269–91.

Bridge, C. (1910) 2018. *Sea-power: And Other Studies*. Smith, Elder & Company. Reprint by Ashed Phoenix Library.

Brito Vieira, M. 2003. 'Mare Liberum vs. Mare Clausum: Grotius, Freitas, and Selden's Debate on Dominion over the Seas'. *Journal of the History of Ideas* 64 (3): 361–77.

Brodie, B. (1943) 1969. *Sea Power in the Machine Age*. New York: Greenwood Press.

Brooks, L.F. 1986. 'Naval Power and National Security: The Case for Maritime Strategy'. *International Security* 11 (2): 58–88.

Brown, J. 2012. 'Pirates and Privateers: Managing the Indian Ocean's Private Security Boom'. *Analysis*, Lowy Institute for International Policy.

Buchanan, E. 2022. 'The Ukraine War and the Future of the Arctic'. *RUSI Commentary*, 18 March 2022. https://rusi.org/explore-our-research/publications/commentary/ukraine-war-and-future-arctic.

Bueger, C. 2015. 'What is Maritime Security?' *Marine Policy* 53: 159–64.

– 2022. 'Making and Breaking Waves: The Evolution of Global Maritime Security Thinking'. *Paper for Proceedings of 2022 Indo-Pacific Sea Power Conference*, Sydney: Sea Power Centre of the Royal Australian Navy, https://bueger.info/wp-content/uploads/2022/05/Bueger-2022-Evolution-of-maritime-security.pdf.

Bueger, C., and T. Edmunds. 2017. 'Beyond Seablindness: A New Agenda for Maritime Security Studies'. *International Affairs* 93 (6): 1293–311.

– 2020. 'Blue Crime: Conceptualising Transnational Organised Crime at Sea'. *Marine Policy* 119: 104067.

– 2021. 'Pragmatic Ordering: Informality, Experimentation, and the Maritime Security Agenda'. *Review of International Studies* 47 (2): 171–91.

Bueger, C., T. Edmunds, and B.J. Ryan. 2019. 'Maritime Security: The Uncharted Politics of the Global Sea'. *International Affairs* 95 (5): 971–8.

Bull, H. 1976a. 'Martin Wight and the Theory of International Relations: The Second Martin Wight Memorial Lecture'. *British Journal of International Studies* 2 (2): 101–16.

– 1976b. 'Sea Power and Political Influence'. *Adelphi Paper*, no. 122.

– (1977) 1995. *The Anarchical Society: A Study of Order in World Politics*. London: Macmillan.

Buzan, B. 1993. 'From International System to International Society: Structural Realism and Regime Theory Meet the English School'. *International Organization* 47 (3): 327–52.

– 2004. *From International to World Society? English School Theory and the Social Structure of Globalisation*. Cambridge: Cambridge University Press.

Buzan, B., O. Wæver, and J. de Wilde. 1997. *Security: A New Framework for Analysis*. Boulder, CO: Lynne Rienner.

Cable, J. 1983. *Britain's Naval Future*. London: Macmillan.

– 1985. *Diplomacy at Sea*. London: Macmillan.

– (1971) 1994. *Gunboat Diplomacy 1919–1991: Political Applications of Limited Naval Force*. 3rd ed. London: Macmillan.

Cahoone, L.E. 1996. *From Modernism to Postmodernism: An Anthology*. Oxford: Balckwell.

Callwell, C.E. (1905) 1996. *Military Operation and Maritime Preponderance: Their Relations and Interdependence*. Edited by C.S. Gray. Annapolis: United States Naval Institute Press. Original edition Edinburgh: William Blackwood and Sons.

Campanella, T. (1601) 1997. *Monarchie d'Espagne: texte inédit*. Paris: PUF.

Campling, L., and A. Colás. 2018. 'Capitalism and the Sea: Sovereignty, Territory and Appropriation in the Global Ocean'. *Environment and Planning D: Society and Space* 36 (4): 776–94.

– 2021. *Capitalism and the Sea*. London: Verso.

Castex, R. (1931–39) 1994. *Strategic Theories*, selections translated and edited by E.C. Kiesling. Annapolis: United States Naval Institute Press. Original edition Paris: Société d'éditions géographiques, maritimes et coloniales.

Chan, G. 2020. *China's Maritime Silk Road: Advancing Global Development?* Cheltenham: Edward Elgar Publishing.

Chan, W.S. 2020. 'Bringing the Ports and Port Diplomacy Back-In: A Comparative Study of the Role of Hong Kong, Macao and Shanghai in Contemporary EU-China Relations'. PhD thesis, Lancaster University.

Coleman, P.T., M. Deutsch, and E.C. Marcus. 2014. *The Handbook of Conflict Resolution: Theory and Practice*. 3rd ed. San Francisco: Jossey-Bass (Wiley).

Colomb, P.H. (1891) 1899. *Naval Warfare: Its Ruling Principles and Practice Historically Treated*. 3rd rev. ed. London: W.H. Allen and Co.

Commission of the European Communities. 2007. *Communication from the Commission to the European Parliament, the Council, the European Economic and Social Committee and the Committee of the Regions: An Integrated Maritime Policy for the European Union*. Brussels. 10.10.2007, COM (2007) 575 final.

Connery, C.L. 1994. 'Pacific Rim Discourse: The U.S. Global Imaginary in the Late Cold War Years'. *boundary 2* 21 (1): 30–56.

– 1995. 'Pacific Rim Discourse: The US Global Imaginary in the Late Cold War Years'. In *Asia/Pacific as Space of Cultural Production*, edited by R. Wilson and A. Dirlik, 30–56. Durham, NC: Duke University Press.

– 2001. 'Ideologies of Land and Sea: Alfred Thayer Mahan, Carl Schmitt, and the Shaping of Global Myth Elements'. *boundary 2* 28 (2): 173–201.

Cooper, D.A. 2011. 'Challenging Contemporary Notions of Middle Power Influence: Implications of the Proliferation Security Initiative for "Middle Power Theory"'. *Foreign Policy Analysis* 7: 317–36.

Corbett, J. (1911) 1988. *Some Principles of Maritime Strategy*. Annapolis: United States Naval Institute. First published, London: Longmans.

Corbett, J., and H.W. Hodges. 1916. 'The Teaching of Naval and Military History'. *History* 1 (1): 12–24.

Council of the European Union. 2014. *Maritime Security Strategy*. Brussels. 11205/14.

Coutau-Bégarie, H. 2002. *Traité de Stratégie*. 7th ed. Paris: Economica.

Cox, R.W. 1980. 'The Crisis of World Order and the Problem of International Organization in the 1980s'. *International Journal* 35 (2): 370–95.

Crespi, F. 1988. 'The Paradox of Power'. In *The Paradox of Democracy*, edited by G. Hermet and H. Trindade, 3–24. Delhi: Gian Publishing House.

Crowe, E.E. 1853. *The Greek and the Turk or Powers and Prospects in the Levant*. London: Richard Bentley.

Crowl, P.A. 1986. 'Alfred Thayer Mahan: The Naval Historian'. In *Makers of Modern Strategy*, edited by P. Paret, 444–80. Oxford: Oxford University Press.

Curto, D.R., and A. Molho, eds. 2002. *Commercial Networks in the Early Modern World*. EUI Working Paper HEC, no. 2002/2. Florence: European University Institute.

Cusumano, E. 2017. 'Emptying the Sea with a Spoon? Non-governmental Providers of Migrants Search and Rescue in the Mediterranean'. *Marine Policy* 75: 91–8.

D'Angeul, P. 1754. *Remarks on the Advantages and Disadvantages of France and Great-Britain With Respect to Commerce, and to the other Means of Increasing the Wealth and Power of a State*. Translated from the original in French. London: T. Osborne.

Damanaki, M. 2014. 'European Maritime Security Strategy: Moving Forward'. Speech at the CHENS (CHiefs of European NavieS) annual meeting, Portsmouth, 23 May 2014, https://ec.europa.eu/commission/presscorner/detail/en/SPEECH_14_408.

de Carvalho, B., and H. Leira, eds. 2022. *The Sea and International Relations*. Manchester: Manchester University Press.

de Graaff, N., and B. Van Apeldoorn. 2018. 'US–China Relations and the Liberal World Order: Contending Elites, Colliding Visions?' *International Affairs*, 94 (1): 113–31.

Dehio, L. 1962. *The Precarious Balance: Four Centuries of European Power Struggle*. New York: Vintage.

Deleuze, G., and F. Guattari. 1988. *A Thousand Plateaus: Capitalism and Schizophrenia*, translated by Brian Massumi. Minneapolis: University of Minnesota Press

de Seyssel, C. (1519) 1558. *La Grande Monarchie de France*. Paris: Etienne Groulleau.

de Souza, P. 2001. Seafaring and Civilization: Maritime Perspectives on World History. London: Profile Books.

d'Oléon, M. 1996. 'Policing the Seas: The Way Ahead'. In *The Role of European Naval Forces after the Cold War*, edited by G. de Nooy, 133–48. The Hague: Kluwer Law International.

Dupont, A., and C.G. Baker. 2014. 'East Asia's Maritime Disputes: Fishing in Troubled Waters'. *The Washington Quarterly* 37 (1): 79–98.

Eccles, H. 1979. *Military Power in a Free Society*. Annapolis: Naval War College Press.

Eckstein, A.M. 2009. 'Rome Dominates the Mediterranean'. In *China Goes to Sea: Maritime Transformation in Comparative Historical Perspectives*, edited by A.S. Erickson, L.J. Goldstein, and C. Lord, 63–92. Annapolis: China Maritime Studies Institute and the Naval Institute Press.

Ellersgaard, C. 2016. 'Elites in Denmark: Power Elites and Ruling Classes in a Welfare State'. PhD thesis, University of Copenhagen.

Falcon y Tella, M.J. 2004. *Civil Disobedience*. Leiden: Martinus Nijhoff.

Federal Department of Foreign Affairs (Switzerland). 2021. *Future Prospects for the Swiss Flag and Fleet at Sea*. Created by the Institute of Shipping Economics and Logistics, Bremen. https://www.eda.admin.ch/smno/en/home/downloads-links.html.

Fieldhouse, J., and W. Pillar. 1984. 'Soviet Maritime Power'. *The RUSI Journal* 129 (2): 3–6.

Fierke, K.M. 2007. *Critical Approaches to International Security*. London: Polity.

Foucault, M. 1982. 'The Subject and Power'. *Critical Inquiry* 8 (4): 777–95.

Fournel, J.-L. 2006. 'L'impossible thalassocratie: la mer dans la pensée politique de Tommaso Campanella'. *Brunania & Campanelliana* 12 (2): 431–49.

Foxcroft, H.C. 1896. 'The Works of George Savile, First Marquis of Halifax'. *The English Historical Review* 11 (44): 703–30.

Freedman, L. 1999. *The Politics of British Defence, 1979–1998*. London: Macmillan.

Frémont, A. 2007. 'Global Maritime Networks, The Case of Maersk'. *Journal of Transport Geography* 15: 431–42.

Friedman, N. 2000. *Seapower and Space: From the Dawn of the Missile Age to Net-Centric Warfare*. London: Chatham Publishing.

– 2001. *Seapower as Strategy: Navies and National Interests*. Annapolis: Naval Institute Press.

– 2007. 'Navies and Technology'. In *The Politics of Maritime Power*, edited by A.T.H. Tan, 45–61. London: Routledge.

Fuchs, D. 2005. 'Commanding Heights? The Strength and Fragility of Business Power in Global Politics'. *Millennium: Journal of International Studies* 33 (3): 771–801.

Fuchs, D., and M. Lederer. 2007. 'The Power of Business'. *Business and Politics* 9 (3): 1–17.

Gade, J.G., and P.S. Hilde. 2016. 'NATO and the Maritime Domain'. In *International Order at Sea*, edited by J. Bekkevold and G. Till, 115–39. London: Palgrave Macmillan.

Germond, B. 2010. 'From Frontier to Boundary and Back Again: The European Union's Maritime Margins'. *European Foreign Affairs Review* 15 (1): 39–55.

– 2014. 'Small Navies in Perspective: Deconstructing the Hierarchy of Naval Forces'. In *Small Navies*, edited by I. Speller, M. Mulqueen, and D. Sanders, 33–50. Farnham: Ashgate (Corbett Centre for Maritime Policy Studies series).

– 2015. *The Maritime Dimension of European Security: Seapower and the European Union*. London: Palgrave Macmillan.

– 2019. 'Seapower and Small Navies: A Collective and Post-Modern Outlook'. In *Europe, Small Navies and Maritime Security*, edited by I. Speller, D. Sanders, and R. McCabe, 26–35. Abingdon: Routledge.

– 2022a. 'Representation: Seapower and the Political Construction of the Ocean'. In *The Routledge Handbook of Ocean Space*, edited by K. Peters, J. Anderson, A. Davies, and P. Steinberg, 46–57. London: Routledge

– 2022b. 'The Security Dimension of Switzerland's Maritime Strategy'. *Current Affairs in Perspective*, no. 10.

– 2022c. 'The Solidaristic Society of Maritime Nations'. *Australian Naval Review*, no. 1: 72–85.

– 2023a. 'The Integrated Review Refresh 2023: A Pragmatic Strategy for a Maritime Nation'. *Navy Lookout*, 17 March 2023. www.navylookout.com/integrated-review-refresh-2023-a-pragmatic-strategy-for-a-maritime-nation.

– 2023b. 'Oral Evidence to The House of Commons'. Environmental Audit Sub-Committee on Polar Research, 25 May 2023. https://committees.parliament.uk/oralevidence/13209/pdf.

Germond-Duret, C. 2016. 'Tradition and Modernity: An Obsolete Dichotomy? Binary Thinking, Indigenous Peoples and Normalisation'. *Third World Quarterly* 37 (9): 1537–58.

– 2022. 'Framing the Blue Economy: Placelessness, Development and Sustainability'. *Development and Change* 53 (2): 308–34.

Gerónymo de Uztáriz, Don. (1742) 1752. *The Theory and Practice of Commerce and Maritime Affairs*. Dublin: G. Faulkner. Written originally in Spanish, translated by John Kippax.

Gilpin, C. 1981. *War and Change in World Politics*. New York: Cambridge University Press.

Glete, J. 2000. *Warfare at Sea, 1500–1650: Maritime Conflicts and the Transformation of Europe*. London: Routledge.

Godwin, P.H.B. 1987. 'Changing Concepts of Doctrine, Strategy, and Operations in the People's Liberation Army 1978–87'. *China Quarterly*, no. 112: 573–90.

Goldman, C. 2021. 'Denmark to Deploy Absalon-Class Danish Frigate to the Gulf of Guinea'. Dryad Global, 19 March 2021. https://channel16. dryadglobal.com/denmark-to-deploy-absalon-class-danish-frigate-to-the-gulf-of-guinea.

Gorshkov, S.G. (1979) 1976. *The Sea Power of the State*. Oxford: Pergamon Press. Original edition, Moscow: Voenizdat.

Gould, A. 2021. 'Sovereign Control and Ocean Governance in the Regulation of Maritime Private Policing'. *Policing and Society* 31 (3): 337–53.

Gray, C.S. 1992. *The Leverage of Sea Power: The Strategic Advantage of Navies in War*. New York: Free Press (Macmillan).

– 1994. *The Navy in the Post-Cold War World: The Uses and Value of Strategic Sea Power*. University Park, PA: Pennsylvania State University Press.

Gresh, G.F. 2020. *To Rule Eurasia's Waves: The New Great Power Competition at Sea*. New Haven: Yale University Press.

Gretton, P. 1965. *Maritime Strategy*. London: Cassell & Company.

Grivel, R. 1869. *De la guerre maritime avant et depuis les nouvelles inventions*. Paris: Arthus Bertrand, J. Dumaine.

Grote, G. (1849) 1857. *History of Greece*. Vol. 5. New York: Harper & Brother.

Grove, E. 1990. *The Future of Sea Power*. Annapolis: Naval Institute Press.

– 2005. *The Royal Navy*. London: Palgrave Macmillan.

Grygiel, J. 2012. 'Geography and Seapower'. In *Twenty-First Century Seapower: Cooperation and Conflict at Sea*, edited by P. Dutton, R.S. Ross and Ø Tunsjø, 18–41. Abingdon: Routledge.

Guilfoyle, D. 2019. 'The Rule of Law and Maritime Security: Understanding Lawfare in the South China Sea'. *International Affairs* 95 (5): 999–1017.

Hadjimichael, M., A. Bruggeman, and M.A. Lange. 2014. 'Tragedy of the Few? A Political Ecology Perspective of the Right to the Sea: The Cyprus Marine Aquaculture Sector'. *Marine Policy* 49: 12–19.

Halewood, L. 2021. '"Peace throughout the Oceans and Seas of the World": British Maritime Strategic Thought and World Order, 1892–1919'. *Historical Research* 94 (265): 554–77.

Hattendorf, J.B. 2000a. *Naval History and Maritime Strategy: Collected Essays*. Malabar, FL: Krieger Publishing.

– ed. 2000b. *Naval Strategy and Policy in the Mediterranean*. London: Frank Cass.

– 2011. *Talking about Naval History*. Newport, RI: Naval War College Press.

Haydon, P.T. 2007. 'Naval Diplomacy: Is it Relevant in the 21st Century?' In *The Politics of Maritime Power*, edited by A.T.H. Tan, 71–4. London: Routledge.

Haywood, R., and R. Spivak. 2012. *Maritime Piracy*. London: Routledge.

Hendriksen, C. 2020. 'Corporate Influence and Environmental Regulation in Shipping: Navigating Norms and Influence Pathways in the International Maritime Organization'. In *MNCs in Global Politics: Pathways of Influence*, edited by J. Mikler and K. Ronit, 77–96. Cheltenham: Edward Elgar Publishing.

Hendrix, H.J. 2020. *To Provide and Maintain a Navy: Why Naval Primacy is American's First Best Strategy*. Annapolis: Focsle LLP Publisher.

Herder, J.G. 1803. *Outlines of a Philosophy of the History of Man*. Translated by T. Churchill. London: J. Johnson, St Paul's Churchyard.

Herodotus. c. 430 BCE. *The Histories*.

Hickey, L.M. 2006. 'Enhancing the Naval Mandate for Law Enforcement: Hot Pursuit or Hot Potato?' *Canadian Military Journal* 7 (1): 42–8.

Higgs, Henry, ed. 1935. *Bibliography of Economics, 1751–1775*. London: Thoemmes Continuum.

Hill, J.R. 1986. *Maritime Strategy for Medium Powers*. Annapolis: Naval Institute Press.

HM Government. 2021. *Global Britain in a Competitive Age: The Integrated Review of Security, Defence, Development and Foreign Policy*. Presented to Parliament by the Prime Minister by Command of Her Majesty, CP 403.

– 2022. *National Strategy for Maritime Security*, Presented to Parliament by the Secretary of State for Transport by Command of Her Majesty, August, CP 724.

Hobson, R., and T. Kristiansen. 2012. 'The National Security of Secondary Maritime Powers within the Classic European States System'. In *Twenty-First Century Seapower: Cooperation and Conflict at Sea*, edited by P. Dutton, R.S. Ross, and Ø. Tunsjø, 9–17. Abingdon: Routledge.

Holmes, J.R., and T. Yoshihara. 2008. *Chinese Naval Strategy: The Turn to Mahan*. Abingdon: Routledge.

House of Commons, Defence Committee. 2021. 'We're Going to Need a Bigger Navy'. Third Report of Session 2021–22. Ordered by the House of Commons to be printed 7 December 2021, HC1069.

– 2022. 'Operation Isotrope: The Use of the Military to Counter Migrant Crossings'. Fourth Report of Session 2021–22. Ordered by the House of Commons to be printed 8 March 2022, HC1069.

Howe, D. 1994. 'Modernity, Postmodernity and Social Work'. *British Journal of Social Work* 24 (5): 513–32.

Hughes, W.P. 2000. *Fleet Tactics and Coastal Combat*. Annapolis: Naval Institute Press.

Hyman, G. 2001. *The Predicament of Postmodern Theology: Radical Orthodoxy or Nihilist Textualism?* Louisville: Westminster John Knox Press.

Jackson, A.P. 2010. 'Keystone Doctrine Development in Five Commonwealth Navies: A Comparative Perspective'. *Papers in Australian Maritime Affairs*, no. 33.

Jane, F.T. (1906) 2013. *Heresies of Sea Power*. Reprint, Cambridge: Cambridge University Press.

Ji, Y. 1995. 'A Test Case for China's Defence and Foreign Policies'. *Contemporary Southeast Asia* 16 (4): 375–403.

Kaczmarska, K. 2015. 'Russia's droit de regard: Pluralist Norms and the Sphere of Influence'. *Global Discourse* 5 (3): 434–48.

Kearsley, H.J. 1992. *Maritime Power and the Twenty-First Century*. Aldershot: Dartmouth Publishing.

Keck, Z. 2014. 'The Philippines Wants Submarines to Deter China'. *National Interest*, 18 December 2014.

Kennedy, G., and W. de Sousa Moreira, eds. 2022. *Power and the Maritime Domain: A Global Dialogue*. London: Routledge.

Kennedy, P. (1976) 2017. *The Rise and Fall of British Naval Mastery*. London: Penguin Books.

– 2022. *Victory at Sea: Naval Power and the Transformation of the Global Order in World War II*. New Haven: Yale University Press.

Kennedy, P., and E. Wilson, eds. 2022. *Navies in Multipolar Worlds: From the Age of Sail to the Present*. Abingdon: Routledge.

Khaldun, I. (1377) 1958. *The Muqaddimah*. Translated by Franz Rosenthal. New York: Pantheon Books.

Kiesling, E.C. 1994. Introduction to R. Castex, *Strategic Theories*, 1–44. Selections translated and edited by E.C. Kiesling. Annapolis: United States Naval Institute Press.

Kipp, J.W. 2009. 'Imperial Russia: Two Models of Maritime Transformation'. In *China Goes to Sea: Maritime Transformation in Comparative Historical Perspectives*, edited by A.S. Erickson, L.J. Goldstein, and C. Lord, 145–70. Annapolis: Naval Institute Press.

Knox-Hayes, J. 2010. 'Constructing Carbon Market Spacetime: Climate Change and the Onset of Neo-Modernity'. *Annals of the Association of American Geographers* 100 (4): 953–62.

Kostecka, D.J. 2011. 'Places and Bases: The Chinese Navy's Emerging Support Network in the Indian Ocean'. *Naval War College Review* 64 (1): 59–78.

Kouar, J. 2010. 'Entretien avec le professeur Hervé Coutau-Bégarie'. *Outre-Terre*, nos. 25–6: 17–19.

Kraska, J. 2009. 'Grasping "the Influence of Law on Sea Power"'. *Naval War College Review* 62 (3): 113–35.

Krause, K., and M.C. Williams. 1996. 'Broadening the Agenda of Security Studies: Politics and Methods'. *Mershon International Studies Review* 40 (2): 229–54.

Kyriazis, N. 2006. 'Seapower and Socioeconomic Change'. *Theory and Society* 35 (1): 71–108.

Kyriazis, N.C., and M.S. Zouboulakis. 2004. 'Democracy, Sea Power and Institutional Change: An Economic Analysis of the Athenian Naval Law'. *European Journal of Law and Economics* 17: 117–32.

Lambert, A. 2000. *War at Sea in the Age of Sail*. London: Cassell.

– 2010. 'Sea Power'. In *The Ashgate Research Companion to Modern Warfare*, edited by G. Kassimeris and J. Buckley, 73–88. Farnham: Ashgate.

– ed. 2017. *21st Century Corbett: Maritime Strategy and Naval Policy for the Modern Era*. Annapolis: Naval Institute Press.

– 2018. *Seapower States*. New Haven: Yale University Press.

– 2021. *The British Way of War: Julian Corbett and the Battle for a National Strategy*. New Haven: Yale University Press.

Larsen, J., and C. Nissen. 2017. *Learning from Danish Counter-Piracy off the Coast of Somalia*. Report 2017, no. 10. Copenhagen: Danish Institute for International Studies.

Lavery, B. 2013. *A Short History of Seafaring*. London: Penguin Random House.

Leggett, D. 2011. 'Navy, Nation and Identity in the Long Nineteenth Century'. *Journal for Maritime Research* 13 (2): 151–63.

Le Mière, C. 2014. *Maritime Diplomacy in the 21st Century*. London: Routledge.

Li, N. 2009. 'The Evolution of China's Naval Strategy and Capabilities: From "Near Coast" and "Near Seas" to "Far Seas"'. *Asian Security* 5 (2): 144–69.

– 2014. 'China's Evolving Naval Strategy and Capabilities in the Hu Jintao Era'. In *Assessing the People's Liberation Army in the Hu Jintao Era*, edited by R. Kamphausen, D. Lai, and T. Tanner, 257–99. Carlisle, PA: US Army War College Press.

Lindberg, M.S. 1998. *Geographical Impact on Coastal Defence Navies*, Basingstoke: Macmillan, 14–37.

Lo, J. 2012. *China as a Sea Power, 1127–1368: A Preliminary Survey of the Maritime Expansion and Naval Exploits of the Chinese People During the Southern Song and Yuan Periods*, edited by B.A. Elleman. Singapore: NUS Press.

Luttwak, E.N. 1974. *The Political Uses of Sea Power*. Baltimore: Johns Hopkins University Press.

Lyotard, J.-F. 1988. 'Reecrire la modernité'. *Cahiers de Philosophie*, no. 5: 193–203.

Mabee, B. 2009. 'Pirates, Privateers and the Political Economy of Private Violence'. *Global Change, Peace & Security* 21 (2): 139–52.

Mackinder, H.J. 1904. 'The Geographical Pivot of History'. *The Geographical Journal* 170 (4): 298–321.

Mahan. A.T. (1890) 2007. *The Influence of Sea Power upon History, 1660–1783*. New York: Cosimo Classics. Original edition, Englewood Cliffs: Prentice-Hall.

Mancke, E. 1999. 'Early Modern Expansion and the Politicization of Oceanic Space'. *Geographical Review* 89 (2): 225–36.

Mansouri, M.T. 2016. 'The Navigation Industry in Ibn Khaldoun's Muqaddimahi'. *Ostour*, no. 4 (June): 46–56.

Maull, H.W. 1990. 'Germany and Japan: The New Civilian Powers'. *Foreign Affairs* 69 (5): 91–106.

Maurer, J.H. 2022. 'Afterword: Reflections on the Great War at Sea'. In *Navies in Multipolar Worlds: From the Age of Sail to the Present*, edited by P. Kennedy and E. Wilson, 235–47. Abingdon: Routledge.

Melissen, J., ed. 1999. *Innovation in Diplomatic Practice*. London: Macmillan.

Mellor, P.A. 1993. 'Reflexive Traditions: Anthony Giddens, High Modernity, and the Contours of Contemporary Religiosity'. *Religious Studies* 29 (1): 111–27.

Mitchell, N.J. 1997. *The Conspicuous Corporation: Business, Public Policy and Representative Democracy*. Ann Arbor: University of Michigan Press.

MoD. 2011. *British Maritime Doctrine*, Joint Doctrine Publication 0-10 (JDP 0-10). Shrivenham: DCDC.

Modelski, G. 1987. *Long Cycles in World Politics*. Seattle: University of Washington Press.

Modelski, G., and W.R. Thompson. 1988. *Seapower in Global Politics, 1494–1993*. London: Macmillan Press.

– 1996. *Leading Sectors and World Powers: The Coevolution of Global Economics and Politics*. Columbia: University of South Carolina Press.

Moineville, H. 1983. *Naval Warfare Today and Tomorrow*. London: Blackwell.

Momigliano, A. 1944. 'Sea-Power in Greek Thought'. *The Classical Review* 58 (1): 1–7.

Morris, M.A. 1987. *Expansion of the Third World Navies*. London: Macmillan.

Mufti, M. 2009. 'Jihad as Statecraft: Ibn Khaldun on the Conduct of War and Empire'. *History of Political Thought* 30 (3): 385–410.

Mullen, M. 2006. 'What I Believe: Eight Tenets That Guide My Vision for the 21st Century Navy'. *US Naval Institute Proceedings* 132 (1). www.usni.org/magazines/proceedings/2006/january/what-i-believe-eight-tenets-guide-my-vision-21st-century-navy.

Münkler, H. 2007. *Empires: The Logic of World Domination from Ancient Rome to the United States*. Cambridge: Polity Press.

NATO. 2022. *Madrid Summit Declaration*. Issued by NATO Heads of State and Government participating in the meeting of the North Atlantic Council in Madrid, 29 June 2022.

Neumann, I. 2011. 'Entry into International Society Reconceptualised: The Case of Russia'. *Review of International Studies* 37 (2): 463–84.

Nye, J.S. 2004. *Soft Power: The Means to Success in World Politics*. Cambridge, MA: Perseus.

Oliver, D., and B. Slack. 2006. 'Rethinking the Port'. *Environment and Planning A* 38 (8): 1409–27.

Orbie, J. 2006. 'Civilian Power Europe: Review of the Original and Current Debates'. *Cooperation and Conflict: Journal of the Nordic International Studies Association* 41 (1): 123–8.

Osborne, P. 1992. 'Modernity is a Qualitative, Not a Chronological, Category'. *New Left Review* 192 (1): 65–84.

Overton, J. 2022. 'For Ukraine, the 1,000-Ship Navy Finally Sets Sail'. Center for International Maritime Security, 13 April 2022. https://cimsec.org/for-ukraine-the-1000-ship-navy-finally-sets-sail.

Pagès, J. 1991. 'La Pensée Navale Athénienne aux Ve et IVe siècles avant J.C.' In *L'évolution de la pensée navale*, edited by H. Coutau-Bégarie. (FEDN) Hautes Etudes Stratégiques, online version.

– 1992. 'La pensée navale Hellénistique'. In *L'évolution de la pensée navale II*, edited by H. Coutau-Bégarie. (FEDN) Hautes Etudes Stratégiques, online version.

– 1993. 'Y a-t-il eu une pensée navale Romaine?' In *L'évolution de la pensée navale III*, edited by H. Coutau-Bégarie. (FEDN) Hautes Etudes Stratégiques, online version.

Peters, K., J. Anderson, A. Davies, and P. Steinberg, eds. 2022. *The Routledge Handbook of Ocean Space*. London: Routledge.

Paine, L. 2013. *The Sea and Civilization: A Maritime History of the World*. London: Atlantic Book.

Pant, H.V. 2012. 'China Shakes up the Maritime Balance in the Indian Ocean'. *Strategic Analysis* 36 (3): 364–8.

Patalano, A. 2018. 'When Strategy is "Hybrid" and not "Grey": Reviewing Chinese Military and Constabulary Coercion at Sea'. *The Pacific Review* 31 (6): 811–39.

– 2022. 'The Global Order at Sea: From a Hierarchy of Power to Hierarchical Legitimacy'. In *Power and the Maritime Domain: A Global Dialogue*, edited by G. Kennedy and W. de Sousa Moreira, 11–23. London: Routledge.

Phillips, C.R. 2000. 'Navies and the Mediterranean in the Early Modern Period'. In *Naval Strategy and Policy in the Mediterranean*, edited by J.B. Hattendorf, 3–29. London: Frank Cass.

Plutarch. c. 100 CE. *The Life of Pompey*.

– c. 100 CE. *The Parallel Lives*.

Posen, B.R. 2003. 'Command of the Commons'. *International Security* 28 (1): 5–53.

Pugh, M. 1996. 'Is Mahan Still Alive? State Naval Power in the
International System'. *Journal of Conflict Studies* 16 (2): 109–23.

Pye, M. 2015. *The Edge of the World: How the North Sea Made Us
Who We Are*. London: Penguin Books. First published, London:
Viking, 2014.

Quilley, G. 2014. 'Sailors on Horseback: The Representation of Seamen
and Social Space in Eighteen-Century British Visual Culture'. In
Framing the Ocean, 1700 to the Present, edited by T. Cusack, 85–100.
London: Ashgate.

Rahman, C. 2008. 'The Global Maritime Partnership Initiative:
Implications for the Royal Australian Navy'. *Papers in Australian
Maritime Affairs*, no. 24. Australia: Sea Power Centre.

Raine, J. 2019. 'War or Peace? Understanding the Grey Zone'. IISS
Analysis Blog, 3 April 2019. www.iiss.org/online-analysis/online-
analysis//2019/04/understanding-the-grey-zone.

Raleigh, W. (c. 1600) 1829. 'A Discourse of the Invention of Ships,
Anchors, Compass, &c.' In *The Works of Sir Walter Ralegh, Kt.*,
vol. 8. Oxford: Oxford University Press, 317–34.

Ratzel, F. 1911. *Das Meer als Quelle der Völkergrösse*. Munich: Verlag
R. Oldenbourg.

RCN (Royal Canadian Navy). 2017. *Canada in a New Maritime World:
LEADMARK 2050*, http://navy-marine.forces.gc.ca/assets/NAVY_
Internet/docs/en/rcn_leadmark-2050.pdf.

Rehman, I. 2017. 'India's Fitful Quest for Seapower'. *India Review*
16 (2): 226–65.

Reilly, J. 2013. 'China's Economic Statecraft: Turning Wealth into Power'.
Analysis. Lowy Institute for International Policy.

Richmond, H. 1934. *Sea Power in the Modern World*. London: G. Bell
and Sons.

– 1946. *Statesmen and Sea Power*. Oxford: Oxford University Press.

Rodger, N.A.M. (1997) 2004. *The Safeguard of the Sea: A Naval History
of Britain*, vol. 1, *660–1649*. London: W.W. Penguin Books.

– (2004) 2005. *The Command of the Ocean: A Naval History of Britain*,
vol. 2, *1649–1815*. London: Penguin Books.

– 2004. "Queen Elizabeth and the Myth of Seapower in English History".
Transactions of the Royal Historical Society 14: 153–74.

– 2012. 'Introduction: Navies and State Formation'. In *Navies and State
Formation: The Schumpeter Hypothesis Revisited and Reflected*,
edited by J.G. Blackhaus, 9–20. Zurich: LIT.

Rosinski, H. 1977. *The Development of Naval Thought: Essays by Herbert Rosinski*. Newport, RI: Naval War College Press.

Roskill, S.W. 1962. *The Strategy of Sea Power*. London: Collins.

Rostow, W.W. 1960. *The Stages of Economic Growth: A Non-Communist Manifesto*. Cambridge: Cambridge University Press.

Sadler, B.D. 2023. *US Naval Power in the 21st Century: A New Strategy for Facing the Chinese and Russian Threat*. Annapolis: Naval Institute Press.

Sagan, S. 1997. 'Why Do States Build Nuclear Weapons?: Three Models in Search of a Bomb'. *International Security* 21 (3): 54–86.

Saunders, R. 2019. 'Myths from a Small Island: The Dangers of a Buccaneering View of British History'. *New Statesman*, 9 October 2019, www.newstatesman.com/politics/2019/10/myths-from-a-small-island-the-dangers-of-a-buccaneering-view-of-british-history.

Schweller, R.L., and X. Pu. 2011. 'After Unipolarity: China's Visions of International Order in an Era of U.S. Decline'. *International Security* 36 (1): 41–72.

Sempa, F.P. 2002. *Geopolitics: From the Cold War to the 21st Century*. London: Transaction Publishers.

Sicking, L. 2004. *Neptune and the Netherlands: State, Economy, and War at Sea in the Renaissance*. Leiden: Brill.

Sivasundaram, S. 2018. 'The Indian Ocean'. In *Oceanic Histories*, edited by D. Armitage, A. Bashford, and S. Sivasundaram, 31–61. Cambridge: Cambridge University Press.

Smith-Windsor, B. 2009. 'Securing the Commons: Towards NATO's New Maritime Strategy'. Research Paper, no. 49. NATO Defense College.

Sørensen, G. 2008. 'The Case for Combining Material Forces and Ideas in the Study of IR'. *European Journal of International Relations* 14 (1): 5–32.

Sparke, M., J.D. Sidaway, T. Bunnell, and C. Grundy-Warr. 2004. 'Triangulating the Borderless World: Geographies of Power in the Indonesia–Malaysia–Singapore Growth Triangle'. *Transactions of the Institute of British Geographers* 29 (4): 485–98.

Speller, I. 2014. *Understanding Naval Warfare*. London: Routledge.

– 2022. 'Modern Maritime Strategy and Naval Warfare'. In *Routledge Handbook of Maritime Security*, edited by R.-L. Boşilcă, S. Ferreira, and B.J. Ryan, 49–61. Abingdon: Routledge.

Spence, D.O. 2015. *A History of the Royal Navy: Empire and Imperialism*. London: Bloomsbury Publishing.

Spykman, N.J. 1944. *The Geography of Peace*. New York: Harcourt.

Starr, C.G. 1978. 'Thucydides on Sea Power'. *Mnemosyne* 31 (4): 343–50.

Stavridis, J. 2017. *Sea Power: The History and Geopolitics of the World's Oceans*. New York: Penguin Books.

Steffen, W., W. Broadgate, L. Deutsch, O. Gaffney, and C. Ludwig. 2015. 'The Trajectory of the Anthropocene: The Great Acceleration'. *The Anthropocene Review* 2 (1): 81–98.

Steinberg, P.E. 1999a. 'The Maritime Mystique: Sustainable Development, Capital Mobility, and Nostalgia in the World Ocean'. *Environment and Planning D: Society and Space* 17 (4): 403–26.

– 1999b. 'Navigating to Multiple Horizons: Toward a Geography of Ocean-Space'. *The Professional Geographer* 51 (3): 366–75.

– 2001. *The Social Construction of the Ocean*. Cambridge: Cambridge University Press.

Steinberg, P.E., and K. Peters. 2015. 'Wet Ontologies, Fluid Spaces: Giving Depth to Volume through Oceanic Thinking'. *Environment and Planning D: Society and Space* 33 (2): 247–64.

Stivachtis, Y.A. 2014. 'The Regional Dimension of International Society'. In *Guide to the English School in International Studies*, edited by C. Navari and D. Green, 109–25. London: John Wiley & Sons.

– 2015. 'Interrogating Regional International Societies, Questioning the Global International Society'. *Global Discourse* 5 (3): 327–40.

Strachan, H. 2005. 'The Lost Meaning of Strategy'. *Survival: Global Politics and Strategy* 47 (3): 33–54.

– 2007. 'Maritime Strategy: Historical Perspectives'. *RUSI Journal* 152 (1): 29–33.

Strange, S. 1976. 'Who Runs World Shipping?' *International Affairs* 52 (3): 346–67.

Suárez-de Vivero, J.L., and J.C. Rodríguez Mateos. 2017. 'Forecasting Geopolitical Risks: Oceans as Source of Instability'. *Marine Policy* 75: 19–28.

– 2014. 'Changing Maritime Scenarios. The Geopolitical Dimension of the EU Atlantic Strategy'. *Marine Policy* 48: 59–72.

Suárez-de Vivero, J.L., J.C. Rodríguez Mateos, and D. Florido del Corral. 2009. 'Geopolitical Factors of Maritime Policies and Marine Spatial Planning: State, Regions, and Geographical Planning Scope'. *Marine Policy* 33 (4): 624–34.

Sumida, J. 1997. *Inventing Grand Strategy and Teaching Command: The Classics Works of Alfred Thayer Mahan Reconsidered*. Baltimore: Johns Hopkins University Press.

– 1999. 'Alfred Thayer Mahan, Geopolitician'. *Journal of Strategic Studies* 22 (2–3): 39–62.

Surminski, S., and A. Williamson. 2014. 'Policy Indexes as Tools for Decision Makers: The Case of Climate Policy'. *Global Policy* 5 (3): 275–85.

Sys, C. 2009. 'Is the Container Liner Shipping Industry an Oligopoly?' *Transport Policy* 16 (5): 259–70.

Tagliacozzo, E. 2018. 'The South China Sea'. In *Oceanic Histories*, edited by D. Armitage, A. Bashford, and S. Sivasundaram, 113–33. Cambridge: Cambridge University Press.

Tanaka, Y. 2004. 'Zonal and Integrated Management Approaches to Ocean Governance: Reflections on a Dual Approach in International Law of the Sea'. *The International Journal of Marine and Coastal Law* 19 (4): 483–514.

– 2008. *A Dual Approach to Ocean Governance: The Case of Zonal and Integrated Management in International Law of the Sea.* Farnham: Ashgate.

Tangredi, S.J. 2002. 'Globalization and Sea Power: Overview and Context'. In *Globalization and Maritime Power*, edited by S.J. Tangredi, 1–24. Washington, DC: National Defense University Press.

– 2013. *Anti-Access Warfare: Countering A2/AD Strategies*. Annapolis: Naval Institute Press.

Taylor, A. 2017. 'Maritime Strategy in the Era of Control and Denial of Visibility'. PhD thesis, Lancaster University.

Thucydides. c. 5th century BCE. *History of the Peloponnesian War.*

Till, G. 1987. *Modern Sea Power*. London: Brassey's.

– 1994. *Seapower: Theory and Practice*. London: Frank Cass.

– 2004. *Seapower: A Guide for the 21st Century*. London: Frank Cass. Re-edited and expanded in 2009, 2013, and 2018.

– 2006. 'Corbett and the Emergence of a British School'. In *The Development of British Naval Thinking*, edited by G. Till, 60–88. Abingdon: Routledge.

– 2007. 'Maritime Strategy in a Globalizing World'. *Orbis* 51 (4): 569–75.

– 2022. *How to Grow a Navy: The Development of Maritime Power.* London: Routledge.

Tritten, J.J. 1989. *Back to Basics: Mahan for the 1990s*. Monterey, CA: Naval Postgraduate School.

Tucker, Josiah. 1749. *Brief Essay on the Advantages and Disadvantages Which Respectively Attend France and Great Britain, With Regards to Trade*. London: T. Tryre

Turnbull, S. 2002. *Fighting Ships of the Far East*, vol. 1: *China and Southeast Asia 202 BC–AD 1419*. Oxford: Osprey Publishing.

Turner, F.J. (1920) 1996. *The Frontier in American History*. New York: Henry Holt. Original edition, New York: Dover.

Turner, O. 2019. 'Global Britain and the Narrative of Empire'. *Political Quarterly* 90 (4): 727–34.

Turner, S. 1974. 'Missions of the U.S. Navy'. *Naval War College Review* (March–April): 2–17.

van Ham, H., and J. Rijsenbrij. 2012. *Development of Containerization: Success through Vision, Drive and Technology*. Amsterdam: IOS Press.

Vince, J. 2014. 'Introduction: Oceans Governance: Where Have We Been and Where Are We Going?' *Australian Journal of Maritime & Ocean Affairs* 6 (1): 3–4.

Vinson, S. 1994. *Egyptian Boats and Ships*. Princes Risborough, UK: Shire Publications.

Waltz, K.N. 1979. *Theory of International Politics*. Long Grove, IL: Waveland Press.

Wegener, W. (1929) 1989. *The Naval Strategy of the World War*. Introduction and translation by Holger H. Herwig. Annapolis: Naval Institute Press.

Wendt, A. 1992. 'Anarchy is What States Make of It: The Social Construction of Power Politics'. *International Organization* 46 (2): 391–425.

Wenmu, Z. 2000. 'Maersk Port Move to Hurt Singapore'. *South China Morning Post*, 22 August 2000. www.ptp.com.my/media-hub/news/maersk-port-move-to-hurt-singapore.

– 2006. 'Sea Power and China's Strategic Choices'. *China Security* (Summer): 17–31.

Willett, L. 2011. 'Pirates and Power Politics'. *RUSI Journal* 156 (6): 20–5.

Wood, A. 2012. *Warships of the Ancient World: 3000–500 BC*. Oxford: Osprey Publishing.

Wood, W.C. 1919. *Flag and Fleet – How the British Navy Won the Freedom of the Seas*. Toronto: Macmillan Company.

Wylie, J.C. 1989. *Military Strategy: A General Theory of Power Control*. Annapolis: Naval Institute Press.

Zambellas, G. 2013. 'Address at BRNS Dartmouth to Celebrate 150 Years of Royal Navy and International Naval Training'. *Navy News*, 30 October 2013.

– 2014. 'The Royal Navy's Approach to Defence Engagement'. In *Naval Diplomacy and Maritime Power Projection*. Proceedings of the Royal Australian Navy Sea Power Conference 2013, edited by A. Forbes, 66–71. Canberra, ACT: Sea Power Centre, Australia.

Zellen, B.S. 2012. *State of Doom*. New York: Continuum.

Index